Free Video  **Free Video**

Essential Test Tips Video from Trivium Test Prep

Dear Customer,

Thank you for purchasing from Trivium Test Prep! We're honored to help you prepare for your SAT exam.

To show our appreciation, we're offering a **FREE** *SAT Essential Test Tips* **Video by Trivium Test Prep**.* Our video includes 35 test preparation strategies that will make you successful on the SAT. All we ask is that you email us your feedback and describe your experience with our product. Amazing, awful, or just so-so: we want to hear what you have to say!

To receive your **FREE** *SAT Essential Test Tips* **Video**, please email us at 5star@triviumtestprep.com. Include "Free 5 Star" in the subject line and the following information in your email:

1. The title of the product you purchased.
2. Your rating from 1 – 5 (with 5 being the best).
3. Your feedback about the product, including how our materials helped you meet your goals and ways in which we can improve our products.
4. Your full name and shipping address so we can send your **FREE** *SAT Essential Test Tips* **Video**.

If you have any questions or concerns please feel free to contact us directly at 5star@triviumtestprep.com.

Thank you!

Trivium Test Prep Team

*To get access to the free video please email us at 5star@triviumtestprep.com, and please follow the instructions above.

SAT PREP 2020-2021 with PRACTICE TESTS

Study Guide and Practice Test Questions
Book for the SAT College Board Exam

Table of Contents

Introduction

Congratulations on choosing to take the SAT! By purchasing this book, you've taken the first step toward getting accepted by the college of your choice.

This guide will provide you with a detailed overview of the SAT so you know exactly what to expect on test day. We'll take you through all the concepts covered on the test and give you the opportunity to test your knowledge with practice questions. Even if it's been a while since you last took a major test, don't worry; we'll make sure you're more than ready!

What is the SAT?

The SAT is an achievement test designed to assess what you've learned in school. Universities will look at your SAT score to help determine if you're ready to tackle college-level material. However, your test score won't be the only thing that schools look at; they'll also consider your high school transcript, letters of recommendation, and school activities. So, while the SAT is an important part of your college application, it's only one part of the application process.

What's on the SAT?

The SAT consists of four sections: reading, writing and language, mathematics, and an optional essay. The reading and writing sections include only multiple-choice questions, while the mathematics section includes multiple-choice, grid-in (shown on the following page), and extended response questions. If you choose to take the Essay section, you'll write a short expository essay.

		SAT Content		
Section	Concepts	Number of Questions	Time	
Reading	understanding and analyzing non-fiction and fiction passages; interpreting graphs and charts; vocabulary in context	52 questions	65 minutes	
Writing and Language	identifying errors in basic grammar, punctuation, usage, and style; rhetorical skills	44 questions	35 minutes	
Mathematics	mathematical reasoning and performing calculations using algebra, geometry, and basic statistics	20 questions (no calculator)	25 minutes	
		38 questions (with calculator)	55 minutes	
Essay	crafting a clear, well-written essay	1 prompt	50 minutes	
Total		154 multiple choice 1 essay	3 hours and 50 minutes	

Grid-in Example

How is the SAT Scored?

Every multiple-choice question on the SAT is worth one point, and there is no penalty for choosing an incorrect answer. Your raw score (the number of questions you get right) will then be scaled from 200 – 800. You'll receive a single score for the combined Reading and Writing sections (called the Evidence-Based Reading and Writing score) and another for the Mathematics section. So, the composite score for all three sections will range from 400 – 1600. The essay is scored separately by two graders on a scale of 1 – 4, for a total score of 2 – 8. Although the essay is optional, some colleges may recommend or require a score for this section.

When you register for the test, you can choose which schools you want to receive your scores; you can also wait until after you receive your scores to have them sent to schools. If you take the test multiple times, you'll also be able to pick the scores from a particular date to send (although you cannot pick individual sections from multiple testing dates).

How is the SAT Administered?

The SAT is a pencil-and-paper test offered at a range of schools and testing centers. The test is offered six times a year, and you must register for the test by the deadline (usually one month before the test date). When registering, you will have to decide whether you want to take the exam with or without the essay. Check with your desired colleges about their application requirements; some institutions prefer or even require the essay section. You can register for the SAT online at https://collegereadiness.collegeboard. org/sat/register. There is no limit on how many times you can take the test.

On the day of your test, arrive early and be sure to bring proper identification and your admission ticket (which is emailed to you after you register). You are required to put away all personal belongings before the test begins. Cell phones and other electronic, photographic, recording, or listening devices are not permitted in the testing center at all. You are allowed pencils, erasers, and a four-function or scientific calculator on your desk during the test. Calculators may only be used during the designated mathematics section. A watch that will not sound during the test is also allowed. For details on what to expect on testing day, refer to the SAT website.

About Accepted, Inc.

Accepted, Inc. uses industry professionals with decades' worth of knowledge in their fields, proven with degrees and honors in law, medicine, business, education, the military, and more, to produce high-quality test prep books for students.

Our study guides are specifically designed to increase any student's score, regardless of his or her current skill level. Our books are also shorter and more concise than typical study guides, so you can increase your score while significantly decreasing your study time.

How to Use This Guide

This guide is not meant to waste your time on superfluous information or concepts you've already learned. Instead, this guide will help you master the most important test topics and also develop critical test-taking skills. To support this effort, the guide provides:

▶ organized concepts with detailed explanations

▶ practice questions with worked-through solutions

▶ key test-taking strategies

▶ simulated one-on-one tutor experience

▶ tips, tricks, and test secrets

Because we have eliminated the filler and fluff, you'll be able to work through the guide at a significantly faster pace than you would with other test prep books. By allowing you to focus only on those concepts that will increase your score, we'll make your study time shorter and more effective.

PART I
Evidence-Based Reading and Writing

Reading: 52 questions ¦ 65 minutes
Writing: 44 questions ¦ 35 minutes

The Evidence-Based Reading and Writing part of the test includes two sections: 1) Reading and 2) Writing and Language. The Reading test will include four single passages and one set of paired passages that cover a range of topics. You'll likely see at least one fictional passage and also excerpts from works on science, history, and social studies. Some of these passages will be accompanied by tables or graphs. Each passage or set of passages will be followed by ten or eleven questions that cover the following topics:

- ▶ the main idea of a passage
- ▶ the role of supporting details in a passage
- ▶ adding supporting details to a passage
- ▶ the structure of a passage
- ▶ the author's purpose
- ▶ logical inferences that can be drawn from a passage
- ▶ comparing passages
- ▶ vocabulary and figurative language

The Writing section tests your knowledge of basic grammar, punctuation, and rhetoric. The test will include four passages with various words, phrases, and sentences underlined. The corresponding questions will ask you to revise the underlined text; you can choose to leave the text as-is or replace it with another option. Topics you'll see on the test include:

- ▶ matching pronouns with their antecedents
- ▶ matching verbs with their subjects
- ▶ ensuring that verbs are in the correct tense
- ▶ correcting sentence structure
- ▶ placing sentences logically within the passage
- ▶ determining if sentences belong within a passage

CHAPTER ONE
Reading Passages

The Main Idea

The main idea of a text is the author's purpose in writing a book, article, story, etc. Being able to identify and understand the main idea is a critical skill necessary to comprehend and appreciate what you're reading.

Consider a political election. A candidate is running for office and plans to deliver a speech asserting her position on tax reform. The topic of the speech—tax reform—is clear to voters, and probably of interest to many. However, imagine that the candidate believes that taxes should be lowered. She is likely to assert this argument in her speech, supporting it with examples proving why lowering taxes would benefit the public and how it could be accomplished. While the topic of the speech would be tax reform, the benefit of lowering taxes would be the main idea. Other candidates may have different perspectives on the topic; they may believe that higher taxes are necessary, or that current taxes are adequate. It is likely that their speeches, while on the same topic of tax reform, would have different main ideas: different arguments likewise supported by different examples. Determining what a speaker, writer, or text is asserting about a specific issue will reveal the MAIN IDEA.

One more quick note: the exam may also ask about a passage's THEME, which is similar to but distinct from its topic. While a TOPIC is usually a specific *person*, *place*, *thing*, or *issue*, the theme is an *idea* or *concept* that the author refers back to frequently. Examples of common themes include ideas like the importance of family, the dangers of technology, and the beauty of nature.

There will be many questions on the exam that require you to differentiate between the topic, theme, and main idea of a passage. Let's look at an example:

QUICK REVIEW

Topic: The subject of the passage.

Theme: An idea or concept the author refers to repeatedly.

Main idea: The argument the writer is making about the topic.

Babe Didrikson Zaharias, one of the most decorated female athletes of the twentieth century, is an inspiration for everyone. Born in 1911 in Beaumont, Texas, Zaharias lived in a time when women were considered second-class to men, but she never let that stop her from becoming a champion. Babe was one of seven children in a poor immigrant family, and was competitive from an early age. As a child she excelled at most things she tried, especially sports, which continued into high school and beyond. After high school, Babe played amateur basketball for two years, and soon after began training in track and field. Despite the fact that women were only allowed to enter in three events, Babe represented the United States in the 1932 Los Angeles Olympics, and won two gold medals and one silver for track and field events.

In the early 1930s, Babe began playing golf which earned her a legacy. The first tournament she entered was a men's only tournament; however she did not make the cut to play. Playing golf as an amateur was the only option for a woman at this time, since there was no professional women's league. Babe played as an amateur for a little over a decade, until she turned pro in 1947 for the Ladies Professional Golf Association (LPGA) of which she was a founding member. During her career as a golfer, Babe won eighty-two tournaments, amateur and professional, including the U.S. Women's Open, All-American Open, and British Women's Open Golf Tournament. In 1953, Babe was diagnosed with cancer, but fourteen weeks later, she played in a tournament. That year she won her third U.S. Women's Open. However by 1955, she didn't have the physicality to compete anymore, and she died of the disease in 1956.

The topic of this passage is obviously Babe Zaharias—the whole passage describes events from her life. Determining the main idea, however, requires a little more analysis. The passage describes Babe Zaharias' life, but the main idea of the paragraph is what it says about her life. To figure out the main idea, consider what the writer is saying about Babe Zaharias. The writer is saying that she's someone to admire—that's the main idea and what unites all the information in the paragraph. Lastly, what might the theme of the passage be? The writer refers to several broad concepts, including never giving up and overcoming the odds, both of which could be themes of the passage.

Two major indicators of the main idea of a paragraph or passage follow below:

▶ It is a general idea; it applies to all the more specific ideas in the passage. Every other sentence in a paragraph should be able to relate in some way to the main idea.

▶ It asserts a specific viewpoint that the author supports with facts, opinions, or other details. In other words, the main idea takes a stand.

EXAMPLE

It's easy to puzzle over the landscapes of our solar system's distant planets—how could we ever know what those far-flung places really look like? However, scientists utilize a number of tools to visualize the surfaces of many planets. The topography of Venus, for example, has been explored by several space probes, including the Russian Venera landers and NASA's Magellan orbiter. These craft used imaging and radar to map the surface of the planet, identifying a whole host of features including volcanoes, craters, and a complex system of channels. Mars has likewise been mapped by space probes, including the famous Mars Rovers, which are automated vehicles that actually landed on the planet's surface. These rovers have been used by NASA and other space agencies to study the geology, climate, and possible biology of the planet.

In addition to these long-range probes, NASA has also used its series of orbiting telescopes to study distant planets. These four massively powerful telescopes include the famous Hubble Space Telescope as well as the Compton Gamma Ray Observatory, Chandra X-Ray Observatory, and the Spitzer Space Telescope. These allow scientists to examine planets using not only visible light but also infrared and near-infrared light, ultraviolet light, x-rays and gamma rays.

Powerful telescopes aren't just found in space: NASA makes use of Earth-bound telescopes as well. Scientists at the National Radio Astronomy Observatory in Charlottesville, VA, have spent decades using radio imaging to build an incredibly detailed portrait of Venus' surface. In fact, Earth-bound telescopes offer a distinct advantage over orbiting telescopes because they allow scientists to capture data from a fixed point, which in turn allows them to effectively compare data collected over a long period of time.

1. Which of the following sentences best describes the main idea of the passage?

A) It's impossible to know what the surfaces of other planets are really like.

B) Telescopes are an important tool for scientists studying planets in our solar system.

C) Venus' surface has many of the same features as the Earth's, including volcanoes, craters, and channels.

D) Scientists use a variety of advanced technologies to study the surface of the planets in our solar system.

TOPIC and SUMMARY SENTENCES

The main idea of a paragraph usually appears within the topic sentence. The **TOPIC SENTENCE** introduces the main idea to readers; it indicates not only the topic of a passage, but also the writer's perspective on the topic.

Notice, for example, how the first sentence in the text about Babe Zaharias states the main idea: *Babe Didrikson Zaharias, one of the most decorated female athletes of the twentieth century, is an inspiration for everyone.*

Even though paragraphs generally begin with topic sentences due to their introductory nature, on occasion writers build up to the topic sentence by using supporting details in order to generate interest or build an argument. Be alert for paragraphs when writers do not include a clear topic sentence at all; even without a clear topic sentence, a paragraph will still have a main idea. You may also see a SUMMARY SENTENCE at the end of a passage. As its name suggests, this sentence sums up the passage, often by restating the main idea and the author's key evidence supporting it.

EXAMPLE

The Constitution of the United States establishes a series of limits to rein in centralized power. Separation of powers distributes federal authority among three competing branches: the executive, the legislative, and the judicial. Checks and balances allow the branches to check the usurpation of power by any one branch. States' rights are protected under the Constitution from too much encroachment by the federal government. Enumeration of powers names the specific and few powers the federal government has. These four restrictions have helped sustain the American republic for over two centuries.

2. In the above paragraph, what are the topic and summary sentences?

IMPLIED MAIN IDEA

A paragraph without a clear topic sentence still has a main idea; rather than clearly stated, it is implied. Determining the implied main idea requires some detective work: you will need to look at the author's word choice and tone in addition to the content of the passage to find his or her main idea. Let's look at an example paragraph.

EXAMPLES

One of my summer reading books was *Mockingjay*. Though it's several hundred pages long, I read it in just a few days. I was captivated by the adventures of the main character and the complicated plot of the book. However, I felt like the ending didn't reflect the excitement of the story. Given what a powerful personality the main character has, I felt like the ending didn't do her justice.

3. Even without a clear topic sentence, this paragraph has a main idea. What is the writer's perspective on the book—what is the writer saying about it?

    A) *Mockingjay* is a terrific novel.

    B) *Mockingjay* is disappointing.

    C) *Mockingjay* is full of suspense.

    D) *Mockingjay* is a lousy novel.

Read the following paragraph:

Fortunately, none of Alyssa's coworkers have ever seen inside the large filing drawer in her desk. Disguised by the meticulous neatness of the rest of her workspace, the drawer betrayed no sign of the chaos within. To even open it, she had to struggle for several minutes with the enormous pile of junk jamming the drawer, until it would suddenly give way, and papers, folders, and candy wrappers spilled out onto the floor. It was an organizational nightmare, with torn notes and spreadsheets haphazardly thrown on top of each other and melted candy smeared across pages. She was worried the odor would soon waft to her coworkers' desks, revealing her secret.

4. Which sentence best describes the main idea of the paragraph above?

   A) Alyssa wishes she could move to a new desk.

   B) Alyssa wishes she had her own office.

   C) Alyssa is glad none of her coworkers know about her messy drawer.

   D) Alyssa is sad because she doesn't have any coworkers.

Supporting Details

SUPPORTING DETAILS provide more support for the author's main idea. For instance, in the Babe Zaharias example, the writer makes the general assertion that *Babe Didrikson Zaharias, one of the most decorated female athletes of the twentieth century, is an inspiration for everyone.* The rest of the paragraph provides supporting details with facts showing why she is an inspiration: the names of the challenges she overcame, and the specific years she competed in the Olympics.

DID YOU KNOW?
The SAT questions almost always refer to specific lines in the text, so you don't need to read the entire passage before you start answering the questions.

Be alert for SIGNAL WORDS, which indicate supporting details and so can be helpful in identifying supporting details. Signal words can also help you rule out sentences that are not the main idea or topic sentence: if a sentence begins with one of these phrases, it will likely be too specific to be a main idea.

Questions on the SAT will ask you to find details that support a particular idea and also to explain why a particular detail was included in the passage. In order to answer these questions, you must have a solid understanding of the passage's main idea. With this knowledge, you can determine how a supporting detail fits in with the larger structure of the passage.

EXAMPLES

It's easy to puzzle over the landscapes of our solar system's distant planets—how could we ever know what those far-flung places really look like? However, scientists utilize a number of tools to visualize the surfaces of many planets. The topography of Venus, for example, has been explored by several space probes, including the Russian Venera landers and NASA's Magellan orbiter. These craft used imaging and radar to map the surface of the planet, identifying a whole host of features including volcanoes, craters, and a complex system of channels. Mars has likewise been mapped by space probes, including the famous Mars Rovers, which are automated vehicles that actually landed on the planet's surface. These rovers have been used by NASA and other space agencies to study the geology, climate, and possible biology of the planet.

In addition to these long-range probes, NASA has also used its series of orbiting telescopes to study distant planets. These four massively powerful telescopes include the famous Hubble Space Telescope as well as the Compton Gamma Ray Observatory, Chandra X-Ray Observatory, and the Spitzer Space Telescope. These allow scientists to examine planets using not only visible light but also infrared and near-infrared light, ultraviolet light, x-rays and gamma rays.

Powerful telescopes aren't just found in space: NASA makes use of Earth-bound telescopes as well. Scientists at the National Radio Astronomy Observatory in Charlottesville, VA, have spent decades using radio imaging to build an incredibly detailed portrait of Venus' surface. In fact, Earth-bound telescopes offer a distinct advantage over orbiting telescopes because they allow scientists to capture data from a fixed point, which in turn allows them to effectively compare data collected over a long period of time.

5. Which sentence from the text best develops the idea that scientists make use of many different technologies to study the surfaces of other planets?

A) These rovers have been used by NASA and other space agencies to study the geology, climate, and possible biology of the planet.

B) It's easy to puzzle over the landscapes of our solar system's distant planets—how could we ever know what those far-flung places really look like?

C) In addition these long-range probes, NASA has also used its series of orbiting telescopes to study distant planets.

D) These craft used imaging and radar to map the surface of the planet, identifying a whole host of features including volcanoes, craters, and a complex system of channels.

6. If true, which sentence could be added to the passage above to support the author's argument that scientists use many different technologies to study the surface of planets?

A) Because the Earth's atmosphere blocks x-rays, gamma rays, and infrared radiation, NASA needed to put telescopes in orbit above the atmosphere.

B) In 2015, NASA released a map of Venus which was created by compiling images from orbiting telescopes and long-range space probes.

C) NASA is currently using the Curiosity and Opportunity rovers to look for signs of ancient life on Mars.

D) NASA has spent over $2.5 billion to build, launch, and repair the Hubble Space Telescope.

7. The author likely included the detail that Earth-bound telescopes offer a distinct advantage over orbiting telescopes because they allow scientists to capture data from a fixed point in order to

A) explain why it has taken scientists so long to map the surface of Venus

B) suggest that Earth-bound telescopes are the most important equipment used by NASA scientists

C) prove that orbiting telescopes will soon be replaced by Earth-bound telescopes

D) demonstrate why NASA scientists rely on many different types of scientific equipment

Text Structure

Authors can structure passages in a number of different ways. These distinct organizational patterns, referred to as TEXT STRUCTURE, use the logical relationships between ideas to improve the readability and coherence of a text. The most common ways passages are organized include:

▸ PROBLEM-SOLUTION: The author presents a problem and then discusses a solution.

▸ COMPARISON-CONTRAST: The author presents two situations and then discusses their similarities and differences.

▸ CAUSE-EFFECT: The author presents an action and then discusses the resulting effects.

▸ DESCRIPTIVE: The author describes an idea, object, person, or other item in detail.

EXAMPLE

The issue of public transportation has begun to haunt the fast-growing cities of the southern United States. Unlike their northern counterparts, cities like Atlanta, Dallas, and Houston have long promoted growth out and not up— these are cities full of sprawling suburbs and single-family homes, not densely concentrated skyscrapers and apartments. What to do then, when all those suburbanites need to get into the central business districts for work? For a long time it seemed highways were the twenty-lane wide expanses of concrete that would allow commuters to move from home to work and back again. But these modern miracles have become time-sucking, pollution-spewing nightmares. They may not like it, but it's time for these cities to turn toward public transport like trains and buses if they are to remain livable.

8. The organization of this passage can best be described as:

A) a comparison of two similar ideas

B) a description of a place

C) a discussion of several effects all related to the same cause

D) a discussion of a problem followed by the suggestion of a solution

The Author's Purpose

Whenever an author writes a text, she always has a purpose, whether that's to entertain, inform, explain, or persuade. A short story, for example, is meant to entertain, while an online news article would be designed to inform the public about a current event. Each of these different types of writing has a specific name:

▶ NARRATIVE WRITING tells a story. (novel, short story, play)

▶ EXPOSITORY WRITING informs people. (newspaper and magazine articles)

▶ TECHNICAL WRITING explains something. (product manual, directions)

▶ PERSUASIVE WRITING tries to convince the reader of something. (opinion column on a blog)

On the exam, you may be asked to categorize a passage as one of these types, either by specifically naming it as such or by identifying its general purpose.

DID YOU KNOW?
When reading, pay attention to characters and people, their titles, dates, places, main ideas, quotations, and italics. Don't be afraid to underline or circle important points in the text.

You may also be asked about primary and secondary sources. These terms describe not the writing itself but the author's relationship to what's being written about. A PRIMARY SOURCE is an unaltered piece of writing that was composed during the time when the events being described took place; these texts are often written by the people directly involved. A SECONDARY SOURCE might address the same topic but provide extra commentary or analysis. These texts are written by outside observers and may even be composed after the event. For example, a book written by a political candidate to inform people about his or her stand on an issue is a primary source. An online article written by a journalist analyzing how that position will affect the election is a secondary source; a book by a historian about that election would be a secondary source, too.

EXAMPLE

Elizabeth closed her eyes and braced herself on the armrests that divided her from her fellow passengers. Take-off was always the worst part for her. The revving of the engines, the way her stomach dropped as the plane lurched upward; it made her feel sick. Then, she had to watch the world fade away beneath her, getting smaller and smaller until it was just her and the clouds hurtling through the sky. Sometimes (but only sometimes) it just had to be endured, though. She focused on the thought of her sister's smiling face and Eher new baby nephew as the plane slowly pulled onto the runway.

9. This passage is reflective of which type of writing?
    A) narrative
    B) expository
    C) technical
    D) persuasive

Facts vs. Opinions

On the SAT you might be asked to identify a statement in a passage as either a fact or an opinion, so you'll need to know the difference between the two. A FACT is a statement or thought that can be proven to be true. The statement *Wednesday comes after Tuesday* is a fact—you can point to a calendar to prove it. In contrast, an OPINION is an assumption that is not based in fact and cannot be proven to be true. The assertion that television is more entertaining than feature films is an opinion—people will disagree on this, and there's no reference you can use to prove or disprove it.

DID YOU KNOW?
Keep an eye out for answer choices that may be facts, but which are not stated or discussed in the passage.

EXAMPLES

Exercise is critical for healthy development in children. Today, there is an epidemic of unhealthy children in the United States who will face health problems in adulthood due to poor diet and lack of exercise in childhood. This is a problem for all Americans, especially with the rising cost of health care.

It is vital that school systems and parents encourage their children to engage in a minimum of thirty minutes of cardiovascular exercise each day, mildly increasing their heart rate for a sustained period. This is proven to decrease the likelihood of developmental diabetes, obesity, and a multitude of other health problems. Also, children need a proper diet rich in fruits and vegetables so that they can grow and develop physically, as well as learn healthy eating habits early on.

10. Which of the following is a fact in the passage, not an opinion?
    A) Fruits and vegetables are the best way to help children be healthy.
    B) Children today are lazier than they were in previous generations.
    C) The risk of diabetes in children is reduced by physical activity.
    D) Children should engage in thirty minutes of exercise a day.

Drawing Conclusions

In addition to understanding the main idea and factual content of a passage, you'll also be asked to take your analysis one step further and anticipate what other information could logically be added to the passage. In a non-fiction passage, for example, you might be asked which statement the author of the passage would agree with. In an excerpt from a fictional work, you might be asked to anticipate what a character would do next.

To answer these questions, you must have a solid understanding of the topic, theme, and main idea of the passage; armed with this information, you can figure out which of the answer choices best fits within those criteria (or alternatively, which ones do not). For example, if the author of the passage is advocating for safer working conditions in textile factories, any supporting details that would be added to the passage should support that idea. You might add sentences that contain information about the number of accidents that occur in textile factories or that outline a new plan for fire safety.

EXAMPLES

Today, there is an epidemic of unhealthy children in the United States who will face health problems in adulthood due to poor diet and lack of exercise during their childhoods. This is a problem for all Americans, as adults with chronic health issues are adding to the rising cost of healthcare. A child who grows up living an unhealthy lifestyle is likely to become an adult who does the same.

Because exercise is critical for healthy development in children, it is vital that school systems and parents encourage their children to engage in a minimum of thirty minutes of cardiovascular exercise each day. Even this small amount of exercise has been proven to decrease the likelihood that young people will develop diabetes, obesity, and other health issues as adults. In addition to exercise, children need a proper diet rich in fruits and vegetables so that they can grow and develop physically. Starting a good diet early also teaches children healthy eating habits they will carry into adulthood.

11. The author of this passage would most likely agree with which statement?
    A) Parents are solely responsible for the health of their children.
    B) Children who do not want to exercise should not be made to.
    C) Improved childhood nutrition will help lower the amount Americans spend on healthcare.
    D) It's not important to teach children healthy eating habits because they will learn them as adults.

Elizabeth closed her eyes and braced herself on the armrests that divided her from her fellow passengers. Take-off was always the worst part for her. The revving of the engines, the way her stomach dropped as the plane lurched upward; it made her feel sick. Then, she had to watch the plane lurched upward; it made her feel sick. Then, she had to watch the world fade away beneath her, getting smaller and smaller until it was just her and the clouds hurtling through the sky. Sometimes (but only sometimes) it just had to be endured, though. She focused on the thought of her sister's smiling face and her new baby nephew as the plane slowly pulled onto the runway.

12. Which of the following is Elizabeth least likely to do in the future?
- **A)** Take a flight to her brother's wedding.
- **B)** Apply for a job as a flight attendant.
- **C)** Never board an airplane again.
- **D)** Get sick on an airplane.

Meaning of Words and Phrases

On the Reading section you may be asked to provide definitions or intended meanings for words within passages. You may have never encountered some of these words before the test, but there are tricks you can use to figure out what they mean.

CONTEXT CLUES

A fundamental vocabulary skill is using context to determine the meaning of a word. There are two types of context that can help you understand unfamiliar words: situational context and sentence context. Regardless of which context you encounter, these types of questions are not really testing your knowledge of vocabulary; rather, they test your ability to comprehend the meaning of a word through its usage.

SITUATIONAL CONTEXT helps you determine the meaning of a word through the setting or circumstances in which that word or phrase occurs. Using **SENTENCE CONTEXT** requires analyzing only the sentence in which the new word appears to understand it. To figure out words using sentence context clues, you should first identify the most important words in the sentence.

There are four types of clues that can help you understand the context, and therefore the meaning of a word:

- ▶ **RESTATEMENT CLUES** occur when the definition of the word is clearly stated in the sentence.
- ▶ **POSITIVE/NEGATIVE CLUES** can tell you whether a word has a positive or negative meaning.
- ▶ **CONTRAST CLUES** include the opposite meaning of a word. Words like *but, on the other hand*, and *however* are tip-offs that a sentence contains a contrast clue.
- ▶ **SPECIFIC DETAIL CLUES** provide a precise detail that can help you understand the meaning of the word.

It is important to remember that more than one of these clues can be present in the same sentence. The more there are, the easier it will be to determine the meaning of the word. For example, the following sentence uses both restatement and positive/negative clues: *Janet suddenly found herself destitute, so poor she could barely afford to eat.* The second part of the sentence clearly indicates that destitute is a negative word. It also restates the meaning: very poor.

EXAMPLES

13. I had a hard time reading her <u>illegible</u> handwriting.
    A) neat
    B) unsafe
    C) sloppy
    D) educated

14. The dog was <u>dauntless</u> in the face of danger, braving the fire to save the girl trapped inside the building.
    A) difficult
    B) fearless
    C) imaginative
    D) startled

15. Beth did not spend any time preparing for the test, but Tyrone kept a <u>rigorous</u> study schedule.
    A) strict
    B) loose
    C) boring
    D) strange

ANALYZING WORDS

As you no doubt know, determining the meaning of a word can be more complicated than just looking in a dictionary. A word might have more than one DENOTATION, or definition; which one the author intends can only be judged by examining the surrounding text. For example, the word *quack* can refer to the sound a duck makes, or to a person who publicly pretends to have a qualification which he or she does not actually possess.

A word may also have different CONNOTATIONS, which are the implied meanings and emotions a word evokes in the reader. For example, a cubicle is a simply a walled desk in an office, but for many the word implies a constrictive, uninspiring workplace. Connotations can vary greatly between cultures and even between individuals.

Lastly, authors might make use of FIGURATIVE LANGUAGE, which is the use of a word to imply something other than the word's literal definition. This is often done by comparing two things. If you say *I felt like a butterfly when I got a new haircut*, the listener knows you don't resemble an insect but instead felt beautiful and transformed.

WORD STRUCTURE

Although you are not expected to know every word in the English language for the SAT, you can use deductive reasoning to determine the answer choice that is the best match for the word in question by breaking down unfamiliar vocabulary. Many complex words can be broken down into three main parts:

PREFIX — ROOT — SUFFIX

ROOTS are the building blocks of all words. Every word is either a root itself or has a root. Just as a plant cannot grow without roots, neither can vocabulary, because a word must have a root to give it meaning. The root is what is left when you strip away all the prefixes and suffixes from a word. For example, in the word *unclear*, if you take away the prefix *un-*, you have the root *clear*.

Roots are not always recognizable words; they generally come from Latin or Greek words like *nat*, a Latin root meaning *born*. The word *native*, which describes a person born in a referenced place, comes from this root, as does the word *prenatal*, meaning before birth. It's important to keep in mind, however, that roots do not always match the exact definitions of words, and they can have several different spellings.

Prefixes are syllables added to the beginning of a word, and suffixes are syllables added to the end of the word. Both carry assigned meanings and can be attached to a word to completely change the word's meaning or to enhance the word's original meaning.

Take the word *prefix* itself as an example: *fix* means to place something securely, and *pre-* means before. Therefore, *prefix* means to place something before or in front of. Now let's look at a suffix: in the word *portable*, *port* is a root which means to move or carry. The suffix *-able* means that something is possible. Thus, *portable* describes something that can be moved or carried.

Although you cannot determine the meaning of a word by a prefix or suffix alone, you can use this knowledge to eliminate answer choices; understanding whether the word is positive or negative can give you the partial meaning of the word.

Comparing Passages

In addition to analyzing single passages, the SAT will also require you to compare two passages. Usually these passages will discuss the same topic, and it will be your task to identify the similarities and differences between the authors' main ideas, supporting details, and tones.

EXAMPLES

Read Passages One and Two, and then answer questions 16 and 17.

Passage One

Today, there is an epidemic of unhealthy children in the United States who will face health problems in adulthood due to poor diet and lack of exercise during their childhoods: in 2012, the Centers for Disease Control found that 18 percent of students aged 6-11 were obese. This is a problem for all Americans, as adults with chronic health issues are adding to the rising cost of healthcare. A child who grows up living an unhealthy lifestyle is likely to become an adult who does the same.

Because exercise is critical for healthy development in children, it is vital that school systems and parents encourage their children to engage in a minimum of thirty minutes of cardiovascular exercise each day. Even this small amount of exercise has been proven to decrease the likelihood that young people will develop diabetes, obesity, and other health issues as adults. In addition to exercise, children need a proper diet rich in fruits and vegetables so that they can grow and develop physically. Starting a good diet early also teaches children healthy eating habits they will carry into adulthood.

Passage Two

When was the last time you took a good, hard look at a school lunch? For many adults, it's probably been years—decades even—since they last thought about students' midday meals. If they did stop to ponder, they might picture something reasonably wholesome if not very exciting: a peanut butter and jelly sandwich paired with an apple, or a traditional plate of meat, potatoes and veggies. At worst, they may think, kids are making due with some pizza and a carton of milk.

The truth, though, is that many students aren't even getting the meager nutrients offered up by a simple slice of pizza. Instead, schools are serving up heaping helpings of previously frozen, recently fried delicacies like french fries and chicken nuggets. These high-carb, low-protein options are usually paired with a limp, flavorless, straight-from-the-freezer vegetable that quickly gets tossed in the trash. And that carton of milk? It's probably a sugar-filled chocolate sludge, or it's been replaced with a student's favorite high-calorie soda.

So what, you might ask. Kids like to eat junk food—it's a habit they'll grow out of soon enough. Besides, parents can always pack lunches for students looking for something better. But is that really the lesson we want to be teaching our kids? Many of those children aren't going to grow out of bad habits; they're going to reach adulthood thinking that ketchup is a vegetable. And students in low-income families are particularly impacted by the sad state of school food. These parents rely on schools to provide a warm, nutritious meal because they don't have the time or money to prepare food at home. Do we really want to be punishing these children with soggy meat patties and salt-soaked potato chips?

16. Both authors are arguing for the importance of improving childhood nutrition. How do the authors' strategies differ?

    A) Passage 1 presents several competing viewpoints while Passage 2 offers a single argument.

    B) Passage 1 uses scientific data while Passage 2 uses figurative language.

    C) Passage 1 is descriptive while Passage 2 uses a cause-effect structure.

    D) Passage 1 has a friendly tone while the tone of Passage 2 is angry.

17. Both authors argue that

    A) children should learn healthy eating habits at a young age.

    B) low-income students are disproportionately affected by the low-quality food offered in schools.

    C) teaching children about good nutrition will lower their chances of developing diabetes as adults.

    D) schools should provide children an opportunity to exercise every day.

Test Your Knowledge

After reading the following passages, choose the best answer to each question and fill in the corresponding oval on your answer document. You may refer to the passages as often as necessary.

Passage A is adapted from "How to Tell a Story" from the book How to Tell a Story and Other Essays *by Mark Twain (1835). Passage B is adapted from "Not That It Matters" from the book* The Pleasure of Writing *by A. A. Milne (1920).*

PASSAGE A

I do not claim that I can tell a story as it ought to be told. I only claim to know how a story ought to be told, for I have been almost daily in the company of the most expert story-tellers for many years.

(5) There are several kinds of stories, but only one difficult kind—the humorous. I will talk mainly about that one. The humorous story is American, the comic story is English, the witty story is French. The humorous story depends for its effect upon the manner of the telling; the comic story and the witty story upon the matter.

The humorous story may be spun out to great length, and may wander around as much as it pleases, and arrive nowhere in particular; but the comic and witty stories (10) must be brief and end with a point. The humorous story bubbles gently along, the others burst.

The humorous story is strictly a work of art—high and delicate art—and only an artist can tell it; but no art is necessary in telling the comic and the witty story; anybody can do it. The art of telling a humorous story—understand, I mean by word of mouth, (15) not print—was created in America, and has remained at home.

The humorous story is told gravely; the teller does his best to conceal the fact that he even dimly suspects that there is anything funny about it; but the teller of the comic story tells you beforehand that it is one of the funniest things he has ever heard, then tells it with eager delight, and is the first person to laugh when he gets through. And (20) sometimes, if he has had good success, he is so glad and happy that he will repeat the "nub" of it and glance around from face to face, collecting applause, and then repeat it again. It is a pathetic thing to see.

Very often, of course, the rambling and disjointed humorous story finishes with a nub, point, snapper, or whatever you like to call it. Then the listener must be alert, for (25) in many cases the teller will divert attention from that nub by dropping it in a carefully casual and indifferent way, with the pretence that he does not know it is a nub.

Artemus Ward used that trick a good deal; then when the belated audience presently caught the joke he would look up with innocent surprise, as if wondering what they

had found to laugh at. Dan Setchell used it before him, Nye and Riley and others use
(30) it today.

But the teller of the comic story does not slur the nub; he shouts it at you—every
time. And when he prints it, in England, France, Germany, and Italy, he italicizes it,
puts some whooping exclamation-points after it, and sometimes explains it in a paren-
thesis. All of which is very depressing, and makes one want to renounce joking and
(35) lead a better life.

Passage B

Sometimes when the printer is waiting for an article which really should have been sent
to him the day before, I sit at my desk and wonder if there is any possible subject in the
whole world upon which I can possibly find anything to say. On one such occasion I
left it to Fate, which decided, by means of a dictionary opened at random, that I should
(40) deliver myself of a few thoughts about goldfish. (You will find this article later on in
the book.) But to-day I do not need to bother about a subject. To-day I am without a
care. Nothing less has happened than that I have a new nib in my pen.

In the ordinary way, when Shakespeare writes a tragedy, or Mr. Blank gives you
one of his charming little essays, a certain amount of thought goes on before pen is put
(45) to paper. One cannot write "Scene I. An Open Place. Thunder and Lightning. Enter
Three Witches," or "As I look up from my window, the nodding daffodils beckon to
me to take the morning," one cannot give of one's best in this way on the spur of the
moment. At least, others cannot. But when I have a new nib in my pen, then I can go
straight from my breakfast to the blotting-paper, and a new sheet of foolscap fills itself
(50) magically with a stream of blue-black words. When poets and idiots talk of the pleasure
of writing, they mean the pleasure of giving a piece of their minds to the public; with
an old nib a tedious business. They do not mean (as I do) the pleasure of the artist in
seeing beautifully shaped "k's" and sinuous "s's" grow beneath his steel. Anybody else
writing this article might wonder "Will my readers like it?" I only tell myself "How
(55) the compositors will love it!"

Questions 1 – 3 refer to Passage A.

1. What organizational method best describes how the author chooses to
explain to the audience his ideas about humorous stories?

A) The author describes the main features of a humorous story in order of
importance in order to define it.

B) The author describes the differences between a humorous story and a
comic or witty story in order to clearly define a humorous story.

C) The author gives an example of a good topic for a humorous story and
describes how it should then be told.

D) The author gives examples of famous tellers of humorous stories in order
to explain how they tell one.

2. It is clear from the passage that the author would agree with which of the following statements?

    A) It is much more challenging to choose a good topic for a witty or comic story than to choose one for a humorous story.

    B) Humorous stories are common and easy to tell—one must simply find an appropriate topic.

    C) One who can tell a humorous story well deserves the respect and appreciation of other storytellers.

    D) The best humorous stories end with a nub because they combine the best components of both kinds of stories.

3. The author suggests that those who tell humorous stories are more skilled, while anyone at all can tell a comic story because:

    A) a humorous story depends in part upon the acting and speaking ability of the teller, while someone telling a comic story only needs to memorize the punch line.

    B) the storyteller has to make up a humorous story, but there are already many good comic stories in existence.

    C) only the storyteller thinks a comic or witty story is funny, which makes him or her seem pathetic; everyone laughs at a humorous story.

    D) a storyteller can laugh at his or her own humorous story without seeming pathetic, but this is not the case for a comic or witty story.

Questions 4 – 6 refer to Passage B.

4. When the author writes *nothing less has happened* in line 42 to describe having a new nib in his pen, he means to convey that:

    A) a new nib in his pen is not very meaningful.

    B) a new nib in his pen is a rare and exciting event.

    C) a new nib being inserted in his pen is the last action he took.

    D) a new nib in his pen will make his writing better.

5. Passage B indicates that compared to other writers, he is:

    A) similar, because he takes great pleasure in speaking his mind to an audience

    B) similar, because he sometimes ignores publication deadlines

    C) dissimilar, because he can write on any subject when he has to

    D) dissimilar, because he takes pleasure in forming the letters over what they say

6. Overall, which of the following best describes how the author feels about writing?

   A) It is a delicate activity subject to mood and environment.

   B) It is a scientific endeavor best approached methodically.

   C) It is a difficult and unpleasant task for many people.

   D) It is a hobby anyone can do successfully with the right equipment or supplies.

Questions 7 – 10 refer to both passages.

7. Which of the following best describes a topic addressed by both passages?

   A) the difficulty of the creative act

   B) the merits of a humorous story

   C) the difficulties of telling a story

   D) the skills of some famous writers

8. Which of the following is the best comparison of the tones in each passage?

   A) Passage A is respectful and admiring, and Passage B is faintly sarcastic.

   B) Passage A is authoritative and direct, and Passage B is whimsical and amused.

   C) Both passages begin with uncertainty but end with a feeling of satisfied discovery.

   D) Both passages begin with contempt for other authors but end with a sense of grudging respect for them.

9. Compared to the author of Passage B, the author of Passage A uses more:

   A) analysis of specific examples of writing

   B) descriptions of writing

   C) comparisons between types of writing

   D) references to specific pieces of writing

10. Which of the following statements about writing and storytelling would both authors be likely to agree with?:

   A) A good story should remain focused on a very specific topic or idea throughout.

   B) Writing a good story and telling a good story are similarly easy to accomplish.

   C) The best authors are those who plan their stories well in advance.

   D) Writing and telling stories are abilities that require both skill and intuition.

Answer Key
EXAMPLES

1. A) can be eliminated because it directly contradicts the rest of the passage, which goes into detail about how scientists have learned about the surfaces of other planets. Answers B) and C) can also be eliminated because they offer only specific details from the passage; while both choices contain details from the passage, neither is general enough to encompass the passage as a whole. **Only answer D) provides an assertion that is both supported by the passage's content and general enough to cover the entire passage.**

2. **The topic sentence is the first sentence in the paragraph.** It introduces the topic of discussion, in this case the constitutional limits on centralized power. The summary sentence is the last sentence in the paragraph. It sums up the information that was just presented: here, that constitutional limits have helped sustain the United States of America for over two hundred years.

3. B) is correct: the novel is disappointing. The process of elimination will reveal the correct answer if that is not immediately clear. While the paragraph begins with positive commentary on the book—*I was captivated by the adventures of the main character and the complicated plot of the book*—this positive idea is followed by the contradictory transition word however. A) cannot be the correct answer because the author concludes that the novel was poor. Likewise, D) cannot be correct because it does not encompass all the ideas in the paragraph; despite the negative conclusion, the author enjoyed most of the book. The main idea should be able to encompass all of the thoughts in a paragraph; choice D) does not apply to the beginning of this paragraph. Finally, choice C) is too specific; it could only apply to the brief description of the plot and adventures of the main character. That leaves choice B) as the best option. The author initially enjoyed the book, but was disappointed by the ending, which seemed unworthy of the exciting plot and character.

4. Clearly, Alyssa has a messy drawer, and **C) is the right answer**. The paragraph begins by indicating her gratitude that her coworkers do not know about her drawer (*Fortunately, none of Alyssa's coworkers have ever seen inside the large filing drawer in her desk*). Plus, notice how the drawer is described: *it was an organizational nightmare*, and it apparently doesn't even function properly: *to even open the drawer, she had to struggle for several minutes...* The writer reveals that it even has an odor, with old candy inside.

    Alyssa is clearly ashamed of her drawer and fearful of being judged by her coworkers about it.

5. You're looking for details from the passage that supports the main idea— scientists make use of many different technologies to study the surfaces of other planets. Answer A) includes a specific detail about rovers, but does not offer any details that support the idea of multiple technologies being used. Similarly, answer D) provides another specific detail about space probes.

Answer B) doesn't provide any supporting details; it simply introduces the topic of the passage. **Only answer C) provides a detail that directly supports the author's assertion that scientists use multiple technologies to study the planets.**

6. You can eliminate answers C) and D) because they don't address the topic of studying the surface of planets. Answer A) can also be eliminated because it only addresses a single technology. **Only choice B) would add support to the author's claim about the importance of using multiple technologies.**

7. **Only answer D) relates directly to the author's main argument.** The author doesn't mention how long it has taken to map the surface of Venus (answer A), nor does he say that one technology is more important than the others (answer B). And while this detail does highlight the advantages of using Earth-bound telescopes, the author's argument is that many technologies are being used at the same time, so there's no reason to think that orbiting telescopes will be replaced (answer C).

8. You can exclude answer choice C) because the author provides no root cause or a list of effects. From there this question gets tricky, because the passage contains structures similar to those described above. For example, it compares two things (cities in the North and South) and describes a place (a sprawling city). However, if you look at the overall organization of the passage, you can see that it starts by presenting a problem (transportation) and then presents a solution (trains and buses), making **answer D) the only choice that encompasses the entire passage**.

9. The passage is telling a story—we meet Elizabeth and learn about her fear of flying—so **it's a narrative text, answer choice A)**. There is no factual information presented or explained, nor is the author trying to persuade the reader of anything.

10. Choice B) can be discarded immediately because it is negative (recall that particularly negative answer statements are generally wrong) and is not discussed anywhere in the passage. Answers A) and D) are both opinions—the author is promoting exercise, fruits, and vegetables as a way to make children healthy. (Notice that these incorrect answers contain words that hint at being an opinion such as best, should, or other comparisons.) **Answer B), on the other hand, is a simple fact stated by the author**; it appears in the passage with the word *proven*, indicating that you don't just need to take the author's word for it.

11. **The author would most likely support answer C)**: he mentions in the first paragraph that poor diets are adding to the rising cost of healthcare. The main idea of the passage is that nutrition and exercise are important for children, so answer B) doesn't make sense—the author would likely support measures to encourage children to exercise. Answers A) and D) can also be eliminated because they are directly contradicted in the text. The author specifically mentions the role of school systems, so he doesn't believe parents are solely

responsible for their children's health. He also specifically states that children who grow up with unhealthy eating habits will become adults with unhealthy eating habits, which contradicts D).

12. It's clear from the passage that Elizabeth hates flying, but it willing to endure it for the sake of visiting her family. Thus, it seems likely that she would be willing to get on a plane for her brother's wedding, making A) and C) incorrect answers. The passage also explicitly tells us that she feels sick on planes, so D) is likely to happen. We can infer, though, that she would not enjoy being on an airplane for work, so she's very unlikely to apply for a job as a flight attendant, which is **choice B)**.

13. Already, you know that this sentence is discussing something that is hard to read. Look at the word that illegible is describing: handwriting. Based on context clues, you can tell that illegible means that her handwriting is hard to read.

    Next, look at the answer choices. Choice A), *neat*, is obviously a wrong answer because neat handwriting would not be difficult to read. Choices B) and D), *unsafe* and *educated*, don't make sense. Therefore, **choice C), *sloppy*, is the best answer**.

14. **Demonstrating bravery in the face of danger would be B), fearless.** In this case, the restatement clue (*braving the fire*) tells you exactly what the word means.

15. In this case, the contrast word *but* tells us that Tyrone studied in a different way than Beth, which means it's a contrast clue. If Beth did not study hard, then Tyrone did. **The best answer, therefore, is choice A).**

16. The first author uses scientific facts (*the Centers for Disease Control found...* and *Even this small amount of exercise has been proven...*) to back up his argument, while the second uses figurative language (the *ironic delicacies* and the metaphor *sugar-filled chocolate sludge*), so **the correct answer is B)**. Answer A) is incorrect because the first author does not present any opposing viewpoints. Answer C) is incorrect because Passage 2 does not have a cause-effect structure. And while the author of the second passage could be described as angry, the first author is not particularly friendly, so you can eliminate answer D) as well.

17. **Both authors argue children should learn healthy eating habits at a young age (answer A).** The author of Passage 1 states that a child who grows up living an unhealthy lifestyle is likely to become an adult who does the same, and the author of Passage 2 states that many of those children aren't going to grow out of bad habits—both of these sentences argue that it's necessary to teach children about nutrition early in life. Answers C) and D) are mentioned only by the author of Passage 1, and answer B) is only discussed in Passage 2.

TEST YOUR KNOWLEDGE

1. **B) is correct.**

2. **C) is correct.**

3. **A) is correct.**

4. **B) is correct.**

5. **D) is correct.**

6. **A) is correct.**

7. **A) is correct.**

8. **B) is correct.**

9. **C) is correct.**

10. **D) is correct.**

CHAPTER TWO
Writing and Language

Parts of Speech

The first step in getting ready for this section of the test is to review parts of speech and the rules that accompany them. The good news is that you have been using these rules since you first began to speak; even if you don't know a lot of the technical terms, many of these rules may be familiar to you.

NOUNS and PRONOUNS

NOUNS are people, places, or things. For example, in the sentence *The hospital was very clean*, the noun is *hospital*; it is a place. Pronouns replace nouns and make sentences sound less repetitive. Take the sentence *Sam stayed home from school because Sam was not feeling well*. The word *Sam* appears twice in the same sentence. To avoid repetition and improve the sentence, use a pronoun instead: *Sam stayed at home because he did not feel well*.

Because pronouns take the place of nouns, they need to agree both in number and gender with the noun they replace. So, a plural noun needs a plural pronoun, and a feminine noun needs a feminine pronoun. In the first sentence of this paragraph, for example, the plural pronoun *they* replaced the plural noun *pronouns*. There will usually be several questions on the English section of the SAT that cover pronoun agreement, so it's good to get comfortable spotting pronouns.

QUICK REVIEW
SINGULAR PRONOUNS
▶ I, me, mine, my
▶ you, your, yours
▶ he, him, his
▶ she, her, hers
▶ it, its

PLURAL PRONOUNS
▶ we, us, our, ours
▶ they, them, their, theirs

EXAMPLES

1. Which sentence below is correct?
   A) If a student forgets their homework, it is considered incomplete.
   B) If a student forgets his or her homework, it is considered incomplete.

2. Which sentence below is correct?
   A) Everybody will receive their paychecks promptly.
   B) Everybody will receive his or her paycheck promptly.

3. Which sentence below is correct?
   A) When a nurse begins work at a hospital, you should wash your hands.
   B) When a nurse begins work at a hospital, he or she should wash his or her hands.

4. Which sentence below is correct?
   A) After the teacher spoke to the student, she realized her mistake.
   B) After Mr. White spoke to his student, she realized her mistake. (she and her referring to student)
   C) After speaking to the student, the teacher realized her own mistake. (her referring to teacher)

VERBS

A **VERB** is the action of a sentence: verbs *do* things. A verb must be conjugated to match the context of the sentence; this can sometimes be tricky because English has many irregular verbs. For example, *run* is an action verb in the present tense that becomes *ran* in the past tense; the linking verb *is* (which describes a state of being) becomes *was* in the past tense.

Table 2.1. Conjugation of the Verb *To Be*			
	PAST	PRESENT	FUTURE
singular	was	is	will be
plural	were	are	will be

QUICK REVIEW
Think of the subject and the verb as sharing a single *s*. If the noun ends with an *s*, the verb shouldn't and vice versa.

Verb tense must make sense in the context of the sentence. For example, the sentence *I was baking cookies and eat some dough* probably sounds strange. That's because the two verbs *was baking* and *eat* are in different tenses. *Was baking* occurred in the past; *eat*, on the other hand, occurs in the present. To correct this error, conjugate *eat* in the past tense: *I was baking cookies and ate some dough.*

Like pronouns, verbs must agree in number with the noun they refer back to. In the example above, the verb *was* refers back to the singular *I*. If the subject of the sentence was plural, it would need to be modified to read *They were baking cookies and ate some dough*. Note that the verb *ate* does not change form; this is common for verbs in the past tense.

QUICK REVIEW

If the subject is separated from the verb, cross out the phrases between them to make conjugation easier.

EXAMPLES

5. Which sentence below is correct?

   A) The cat chase the ball while the dogs runs in the yard.

   B) The cat chases the ball while the dogs run in the yard.

6. Which sentence below is correct?

   A) The cars that had been recalled by the manufacturer was returned within a few months.

   B) The cars that had been recalled by the manufacturer were returned within a few months.

7. Which sentence below is correct?

   A) The deer hid in the trees.

   B) The deer are not all the same size.

8. Which sentence below is correct?

   A) The doctor and nurse work in the hospital.

   B) Neither the nurse nor her boss was scheduled to take a vacation.

   C) Either the patient or her parents complete her discharge paperwork.

9. Which sentence below is correct?

   A) Because it will rain during the party last night, we had to move the tables inside.

   B) Because it rained during the party last night, we had to move the tables inside.

ADJECTIVES and ADVERBS

ADJECTIVES are words that describe a noun. Take the sentence *The boy hit the ball*. If you want to know more about the noun *ball*, then you could use an adjective to describe him: *The boy hit the red ball*. An adjective simply provides more information about a noun in a sentence.

Like adjectives, **ADVERBS** provide more information about a part of a sentence. Adverbs can describe verbs, adjectives, and even other adverbs. For example, in the sentence

Writing and Language 29

The doctor had recently hired a new employee, the adverb *recently* tells us more about how the action *hired* took place. Often, but not always, adverbs end in *–ly*. Remember that adverbs can never describe nouns—only adjectives can.

Adjectives, adverbs, and *modifying phrases* (groups of words that together modify another word) should always be placed as close as possible to the word they modify. Separating words from their modifiers can result in incorrect or confusing sentences.

EXAMPLES

10. Which sentence below is correct?
    A) Running through the hall, the bell rang and the student knew she was late.
    B) Running through the hall, the student heard the bell ring and knew she was late.

11. Which sentence below is correct?
    A) The terrifyingly lion's loud roar scared the zoo's visitors.
    B) The lion's terrifyingly loud roar scared the zoo's visitors.

OTHER PARTS of SPEECH

PREPOSITIONS generally help describe relationships in space and time; they may express the location of a noun or pronoun in relation to other words and phrases in a sentence.

For example, in the sentence *The nurse parked her car in a parking garage*, the preposition *in* describes the position of the car in relation to the garage. The noun that follows the preposition is called its *object*. In the example above, the object of the preposition *in* is the noun *parking garage*.

DID YOU KNOW?
Just a few other prepositions include *after, between, by, during, of, on, to,* and *with*.

CONJUNCTIONS connect words, phrases, and clauses. The conjunctions summarized in the acronym FANBOYS—for, and, nor, but, or, yet, so—are called **COORDINATING CONJUNCTIONS** and are used to join independent clauses. For example, in the sentence *The nurse prepared the patient for surgery, and the doctor performed the surgery*, the conjunction *and* joins the two independent clauses together. **SUBORDINATING CONJUNCTIONS**, like *although, because,* and *if,* join together an independent and dependent clause. In the sentence *She had to ride the subway because her car was broken*, the conjunction *because* joins together the two clauses. (Independent and dependent clauses are covered in more detail below.)

QUICK REVIEW
See *Phrases and Clauses* below for more on independent and dependent clauses.

INTERJECTIONS, like *wow* and *hey*, express emotion and are most commonly used in conversation and casual writing. They are often followed by *exclamation points*.

Constructing Sentences
PHRASES and CLAUSES

A **PHRASE** is a group of words acting together that contain either a subject or verb, but not both. Phrases can be constructed from several different parts of speech. For example, a prepositional phrase includes a preposition and the object of that preposition (e.g., *under the table*), and a verb phrase includes the main verb and any helping verbs (e.g., *had been running*). Phrases cannot stand alone as sentences.

A **CLAUSE** is a group of words that contains both a subject and a verb. There are two types of clauses: **INDEPENDENT CLAUSES** can stand alone as sentences, and **DEPENDENT CLAUSES** cannot stand alone. Again, dependent clauses are recognizable as they begin with subordinating conjunctions.

EXAMPLES

12. Classify each of the following as a phrase, independent clause, or dependent clause:

1) I have always wanted to drive a bright red sports car

2) under the bright sky filled with stars

3) because my sister is running late

TYPES of SENTENCES

A sentence can be classified as simple, compound, complex, or compound-complex based on the type and number of clauses it has.

Table 2.2. Sentence Classification

SENTENCE TYPE	NUMBER OF INDEPENDENT CLAUSES	NUMBER OF DEPENDENT CLAUSES
simple	1	0
compound	2+	0
complex	1	1+
compound-complex	2+	1+

A **SIMPLE SENTENCE** consists of only one independent clause. Because there are no dependent clauses in a simple sentence, it can be as short as two words, a subject and a verb (e.g., *I ran.*). However, a simple sentence may also contain prepositions, adjectives, and adverbs. Even though these additions can extend the length of a simple sentence, it is still considered a simple sentence as long as it doesn't contain any dependent clauses.

COMPOUND SENTENCES have two or more independent clauses and no dependent clauses. Usually a comma and a coordinating conjunction (*for, and, nor, but, or, yet,* and *so*) join the independent clauses, though semicolons can be used as well. For example, the sentence *My computer broke, so I took it to be repaired* is compound.

DID YOU KNOW?
Joining two independent clauses with only a comma and no coordinating conjunction is a punctuation error called a comma splice—be on the lookout for these.

COMPLEX SENTENCES have one independent clause and at least one dependent clause. In the complex sentence *If you lie down with dogs, you'll wake up with fleas*, the first clause is dependent (because of the subordinating conjunction *if*), and the second is independent.

COMPOUND-COMPLEX SENTENCES have two or more independent clauses and at least one dependent clause. For example, the sentence *City traffic frustrates David because the streets are congested, so he is seeking an alternate route home*, is compound-complex. *City traffic frustrates David* is an independent clause, as is *he is seeking an alternate route home*; however the subordinating conjunction *because* indicates that *because the streets are so congested* is a dependent clause.

EXAMPLES

13. Classify the following sentence: *San Francisco is one of my favorite places in the United States.*
    A) A simple sentence
    B) A compound sentence
    C) A complex sentence
    D) A compound-complex sentence

14. Classify the following sentence: *I love listening to the radio in the car because I enjoy loud music on the open road.*
    A) A simple sentence
    B) A compound sentence
    C) A complex sentence
    D) A compound-complex sentence

15. Classify the following sentence: *I wanted to get a dog, but I got a fish because my roommate is allergic to pet dander.*
    A) A simple sentence
    B) A compound sentence
    C) A complex sentence
    D) A compound-complex sentence

16. Classify the following sentence: *The game was cancelled, but we will still practice on Saturday.*

   A) A simple sentence

   B) A compound sentence

   C) A complex sentence

   D) A compound-complex sentence

CLAUSE PLACEMENT

In addition to the classifications above, sentences can also be defined by the location of the main clause. In a periodic sentence, the main idea of the sentence is held until the end. In a cumulative sentence, the independent clause comes first, and any modifying words or clauses follow it. (Note that this type of classification—periodic or cumulative—is not used in place of the simple, compound, complex, or compound-complex classifications. A sentence can be both cumulative and complex, for example.)

EXAMPLES

17. Classify the following sentence: *The GED, the TASC, the SAT, the ACT—this dizzying array of exams proved no match for the determined students.*

   A) A cumulative sentence

   B) A periodic sentence

18. Classify the following sentence: *Jessica was well-prepared for the test, for she had studied for weeks, taken practice exams, and reviewed the material with other students.*

   A) A cumulative sentence

   B) A periodic sentence

Punctuation

The basic rules for using the major punctuation marks are given in Table 2.3.

Table 2.3. Basic Punctuation Rules		
PUNCTUATION	PURPOSE	EXAMPLE
period	ending sentences	Periods go at the end of complete sentences.
question mark	ending questions	What's the best way to end a sentence?

Table 2.3. Basic Punctuation Rules (continued)

PUNCTUATION	PURPOSE	EXAMPLE
exclamation point	indicating interjections or commands; ending sentences that show extreme emotion	Help! I'll never understand how to use punctuation!
comma	joining two independent clauses (always with a coordinating conjunction)	Commas can be used to join independent clauses, but they must always be followed by a coordinating conjunction in order to avoid a comma splice.
	setting apart introductory and nonessential words and phrases	Commas, when used properly, set apart extra information in a sentence.
	separating three or more items in a list	My favorite punctuation marks include the colon, semicolon, and period.
semicolon	joining together two independent clauses (never with a conjunction)	I love semicolons; they make sentences so concise!
colon	introducing a list, explanation, or definition	When I see a colon I know what to expect: more information.
apostrophe	form contractions	It's amazing how many people can't use apostrophes correctly.
	show possession	The students' grammar books are out of date, but the school's principal cannot order new ones yet.
quotation marks	indicate a direct quote	I said to her, "Tell me more about parentheses."

EXAMPLES

19. Which sentence below is correct?
    A) Her roommate asked her to pick up milk, and a watermelon from the grocery store.
    B) Her roommate asked her to pick up milk and a watermelon from the grocery store.

20. Which sentence below is correct?
    A) The softball coach—who had been in the job for only a year, quit unexpectedly on Friday.
    B) The softball coach—who had been in the job for only a year—quit unexpectedly on Friday.
    C) The softball coach, who had been in the job for only a year, quit unexpectedly on Friday

Point of View

A sentence's **POINT OF VIEW** is the perspective from which it is written. Point of view is described as either first, second, or third person.

Table 2.4. Point of View

PERSON	PRONOUNS	WHO'S ACTING?	EXAMPLE
first	I, we	the writer	I take my time when shopping for shoes.
second	you	the reader	You prefer to shop online.
third	he, she, it, they	the subject	She buys shoes from her cousin's store.

First person perspective appears when the writer's personal experiences, feelings, and opinions are an important element of the text. Second person perspective is used when the author directly addresses the reader. Third person perspective is most common in formal and academic writing; it creates distance between the writer and the reader. A sentence's point of view must remain consistent.

EXAMPLES

22. Which sentence below is correct?

    A) If someone wants to be a professional athlete, you have to practice often.

    B) If you want to be a professional athlete, you have to practice often.

    C) If someone wants to be a professional athlete, he or she has to practice often.

Active and Passive Voice

Sentences can be written in active voice or passive voice. **ACTIVE VOICE** means that the subjects of the sentences are performing the action of the sentence. In a sentence written in **PASSIVE VOICE**, the subjects are being acted on. The sentence *Justin wrecked my car* is in the active voice because the subject (*Justin*) is doing the action (*wrecked*). The sentence can be rewritten in passive voice by using a to be verb: *My car was wrecked by Justin.* Now the subject of the sentence (*car*) is being acted on. It's also possible to write the sentence so that the person performing the action is not identified: *My car was wrecked.*

Generally, good writing will avoid using passive voice. However, when it is unclear who or what performed the action of the sentence, passive voice may be the only option.

EXAMPLES

23. Rewrite the following sentence in active voice: *I was hit with a stick by my brother.*

24. Rewrite the following sentence in passive voice: *My roommate made coffee this morning.*

Transitions

TRANSITIONS connect two ideas and also explain the logical relationship between them. For example, the transition *because* tells you that two things have a cause and effect relationship, while the transitional phrase *on the other hand* introduces a contradictory idea. On the SAT English section you may be asked to identify the best transition for a particular sentence, and you will definitely need to make good use of transitions in your essay.

DID YOU KNOW?
Don't be afraid to choose "No Change"—it will be the correct choice around a quarter of the time!

Table 2.5. Common Transitions	
CAUSE AND EFFECT	AS A RESULT, BECAUSE, CONSEQUENTLY, DUE TO, IF/THEN, SO, THEREFORE, THUS
Similarity	also, likewise, similar, between
Contrast	but, however, in contrast, on the other hand, nevertheless, on the contrary, yet
Concluding	briefly, finally, in conclusion, in summary, to conclude
Addition	additionally, also, as well, further, furthermore, in addition, moreover
Examples	in other words, for example, for instance, to illustrate
Time	after, before, currently, later, recently, since, subsequently, then, while

EXAMPLES

Choose the transition that would best fit in the blank.

25. Clara's car breaks down frequently. _____, she decided to buy a new one.

    A) however

    B) for example

    C) while

    D) therefore

26. Chad scored more points than any other player on his team. _____, he is often late to practice, so his coach won't let him play in the game Saturday.

    A) however

    B) for example

    C) while

    D) therefore

27. Miguel will often eat his lunch outside. _____, on Wednesday he took his sandwich to the park across from his office.

    A) however

    B) for example

    C) while

    D) therefore

28. Alex set the table _____ the lasagna finished baking in the oven.

    A) however

    B) for example

    C) while

    D) therefore

Wordiness and Redundancy

Sometimes sentences can be grammatically correct but still be confusing or poorly written. Often this problem arises when sentences are wordy or contain redundant phrasing (i.e., when several words with similar meanings are used). Often such phrases are used to make the writing seem more serious or academic when actually they can confuse the reader. On the test, you might be asked to clarify or even remove such phrases.

Some examples of excessive wordiness and redundancy include:

▶ I'll meet you in the *place where I parked my car.* → I'll meet you in the *parking lot.*

▶ *The point I am trying to make is that* the study was flawed. → The study was flawed.

▶ A memo was sent out *concerning the matter of* dishes left in the sink. → A memo was sent out *about* dishes left in the sink.

▶ The email was *brief and to the point.* → The email was *terse.*

▶ I don't think I'll ever *understand or comprehend* Italian operas. → I don't think I'll ever *understand* Italian operas.

EXAMPLES

Rewrite each of the following sentences to eliminate wordiness and redundancy.

29. The game was canceled due to the fact that a bad storm was predicted.

30. The possibility exists that we will have a party for my mother's birthday.

31. With the exception of our new puppy, all of our dogs have received their vaccinations.

32. We threw away the broken microwave that didn't work.

33. It was an unexpected surprise when we won the raffle.

Test Your Knowledge

In the following passages, there are numbered and underlined words and phrases that correspond with the questions in the right-hand column. You are to choose the answer that best completes the statement grammatically, stylistically, and/or logically. If you think the original version is best, select "NO CHANGE."

THE BRAT PACK

Anyone who has been given a nickname knows that these (1)informal labels can sometimes be difficult to shake. In the 1980s, one group of young actors earned a group nickname—the Brat Pack—that would follow them for decades. While some members of the Brat Pack still went on to have successful

(2)careers; others struggled to make their own names stand out against the backdrop of the group.

The members of the Brat Pack earned their fame by appearing together in a series of films made for teen and young adult audiences. (3)Though the first one of these

movies (4)were made in the early 1980s, the Brat Pack label did not appear until 1985, when New York magazine writer David Blum wrote an article about his experience socializing with some of the group members. The article (5)is portraying these young actors as immature, unprofessional, and spoiled, and though Blum's experience with them was limited to one night with just three individuals, his label quickly caught on and tarnished the reputations of many of the other young actors who worked

1. Which of the following options is the LEAST appropriate alternative to the underlined portion?
   A) casual designations
   B) unofficial epithets
   C) improper titles
   D) unconventional tags

2. A) NO CHANGE
   B) careers, others
   C) careers, but others
   D) careers. Others

3. A) NO CHANGE
   B) The first of
   C) Because the first of
   D) Consequently, the first of

4. A) NO CHANGE
   B) was
   C) is
   D) are

5. A) NO CHANGE
   B) would portray
   C) was portraying
   D) portrayed

alongside the three. Many of these individuals struggled professionally as a result of the negative label, and most of them denied being a part of any such group.

Today, despite the initial repercussions of the unfortunate nickname, the Brat Pack label is still in use, largely because of the (6)ongoing and perpetual relevance and significance of the Brat Pack films. Most of these films are coming-of-age stories, in which one or more of the characters gains experience or learns an important lesson about adult life.

(7)For example, in the most famous of these films, *The Breakfast Club*, the five main characters,

6. **A)** NO CHANGE
   B) perpetually ongoing
   C) never-ending, perpetual
   D) ongoing

7. At this point in the paragraph, the writer is considering adding the following statement: *In literary criticism, novels that center on coming-of-age stories are referred to as Bildungsroman.* Should this addition be made?
   A) Yes; it provides more information about the types of movies the Brat Pack made.
   B) Yes; it helps the reader to understand the literary trend of coming-of-age stories.
   C) No; it distracts from the main idea of the passage.
   D) No; the Brat Pack did not write novels.

(8)whom are all from different social circles at one high school, learn to look past labels and appearances and find that they have more in common than they ever imagined.

8. **A)** NO CHANGE
   B) who
   C) which
   D) and

Because of the talent and the relatability of the Brat Pack members, (9)these characters and their stories continue to appeal to young people and influence popular culture in the new millennium.

(10)Thus, the Brat Pack nickname has been freed of its negative connotations by the actors who once despised and wore the label.

9. Given that all of the following options are true, which one most effectively supports the claim made in the first sentence of the previous paragraph?
   A) NO CHANGE
   B) These movies were hugely successful in appealing to all age groups.
   C) These movies drew in enormous box-office profits.
   D) These movies propelled a few of their stars into hugely successful careers.

10. A) NO CHANGE
    B) Thus, the Brat Pack label that was worn by the actors has been freed of the negative connotations it had, making it less despised.
    C) Thus, the label that was once despised by the actors, the Brat Pack, has been altogether freed of its negative connotations.
    D) Thus, the Brat Pack nickname, which was once so despised by the actors who wore the label, has been altogether freed of its negative connotations.

Answer Key
EXAMPLES

1. **B) is correct.** *Student* is a singular noun, but *their* is a plural pronoun, making the first sentence grammatically incorrect. To correct it, replace *their* with the singular pronoun *his* or *her*.

2. **B) is correct.** *Everybody* is a singular noun, but *their* is a plural pronoun; the first sentence is grammatically incorrect. To correct it, replace *their* with the singular pronoun *his* or *her*.

3. **B) is correct.** This sentence begins in third-person perspective and finishes in second-person perspective. To correct it, ensure the sentence finishes with third-person perspective.

4. **B) and C) are correct.** This sentence refers to a teacher and a student. But to whom does *she* refer, the teacher or the student? To improve clarity, use specific names or state more clearly who spotted the mistake.

5. **B) is correct.** *Cat* is singular, so it takes a singular verb (which confusingly ends with an s); *dogs* is plural, so it needs a plural verb.

6. **B) is correct.** Sometimes the subject and verb are separated by clauses or phrases. Here, the subject *cars* is separated from the verb phrase *were returned*, making it more difficult to conjugate the verb correctly; this results in a number error.

7. **A) and B) are correct.** The subject of these sentences is a collective noun, which describes a group of people or things. This noun can be singular if it is referring to the group as a whole or plural if it refers to each item in the group as a separate entity.

8. **A) , B), and C are correct.** When the subject contains two or more nouns connected by *and*, that subject is plural and requires a plural verb. Singular subjects joined by *or, either/or, neither/nor*, or *not only/but also* remain singular; when these words join plural and singular subjects, the verb should match the closest subject.

9. **B) is correct.** All the verb tenses in a sentence need to agree both with each other and with the other information in the sentence. In the first sentence above, the tense doesn't match the other information in the sentence: *last night* indicates the past (rained) not the future (will rain).

10. **B) is correct.** The phrase *running through the hall* should be placed next to *student*, the noun it modifies.

11. **B) is correct.** While the lion may indeed be terrifying, the word *terrifyingly* is an adverb and so can only modify a verb, an adjective or another adverb, not the noun *lion*. In the second sentence, *terrifyingly* is modifying the adjective *loud*, telling us more

about the loudness of the lion's roar—so loud, it was terrifying.

12. **1 is an independent clause**—it has a subject (*I*) and a verb (*have wanted*) and has no subordinating conjunction. **2 is a phrase** made up of a preposition (*under*), its object (*sky*), and words that modify sky (*bright, filled with stars*), but lacks a conjugated verb. **3 is a dependent clause**—it has a subject (*sister*), a verb (*is running*), and a subordinating conjunction (*because*).

13. **A) is correct.** Although the sentence is lengthy, it is simple because it contains only one subject and verb (*San Francisco... is*) modified by additional phrases.

14. **C) is correct.** The sentence has one independent clause (*I love... car*) and one dependent (*because I... road*), so it is complex.

15. **D) is correct.** This sentence has three clauses: two independent (*I wanted... dog* and *I got a fish*) and one dependent (*because my... dander*), so it is compound-complex.

16. **B) is correct.** This sentence is made up of two independent clauses joined by a conjunction (*but*), so it is compound.

17. **B) is correct.** In this sentence the main independent clause—*this... students*—is held until the very end, so it's periodic. Furthermore, despite its length the sentence is simple because it has only one subject (*dizzying array*) and verb (*proved*).

18. **A) is correct.** Here, the main clause *Jessica...test* begins the sentence; the other clauses modify the main clause, providing more information about the main idea and resulting in a cumulative sentence. In addition, the sentence is compound as it links two independent clauses together with a comma and the coordinating conjunction *for*.

19. **B) is correct.** Commas are only needed when joining three items in a series; this sentence only has two (milk and watermelon).

20. **B) and C) are correct.** When setting apart nonessential words and phrases, you can use either dashes or commas, but not both.

21. **B) is correct.** Prepositional phrases are usually essential to the meaning of the sentence, so they don't need to be set apart with commas. Here, the prepositional phrase *with extra cheese* helps the reader understand that the speaker wants a particularly unhealthy meal; however, the friend is encouraging a healthier option. Removing the prepositional phrase would limit the contrast between the burger and the salad. Note that the second comma remains because it is separating two independent clauses.

22. **B) and C) are correct.** In the first sentence, the person shifts from third (*someone*) to second (*you*). It needs to be rewritten to be consistent.

23. First, identify the person or object performing the action (usually given in a prepositional phrase—here, *by my brother*) and make

it the subject; the subject of the original sentence (*I*) becomes the object. Remove the *to be* verb: *My brother hit me with a stick.*

24. Here, the object (*coffee*) becomes the subject; move the original subject (*my roommate*) to a prepositional phrase at the end of the sentence. Add the *to be* verb: *The coffee was made this morning by my roommate.*

25. **D) is correct.** The sentence is describing a cause (*her car breaks down*) and an effect (*she'll buy a new one*), so the correct transition is *therefore*.

26. **A) is correct.** The sentence includes a contrast: it would make sense for Chad to play in the game, but he isn't, so the best transition is *however*.

27. **B) is correct.** In the sentence, the clause after the transition is an example, so the best transition is *for example*.

28. **C) is correct.** In the sentence, two things are occurring at the same time, so the best transition is *while*.

29. The game was canceled because a bad storm was predicted.

    Replace the long phrase *due to the fact that* with the much shorter *because*.

30. We might have a party for my mother's birthday.

    By rearranging the sentence, we can replace the phrase *the possibility exists that* with the word *might*.

31. All of our dogs have been vaccinated except our new puppy.

    The sentence can be rearranged to replace *with the exception of* with *except*. The phrase *receive their vaccinations* has also been shortened to *been vaccinated*.

32. We threw away the broken microwave.

    If something is broken that means it doesn't work, so the phrase *that didn't work* can be removed.

33. It was a surprise when we won the raffle.

    By definition, a surprise is always unexpected, so the word *unexpected* can be removed.

TEST YOUR KNOWLEDGE

1. **C) is correct.**

2. **B) is correct.**

3. **A) is correct.**

4. **B) is correct.**

5. **D) is correct.**

6. **D) is correct.**

7. **C) is correct.**

8. **B) is correct.**

9. **A) is correct.**

10. **D) is correct.**

PART II
Mathematics

20 questions ¦ 25 minutes (without calculator)

38 questions ¦ 55 minutes (with calculator)

The Mathematics section of the SAT tests your knowledge of math concepts taught through the tenth grade, including geometry, algebra, statistics, probability, and trigonometry. The majority of the questions will require you to use complex reasoning to work through multiple steps—you won't simply be performing calculations. Instead, you can expect to perform tasks like building equations from word problems, comparing expressions, and interpreting figures.

The first twenty questions of the Mathematics section have to be done without a calculator; you may use a calculator on the final thirty-eight questions. You can use any calculator that can't access the internet, including graphing calculators. Note that you cannot use the calculator on your tablet or phone.

There are two types of questions on the Mathematics section: multiple-choice (forty-five questions) and grid-in (thirteen questions). For the grid-in questions, you will be required to provide an answer—no answer choices will be provided for you. A couple of notes about grid-in answers:

▶ Answers cannot be given as mixed numbers—you must convert the answer to a decimal or improper fraction.

▶ Decimal numbers must be rounded to fit in the grid. Do not include the zero before the decimal point; instead you can place the decimal point in the left-most column.

▶ There are no negative answers on the grid-in questions.

▶ You will only receive credit for answers that are bubbled in; you will NOT get credit if you only write the answer in the box at the top of the grid.

CHAPTER THREE
Numbers and Operations

In order to do any type of math—whether it's basic geometry or advanced calculus—you need to have a solid understanding of numbers and operations. The specific operations the SAT will test you on are covered in this chapter. However, we won't be covering basic arithmetic operations like adding fractions or long division, since you'll be able to perform these on your calculator during the test.

Types of Numbers

INTEGERS are whole numbers, including the counting numbers, the negative counting numbers and zero. 3, 2, 1, 0, –1, –2, –3 are examples of integers. RATIONAL NUMBERS are made by dividing one integer by another integer. They can be expressed as fractions or as decimals. 3 divided by 4 makes the rational number $\frac{3}{4}$ or 0.75. IRRATIONAL NUMBERS are numbers that cannot be written as fractions; they are decimals that go on forever without repeating. The number π (3.14159...) is an example of an irrational number.

Imaginary numbers are numbers that, when squared, give a negative result. Imaginary numbers use the symbol i to represent $\sqrt{-1}$, so $3i = 3\sqrt{-1}$ and $(3i)^2 = -9$. COMPLEX NUMBERS are combinations of real and imaginarnumbers, written in the form $a + bi$, where a is the real number and b is the imaginary number. An example of a complex number is $4 + 2i$. When adding complex numbers, add the real and imaginary numbers separately: $(4 + 2i) + (3 + i) = 7 + 3i$.

Working with Positive and Negative Numbers

Adding, multiplying, and dividing numbers can yield positive or negative values depending on the signs of the original numbers. Knowing these rules can help determine if your answer is correct.

$(+) + (-) =$ the sign of the larger number

$(-) + (-) =$ negative number

$(-) \times (-) =$ positive number

$(-) \times (+) =$ negative number

$(-) \div (-) =$ positive number

$(-) \div (+) =$ negative number

Order of Operations

Operations in a mathematical expression are always performed in a specific order, which is described by the acronym PEMDAS:

1. Parentheses
2. Exponents
3. Multiplication
4. Division

5. Addition

6. Subtraction

Perform the operations within parentheses first, and then address any exponents. After those steps, perform all multiplication and division. These are carried out from left to right as they appear in the problem. Finally, do all required addition and subtraction, also from left to right as each operation appears in the problem.

EXAMPLES

8. Solve $[-(2)^2 - (4 + 7)]$

9. Solve $(5)^2 \div 5 + 4 \times 2$

10. Solve the expression $15 \times (4 + 8) - 33$

11. Solve the expression $\left(\frac{5}{2} \times 4\right) + 23 - 4^2$

Units of Measurement

You are expected to memorize some units of measurement. These are given below. When doing unit conversion problems (i.e., when converting one unit to another), find the conversion factor, then apply that factor to the given measurement to find the new units.

Table 3.1. Unit Prefixes		
PREFIX	SYMBOL	MULTIPLICATION FACTOR
tera	T	1,000,000,000,000
giga	G	1,000,000,000
mega	M	1,000,000
kilo	k	1,000
hecto	h	100
deca	da	10
base unit	--	--
deci	d	0.1
centi	c	0.01
milli	m	0.001
micro	μ	0.0000001
nano	n	0.0000000001
pico	p	0.0000000000001

Table 3.2. Units and Conversion Factors

DIMENSION	AMERICAN	SI
length	inch/foot/yard/mile	meter
mass	ounce/pound/ton	gram
volume	cup/pint/quart/gallon	liter
force	pound-force	newton
pressure	pound-force per square inch	pascal
work and energy	cal/British thermal unit	joule
temperature	Fahrenheit	kelvin
charge	faraday	coulomb

CONVERSION FACTORS

1 in = 2.54 cm	1 lb = 0.454 kg
1 yd = 0.914 m	1 cal = 4.19 J
1 mile = 1.61 km	$1 °F = \frac{5}{9} (°F - 32)$
1 gallon = 3.785 L	$1 cm^3 = 1 mL$
1 oz = 28.35 g	1 hour = 3600 s

EXAMPLES

12. A fence measures 15 ft. long. How many yards long is the fence?

13. A pitcher can hold 24 cups. How many gallons can it hold?

14. A spool of wire holds 144 in. of wire. If Mario has 3 spools, how many feet of wire does he have?

15. A ball rolling across a table travels 6 inches per second. How many feet will it travel in 1 minute?

16. How many millimeters are in 0.5 meters?

17. A lead ball weighs 38 g. How many kilograms does it weigh?

18 How many cubic centimeters are in 10 L?

19. Jennifer's pencil was initially 10 centimeters long. After she sharpened it, it was 9.6 centimeters long. How many millimeters did she lose from her pencil by sharpening it?

Decimals and Fractions
ADDING and SUBTRACTING DECIMALS

When adding and subtracting decimals, line up the numbers so that the decimals are aligned. You want to subtract the ones place from the ones place, the tenths place from the tenths place, etc.

EXAMPLES

20. Find the sum of 17.07 and 2.52.

21. Jeannette has 7.4 gallons of gas in her tank. After driving, she has 6.8 gallons. How many gallons of gas did she use?

MULTIPLYING and DIVIDING DECIMALS

When multiplying decimals, start by multiplying the numbers normally. You can then determine the placement of the decimal point in the result by adding the number of digits after the decimal in each of the numbers you multiplied together.

When dividing decimals, you should move the decimal point in the divisor (the number you're dividing by) until it is a whole number. You can then move the decimal in the dividend (the number you're dividing into) the same number of places in the same direction. Finally, divide the new numbers normally to get the correct answer.

EXAMPLES

22. What is the product of 0.25 and 1.4?

23. Find 0.8 ÷ 0.2.

24. Find the quotient when 40 is divided by 0.25.

WORKING with FRACTIONS

FRACTIONS are made up of two parts: the **NUMERATOR**, which appears above the bar, and the **DENOMINATOR**, which is below it. If a fraction is in its **SIMPLEST FORM**, the numerator and the denominator share no common factors. A fraction with a numerator larger than its denominator is an **IMPROPER FRACTION**; when the denominator is larger, it's a **PROPER FRACTION**.

Improper fractions can be converted into proper fractions by dividing the numerator by the denominator. The resulting whole number is placed to the left of the fraction, and the remainder becomes the new numerator; the denominator does not change. The new number is called a **MIXED NUMBER** because it contains a whole number and a fraction. Mixed numbers can be turned into improper fractions through the reverse process: multiply the whole number by the denominator and add the numerator to get the new numerator.

EXAMPLES

25. Simplify the fraction $\frac{121}{77}$.

26. Convert $\frac{37}{5}$ into a proper fraction.

MULTIPLYING and DIVIDING FRACTIONS

To multiply fractions, convert any mixed numbers into improper fractions and multiply the numerators together and the denominators together. Reduce to lowest terms if needed.

DID YOU KNOW?
Inverting a fraction changes multiplication to division:
$\frac{a}{b} \div \frac{c}{d} = \frac{a}{b} \times \frac{d}{c} = \frac{d}{bc}$

To divide fractions, first convert any mixed fractions into single fractions. Then, invert the second fraction so that the denominator and numerator are switched. Finally, multiply the numerators together and the denominators together.

EXAMPLES

27. Find $\frac{7}{8} \div \frac{1}{4}$.

28. What is the product of $\frac{1}{12}$ and $\frac{6}{8}$?

29. What is the quotient of $\frac{2}{5} \div 1\frac{1}{5}$?

30. A recipe calls for $\frac{1}{4}$ cup of sugar. If 8.5 batches of the recipe are needed, how many cups of sugar will be used?

ADDING and SUBTRACTING FRACTIONS

Adding and subtracting fractions requires a **COMMON DENOMINATOR**. To find the common denominator, you can multiply each fraction by the number 1. With fractions, any number over itself (e.g., $\frac{5}{5}$, $\frac{12}{12}$, etc.) is equivalent to 1, so multiplying by such a fraction can change the denominator without changing the value of the fraction. Once the denominators are the same, the numerators can be added or subtracted.

DID YOU KNOW?
The phrase *simplify the expression* just means you need to perform all the operations in the expression.

To add mixed numbers, you can first add the whole numbers and then the fractions. To subtract mixed numbers, convert each number to an improper fraction, then subtract the numerators.

EXAMPLES

31. Simplify the expression $\frac{2}{3} - \frac{1}{5}$.

32. Find $2\frac{1}{3} - \frac{3}{2}$.

33. Find the sum of $\frac{9}{16}$, $\frac{1}{2}$, and $\frac{7}{4}$.

34. Sabrina has $\frac{2}{3}$ of a can of red paint. Her friend Amos has $\frac{1}{6}$ of a can. How much red paint do they have combined?

CONVERTING FRACTIONS to DECIMALS

Calculators are not allowed on a portion of the SAT, which can make handling fractions and decimals intimidating for many test takers. However, there are several helpful techniques you can use to navigate between the two forms.

The first thing to do is simply memorize common decimals and their fractional equivalents; a list of these is given below. With these values, it's possible to convert more complicated fractions as well. For example, $\frac{2}{5}$ is just $\frac{1}{5}$ multiplied by 2, so $\frac{2}{5} = 0.2 \times 2 = 0.4$.

Table 3.3. Fractions to Decimals

Fraction	Decimal
$\frac{1}{2}$	0.5
$\frac{1}{3}$	$0.\overline{33}$
$\frac{1}{4}$	0.25
$\frac{1}{5}$	0.2
$\frac{1}{6}$	$0.1\overline{66}$
$\frac{1}{7}$	$0.\overline{142857}$
$\frac{1}{8}$	0.125
$\frac{1}{9}$	$0.\overline{11}$
$\frac{1}{10}$	0.1

Knowledge of common decimal equivalents to fractions can also help you estimate. This skill can be particularly helpful on multiple-choice tests like the SAT, where excluding incorrect answers can be just as helpful as knowing how to find the right one. For example, to find $\frac{5}{8}$ in decimal form for an answer, you can eliminate any answers less than 0.5 because $\frac{4}{8}$ = 0.5. You may also know that $\frac{6}{8}$ is the same as $\frac{3}{4}$ or 0.75, so anything above 0.75 can be eliminated as well.

Another helpful trick is to check if the denominator is easily divisible by 100; for example in the fraction $\frac{9}{20}$, you know 20 goes into 100 five times, so you can multiply the top and bottom by 5 to get $\frac{45}{100}$ or 0.45.

If none of these techniques work, you'll need to find the decimal by dividing the denominator by the numerator using long division.

EXAMPLES

35. Write $\frac{8}{18}$ as a decimal.

36. Write the fraction $\frac{3}{16}$ as a decimal.

CONVERTING DECIMALS to FRACTIONS

Converting a decimal into a fraction is more straightforward than the reverse process is. To convert a decimal, simply use the numbers that come after the decimal as the numerator in the fraction. The denominator will be a power of 10 that matches the place value for the original decimal. For example, the numerator for 0.46 would be 100 because the last number is in the hundredths place; likewise, the denominator for 0.657 would be 1000 because the last number is in the thousandths place. Once this fraction has been set up, all that's left is to simplify it.

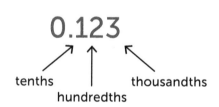

Figure 3.1. Decimal Places

EXAMPLE

37. Convert 0.45 into a fraction.

Ratios

A ratio describes the quantity of one thing in relation to the quantity of another. Unlike fractions, ratios do not give a part relative to a whole; instead, they compare two values. For example, if you have 3 apples and 4 oranges, the ratio of apples to oranges is 3 to 4. Ratios can be written using words (3 to 4), fractions $\left(\frac{3}{4}\right)$, or colons (3:4).

It's helpful to rewrite a ratio as a fraction expressing a part to a whole. For instance, in the example above you have 7 total pieces of fruit, so the fraction of your fruit that is apples is $\frac{3}{7}$, while oranges make up $\frac{4}{7}$ of your fruit collection.

When working with ratios, always consider the units of the values being compared. On the SAT, you may be asked to rewrite a ratio using the same units on both sides. For example, you might have to rewrite the ratio 3 minutes to 7 seconds as 180 seconds to 7 seconds.

EXAMPLES

38. There are 90 voters in a room, and each is either a Democrat or a Republican. The ratio of Democrats to Republicans is 5:4. How many Republicans are there?

39. The ratio of students to teachers in a school is 15:1. If there are 38 teachers, how many students attend the school?

Proportions

A proportion is an equation that equates two ratios. Propo tions are usually written as two fractions joined by an equal sign $\left(\frac{a}{b} = \frac{c}{d}\right)$, but they can also be written using colons (a:b::c:d). Note that in a proportion, the units must be the same in both numerators and in both denominators.

Often you will be given three of the values in a proportion and asked to find the fourth. In these types of problems, you can solve for the missing variable by cross-multiplying—multiply the numerator of each fraction by the denominator of the other to get an equation with no fractions as shown below. You can then solve the equation using basic algebra. (For more on solving basic equations, see *Algebraic Expressions and Equations*.)

$$\frac{a}{b} = \frac{c}{d} \rightarrow ad = bc$$

EXAMPLES

40. A train traveling 120 miles takes 3 hours to get to its destination. How long will it take for the train to travel 180 miles?

41. One acre of wheat requires 500 gallons of water. How many acres can be watered with 2600 gallons?

42. If 35:5::49:x, find x.

Percentages

A percent is the ratio of a part to the whole. Questions may give the part and the whole and ask for the percent, or give the percent and the whole and ask for the part, or give the part and the percent and ask for the value of the whole. The equation for percentages can be rearranged to solve for any of these:

$$percent = \frac{part}{whole}$$

$$part = whole \times percent$$

$$whole = \frac{part}{percent}$$

In the equations above, the percent should always be expressed as a decimal. In order to convert a decimal into a percentage value, simply multiply it by 100. So, if you've read 5 pages (the part) of a 10-page article (the whole), you've read $\frac{5}{10}$ = .50 or 50%. (The percent sign (%) is used once the decimal has been multiplied by 100.)

Note that when solving these problems, the units for the part and the whole should be the same. If you're reading a book, saying you've read 5 pages out of 15 chapters doesn't make any sense.

EXAMPLES

43. 45 is 15% of what number?

44. Jim spent 30% of his paycheck at the fair. He spent $15 for a hat, $30 for a shirt, and $20 playing games. How much was his check? (Round to nearest dollar.)

45. What percent of 65 is 39?

46. Greta and Max sell cable subscriptions. In a given month, Greta sells 45 subscriptions and Max sells 51. If 240 total subscriptions were sold in that month, what percent were not sold by Greta or Max?

47. Grant needs to score 75% on an exam. If the exam has 45 questions, at least how many does he need to answer correctly to get this score?

PERCENT CHANGE

Percent change problems ask you to calculate how much a given quantity has changed. The problems are solved in a similar way to regular percent problems, except that instead of using the *part* you'll use the *amount of change*. Note that the sign of the *amount of change* is important: if the original amount has increased the change will be positive; if it has decreased the change will be negative. Again, in the equations below the percent is a decimal value; you need to multiply by 100 to get the actual percentage.

$$\text{percent change} = \frac{\text{amount of change}}{\text{original amount}}$$

$$\text{amount of change} = \text{original amount} \times \text{percent change}$$

$$\text{original amount} = \frac{\text{amount of change}}{\text{percent change}}$$

EXAMPLES

48. A computer software retailer marks up its games by 40% above the wholesale price when it sells them to customers. Find the price of a game for a customer if the game costs the retailer $25.

49. A golf shop pays its wholesaler $40 for a certain club, and then sells it to a golfer for $75. What is the markup rate?

50. A shoe store charges a 40% markup on the shoes it sells. How much did the store pay for a pair of shoes purchased by a customer for $63?

51. An item originally priced at $55 is marked 25% off. What is the sale price?

52. James wants to put an 18 foot by 51 foot garden in his backyard. If he does, it will reduce the size of his yard by 24%. What will be the area of the remaining yard space?

Comparison of Rational Numbers

Number comparison problems present numbers in different formats and ask which is larger or smaller, or whether the numbers are equivalent. The important step in solving these problems is to convert the numbers to the same format so that it is easier to compare them. If numbers are given in the same format, or after converting them, determine which number is smaller or if the numbers are equal. Remember that for negative numbers, higher numbers are actually smaller.

EXAMPLES

53. Is $4\frac{3}{4}$ greater than, equal to, or less than $\frac{18}{4}$?

54. Which of the following numbers has the greatest value: 104.56, 104.5, or 104.6?

55. Is 65% greater than, less than, or equal to $\frac{13}{20}$?

Exponents and Radicals

Exponents tell us how many times to multiply a base number by itself. In the example 2^4, 2 is the base number and 4 is the exponent. $2^4 = 2 \times 2 \times 2 \times 2 = 16$. Exponents are also called powers: 5 to the third power = $5^3 = 5 \times 5 \times 5 = 125$. Some exponents have special names: x to the second power is also called "x squared" and x to the third power is also called "x cubed." The number 3 squared = $3^2 = 3 \times 3 = 9$.

Radicals are expressions that use roots. Radicals are written in the form $\sqrt[a]{x}$ where a = the **RADICAL POWER** and x = **THE RADICAND**. The solution to the radical $\sqrt[3]{8}$ is the number that, when multiplied by itself 3 times, equals 8. $\sqrt[3]{8} = 2$ because $2 \times 2 \times 2 = 8$. When the radical power is not written we assume it is 2, so $\sqrt{9} = 3$ because $3 \times 3 = 9$. Radicals can also be written as exponents, where the power is a fraction. For example, $x^{\frac{1}{3}} = \sqrt[3]{x}$.

Review more of the rules for working with exponents and radicals in the table below.

Table 3.4. Exponents and Radicals Rules	
RULE	**EXAMPLE**
$x^0 = 1$	$5^0 = 1$
$x^1 = x$	$5^1 = 5$
$x^a \times x^b = x^{a+b}$	$5^2 \times 5^3 = 5^5 = 3125$
$(xy)^a = x^a y^a$	$(5 \times 6)^2 = 5^2 \times 6^2 = 900$
$(x^a)^b = x^{ab}$	$(5^2)^3 = 5^6 = 15,625$
$\left(\frac{x}{y}\right)^a = \frac{x^a}{y^b}$	$\left(\frac{5}{6}\right)^2 = \frac{5^2}{6^2} = \frac{25}{36}$
$\frac{x^a}{x^b} = x^{a-b} \ (x \neq 0)$	$\frac{5^4}{5^3} = 5^1 = 5$
$x^{-a} = \frac{1}{x^a} \ (x \neq 0)$	$5^{-2} = \frac{1}{5^2} = \frac{1}{25}$
$x^{\frac{1}{a}} = \sqrt[a]{x}$	$25^{\frac{1}{2}} = \sqrt[2]{25} = 5$
$\sqrt[a]{x \times y} = \sqrt[a]{x} \times \sqrt[a]{y}$	$\sqrt[3]{8 \times 27} = \sqrt[3]{8} \times \sqrt[3]{27} = 2 \times 3 = 6$
$\sqrt[a]{\frac{x}{y}} = \frac{\sqrt[a]{x}}{\sqrt[a]{y}}$	$\sqrt[3]{\frac{27}{8}} = \frac{\sqrt[3]{27}}{\sqrt[3]{8}} = \frac{3}{2}$
$\sqrt[a]{x^b} = x^{\frac{b}{a}}$	$\sqrt[2]{5^4} = 5^{\frac{4}{2}} = 5^2 = 25$

56. Simplify the expression $2^4 \times 2^2$

57. Simplify the expression $(3^4)^{-1}$

58. Simplify the expression $\left(\frac{9}{4}\right)^{\frac{1}{2}}$

Matrices

A **MATRIX** is an array of numbers aligned into horizontal rows and vertical columns. A matrix is described by the number of rows (m) and columns (n) it contains. For example, a matrix with 3 rows and 4 columns is a 3×4 matrix, as shown below.

$$\begin{bmatrix} 2 & -3 & 5 & 0 \\ 4 & -6 & 2 & 11 \\ 3.5 & 7 & 2.78 & -1.2 \end{bmatrix}$$

To add or subtract 2 matrices, simply add or subtract the corresponding numbers in each matrix. Only matrices with the same dimensions can be added or subtracted, and the resulting matrix will also have the same dimensions.

In order to multiple 2 matrices, the number of columns in the first must equal the number of rows in the second. To multiply the matrices, multiply the numbers in each row of the first by the numbers in the column of the second and add. The resulting matrix will have the same number of rows as the first matrix and same number of columns as the second. Note that the order of the matrices is important when they're being multiplied: **AB** is not the same as **BA**.

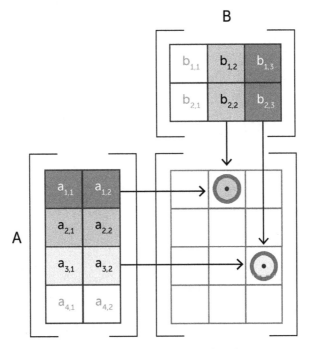

Figure 3.2. Matrix Multiplication

To multiply a matrix by a single number or variable, simply multiple each value within the matrix by that number or variable.

EXAMPLES

59. Simplify: $\begin{bmatrix} 6 & 4 & -8 \\ -3 & 1 & 0 \end{bmatrix} + \begin{bmatrix} 5 & -3 & -2 \\ -3 & 4 & 9 \end{bmatrix}$

60. Solve for x and y: $\begin{bmatrix} x & 6 \\ 4 & y \end{bmatrix} + \begin{bmatrix} 3 & 2 \\ 8 & -1 \end{bmatrix} = \begin{bmatrix} 11 & 8 \\ 12 & 4 \end{bmatrix}$

61. If $\mathbf{A} = \begin{bmatrix} 1 & 3 & 0 \\ 6 & 2 & 4 \end{bmatrix}$ and $\mathbf{B} = \begin{bmatrix} 5 & 3 \\ 2 & 1 \\ 4 & 7 \end{bmatrix}$, what is $\mathbf{AB}$?

62. Simplify: $6x \begin{bmatrix} 2 & -3 \\ 6 & 4 \end{bmatrix}$

Answer Key

1. $\sqrt{5}$ is an irrational number because it cannot be written as a fraction of two integers. It is a decimal that goes on forever without repeating.

2. $-\sqrt{64}$ can be rewritten as the negative whole number -8, so it is an **integer**.

3. Subtract the real and imaginary numbers separately.

    $3 - 1 = 2$

    $5i - (-2i) = 5i + 2i = 7i$

    Solve $(3 + 5i) - (1 - 2i) = 2 + 7i$

4. $(-) \times (+) = (-)$

    $-10 \times 47 = $ **−470**

5. $(-) + (-) = (-)$

    $-65 + -32 = $ **−97**

6. $(-) \times (+) = (-)$

    $-7 \times 4 = -28$, which is **less than −7**

7. $(-) \div (+) = (-)$

    $-16 \div 2.5 = $ **−6.4**

8. First, complete operations within parentheses:

    $-(2)^2 - (11)$

    Second, calculate the value of exponential numbers:

    $-(4) - (11)$

    Finally, do addition and subtraction:

    $-4 - 11 = $ **−15**

9. First, calculate the value of exponential numbers:

    $(25) \div 5 + 4 \times 2$

    Second, calculate division and multiplication from left to right:

    $5 + 8$

    Finally, do addition and subtraction:

    $5 + 8 = $ **13**

10. First, complete operations within parentheses:

    $15 \times (12) - 3^3$

    Second, calculate the value of exponential numbers:

    $15 \times (12) - 27$

    Third, calculate division and multiplication from left to right:

    $180 - 27$

    Finally, do addition and subtraction from left to right:

    $180 - 27 = $ **153**

11. First, complete operations within parentheses:

    $(10) + 23 - 4^2$

    Second, calculate the value of exponential numbers:

    $(10) + 23 - 16$

    Finally, do addition and subtraction from left to right:

    $(10) + 23 - 16$

    $33 - 16 = $ **17**

12. 1 yd. = 3 ft.

    $\frac{15}{3} = $ **5 yd.**

13. 1 gal. = 16 cups

    $\frac{24}{16} = $ **1.5 gal.**

14. 12 in. = 1 ft.

    $\frac{144}{12} = 12$ ft.

    12 ft. × 3 spools = **36 ft. of wire**

15. This problem can be worked in two steps: finding how many inches are covered in 1 minute, and then converting that value to feet. It can also be worked the opposite way, by finding how many feet it travels in 1 second and then converting that to feet traveled per minute. The first method is shown below.

1 min. = 60 sec.

$\frac{6 \text{ in.}}{\text{sec.}} \times 60 \text{ s} = 360 \text{ in.}$

1 ft. = 12 in.

$\frac{360 \text{ in.}}{12 \text{ in.}} = \textbf{30 ft.}$

16. 1 meter = 1000 mm

0.5 meters = **500 mm**

17. 1 kg = 1000 g

$\frac{38 \text{ g}}{1000 \text{ g}} = \textbf{0.038 kg}$

18. 1 L = 1000 cm³

10 L = 1000 cm³ × 10

10 L = **10,000 cm³**

19. 1 cm = 10 mm

10 cm − 9.6 cm = 0.4 cm lost

0.4 cm = 10 mm × 0.4 = **4 mm were lost**

20. 17.07
+ 2.52
= **19.59**

21. 7.4
− 6.8
= **0.6 gal.**

22. 25 × 14 = 350

There are 2 digits after the decimal in 0.25 and one digit after the decimal in 1.4. Therefore the product should have 3 digits after the decimal: **0.350 is the correct answer.**

23. Change 0.2 to 2 by moving the decimal one space to the right.

Next, move the decimal one space to the right on the dividend. 0.8 becomes 8.

Now, divide 8 by 2. 8 ÷ 2 = **4**

24. First, change the divisor to a whole number: 0.25 becomes 25.

Next, change the dividend to match the divisor by moving the decimal two spaces to the right, so 40 becomes 4000.

Now divide: 4000 ÷ 25 = **160**

25. 121 and 77 share a common factor of 11. So, if we divide each by 11 we can simplify the fraction:

$\frac{121}{77} = \frac{11}{11} \times \frac{11}{7} = \frac{\textbf{11}}{\textbf{7}}$

26. Start by dividing the numerator by the denominator:

37 ÷ 5 = 7 with a remainder of 2.

Now build a mixed number with the whole number and the new numerator:

$\frac{37}{5} = \textbf{7}\frac{\textbf{2}}{\textbf{5}}$

27. For a fraction division problem, invert the second fraction and then multiply and reduce:

$\frac{7}{8} \div \frac{1}{4} = \frac{7}{8} \times \frac{4}{1} = \frac{28}{8} = \frac{\textbf{7}}{\textbf{2}}$

28. This is a fraction multiplication problem, so simply multiply the numerators together and the denominators together and then reduce:

$\frac{1}{12} \times \frac{6}{8} = \frac{6}{96} = \frac{\textbf{1}}{\textbf{16}}$

Sometimes it's easier to reduce fractions before multiplying if you can:

$\frac{1}{12} \times \frac{6}{8} = \frac{1}{12} \times \frac{3}{4} = \frac{3}{48} = \frac{\textbf{1}}{\textbf{16}}$

29. This is a fraction division problem, so the first step is to convert the mixed number to an improper fraction:

$$1\frac{1}{5} = \frac{5 \times 1}{5} + \frac{1}{5} = \frac{6}{5}$$

Now, divide the fractions. Remember to invert the second fraction, and then multiply normally:

$$\frac{2}{5} \div \frac{6}{5} = \frac{2}{5} \times \frac{5}{6} = \frac{10}{30} = \mathbf{\frac{1}{3}}$$

30. This is a fraction multiplication problem: $\frac{1}{4} \times 8\frac{1}{2}$.

First, we need to convert the mixed number into an improper fraction:

$$8\frac{1}{2} = 8 \times 2 \text{\_\_\_\_} 2 + \frac{1}{2} = \frac{17}{2}$$

Now, multiply the fractions across the numerators and denominators, and then reduce:

$$\frac{1}{4} \times 8\frac{1}{2} = \frac{1}{4} \times \frac{17}{2} = \mathbf{\frac{17}{8}} \textbf{ cups of sugar}$$

31. First, multiply each fraction by a factor of 1 to get a common denominator.

How do you know which factor of 1 to use? Look at the other fraction and use the number found in that denominator:

$$\frac{2}{3} - \frac{1}{5} = \frac{2}{3}\left(\frac{5}{5}\right) - \frac{1}{5}\left(\frac{3}{3}\right) = \frac{10}{15} - \frac{3}{15}$$

Once the fractions have a common denominator, simply subtract the numerators:

$$\frac{10}{15} - \frac{3}{15} = \mathbf{\frac{7}{15}}$$

32. This is a fraction subtraction problem with a mixed number, so the first step is to convert the mixed number to an improper fraction:

$$2\frac{1}{3} = \frac{2 \times 3}{3} + \frac{1}{3} = \frac{7}{3}$$

Next, convert each fraction so they share a common denominator:

$$\frac{7}{3} \times \frac{2}{2} = \frac{14}{6}$$
$$\frac{3}{2} \times \frac{3}{3} = \frac{9}{6}$$

Now, subtract the fractions by subtracting the numerators:

$$\frac{14}{6} - \frac{9}{6} = \mathbf{\frac{5}{6}}$$

33. For this fraction addition problem, we need to find a common denominator. Notice that 2 and 4 are both factors of 16, so 16 can be the common denominator:

$$\frac{1}{2} \times \frac{8}{8} = \frac{8}{16}$$
$$\frac{7}{4} \times \frac{4}{4} = \frac{28}{16}$$
$$\frac{9}{16} + \frac{8}{16} + \frac{28}{16} = \mathbf{\frac{45}{16}}$$

34. To add fractions, make sure that they have a common denominator. Since 3 is a factor of 6, 6 can be the common denominator:

$$\frac{2}{3} \times \frac{2}{2} = \frac{4}{6}$$

Now, add the numerators:

$$\frac{4}{6} + \frac{1}{6} = \mathbf{\frac{5}{6}} \textbf{ of a can}$$

35. The first step here is to simplify the fraction:

$$\frac{8}{18} = \frac{4}{9}$$

Now it's clear that the fraction is a multiple of $\frac{1}{9}$, so you can easily find the decimal using a value you already know:

$$\frac{4}{9} = \frac{1}{9} \times 4 = 0.\overline{11} \times 4 = \mathbf{0.\overline{44}}$$

36. None of the tricks above will work for this fraction, so you need to do long division:

```
        0.1875
16 ) 3.0000
   − 1.6000
     1.40
   − 1.28
     0.120
   − 0.112
     0.0080
   − 0.0080
     0.0000
```

The decimal will go in front of the answer, so now you know that $\frac{3}{16}$ = **0.1875.**

37. The last number in the decimal is in the hundredths place, so we can easily set up a fraction:

$$0.45 = \frac{45}{100}$$

The next step is simply to reduce the fraction down to the lowest common denominator. Here, both 45 and 100 are divisible by 5. 45 divided by 5 is 9, and 100 divided by 5 is 20. Therefore, you're left with:

$$\frac{45}{100} = \mathbf{\frac{9}{20}}$$

38. We know that there are 5 Democrats for every 4 Republicans in the room, which means for every 9 people, 4 are Republicans.

$$5 + 4 = 9$$

Fraction of Democrats: $\frac{5}{9}$
Fraction of Republicans: $\frac{4}{9}$
If $\frac{4}{9}$ of the 90 voters are Republicans, then:

$\frac{4}{9} \times 90 = \mathbf{40\ voters\ are}$
Republicans

39. To solve this ratio problem, we can simply multiply both sides of the ratio by the desired value to find the number of students that correspond to having 38 teachers:

$\frac{15\ stdents}{1\ teacher} \times 38$ teachers = 570 students

The school has **570 students.**

40. Start by setting up the proportion:

$$\frac{120\ i}{3\ hrs} = \frac{180 mi}{x\ hr}$$

Note that it doesn't matter which value is placed in the numerator or denominator, as long as it is the same on both sides. Now, solve for the missing quantity through cross-multiplication:

$$120\ mi \times x\ hr = 3\ hrs \times 180\ mi$$

Now solve the equation:

$$x\ hours = \frac{3\ hrs \times 18\ mi}{120\ mi}$$

$$x = \mathbf{4.5\ hrs}$$

41. Set up the equation:

$$\frac{1\ acre}{500\ gal} = \frac{x\ acres}{2600\ gal}$$

Then solve for x:

$$x\ acres = \frac{1\ acre \times 2600\ gal}{500\ gal}$$

$$x = \frac{26}{5}\ acres\ or\ \mathbf{5.2\ acres}$$

42. This problem presents two equivalent ratios that can be set up in a fraction equation:

$$\frac{35}{5} = \frac{49}{x}$$

You can then cross-multiply to solve for x:

$$35x = 49 \times 5$$

$$\mathbf{x = 7}$$

43. Set up the appropriate equation and solve. Don't forget to change 15% to a decimal value:

$$whole = \frac{part}{percent} = \frac{45}{0.15} = \mathbf{300}$$

44. Set up the appropriate equation and solve:

$$whole = \frac{part}{percent} = \frac{15 + 30 + 20}{.30} =$$
$217.00

45. Set up the equation and solve:

$$percent = \frac{part}{whole} = \frac{39}{65} = \mathbf{0.6\ or\ 60\%}$$

46. You can use the information in the question to figure out what percentage of subscriptions were sold by Max and Greta:

$$percent = \frac{part}{whole} = \frac{51 + 45}{240} = \frac{96}{240} =$$
0.4 or 40%

However, the question asks how many subscriptions weren't sold by Max or Greta. If they sold 40%, then the other salespeople sold 100% − 40% = **60%**.

47. Set up the equation and solve. Remember to convert 75% to a decimal value:
part = whole × percent = 45 × 0.75 = 33.75, so **he needs to answer at least 34 questions correctly.**

48. Set up the appropriate equation and solve:
amount of change = original amount × percent change →
25 × 0.4 = 10
If the amount of change is 10, that means the store adds a markup of $10, so the game costs:
$25 + $10 = **$35**

49. First, calculate the amount of change:
75 − 40 = 35
Now you can set up the equation and solve. (Note that markup rate is another way of saying percent change):
$$\text{percent change} = \frac{\text{amount of change}}{\text{original amount}}$$
$$\rightarrow \quad \frac{35}{40} = 0.875 = \textbf{87.5\%}$$

50. You're solving for the original price, but it's going to be tricky because you don't know the amount of change; you only know the new price. To solve, you need to create an expression for the amount of change:
If original amount = x
Then amount of change = 63 − x
Now you can plug these values into your equation:
$$\text{original amount} = \frac{\text{amount of change}}{\text{percent change}}$$
$$x = \frac{63\ x}{0.4}$$

The last step is to solve for x:
0.4x = 63 − x
1.4x = 63
x = 45 → **The store paid $45 for the shoes.**

51. You've been asked to find the sale price, which means you need to solve for the amount of change first:
amount of change = original amount × percent change =
55 × 0.25 = 13.75
Using this amount, you can find the new price. Because it's on sale, we know the item will cost less than the original price:
55 − 13.75 = 41.25
The sale price is **$41.25**.

52. This problem is tricky because you need to figure out what each number in the problem stands for. 24% is obviously the percent change, but what about the measurements in feet? If you multiply these values you get the area of the garden (for more on area see *Area and Perimeter*):
18 ft. × 51 ft. = 918 ft.^{2}
This 918 ft.^{2} is the amount of change—it's how much area the yard lost to create the garden. Now you can set up an equation:
$$\text{original amount} = \frac{\text{amount of change}}{\text{percent change}}$$
$$= \frac{918}{.24} = 3825$$
If the original lawn was 3825 ft.^{2} and the garden is 918 ft.^{2}, then the remaining area is:
3825 − 918 = 2907
The remaining lawn covers 2907 ft.^{2}

53. These numbers are in different formats—one is a mixed fraction and the other is just a fraction. So, the first step is to convert the mixed fraction to a fraction:

$$4\frac{3}{4} = 4 \times \frac{4}{4} + \frac{3}{4} = \frac{19}{4}$$

Once the mixed number is converted, it is easier to see that

$$\frac{19}{4} \text{ is greater than } \frac{18}{4}.$$

54. These numbers are already in the same format, so the decimal values just need to be compared. Remember that zeros can be added after the decimal without changing the value, so the three numbers can be rewritten as:

104.56

104.50

104.60

From this list, it is clearer that **104.60 is the greatest** because 0.60 is larger than 0.50 and 0.56.

55. The first step is to convert the numbers into the same format—65% is the same as $\frac{65}{100}$.

Next, the fractions need to be converted to have the same denominator because it is difficult to compare fractions with different denominators. Using a factor of $\frac{5}{5}$ on the second fraction will give common denominators:

$\frac{13}{20} \times \frac{5}{5} = \frac{65}{100}$. Now it is easy to see that **the numbers are equivalent.**

56. When multiplying exponents in which the base number is the same, simply add the powers:

$$2^4 \times 2^2 = 2^{(4+2)} = 2^6$$

$$2^6 = 2 \times 2 \times 2 \times 2 \times 2 \times 2 = \mathbf{64}$$

57. When an exponent is raised to a power, multiply the powers:

$$(3^4)^{-1} = 3^{-4}$$

When the exponent is a negative number, rewrite as the reciprocal of the positive exponent:

$$3^{-4} = \frac{1}{3^4}$$

$$\frac{1}{3^4} = \frac{1}{3 \times 3 \times 3 \times 3} = \frac{\mathbf{1}}{\mathbf{81}}$$

58. When the power is a fraction, rewrite as a radical:

$$\left(\frac{9}{4}\right)^{\frac{1}{2}} = \sqrt{\frac{9}{4}}$$

Next, distribute the radical to the numerator and denominator:

$$\sqrt{\frac{9}{4}} = \frac{\sqrt{9}}{\sqrt{4}} = \frac{\mathbf{3}}{\mathbf{2}}$$

59. Add each corresponding number:

$$\begin{bmatrix} 6+5 & 4+(-3) & (-8)+(-2) \\ (-3)+(-3) & 1+4 & 0+9 \end{bmatrix} = \begin{bmatrix} \mathbf{11} & \mathbf{1} & \mathbf{-10} \\ \mathbf{-6} & \mathbf{5} & \mathbf{9} \end{bmatrix}$$

60. Add each corresponding number to create 2 equations:

$$\begin{bmatrix} x+3 & 6+2 \\ 4+8 & y+(-1) \end{bmatrix} = \begin{bmatrix} 11 & 8 \\ 12 & 4 \end{bmatrix}$$

$x + 3 = 11$

$y - 1 = 4$

Now, solve each equation:

$\mathbf{\textit{x} = 8, \textit{y} = 5}$

61. First, check to see that they can be multiplied: **A** has 3 columns and **B** has 3 rows, so they can. The resulting matrix will be 2 × 2. Now multiply the numbers in the first row of **A** by the numbers in the first column of **B** and add the results:

$$\begin{bmatrix} 1 & 3 & 0 \\ 6 & 2 & 4 \end{bmatrix} \times \begin{bmatrix} 5 & 3 \\ 2 & 1 \\ 4 & 7 \end{bmatrix} = \begin{bmatrix} (1 \times 5)+(3 \times 2)+(0 \times 4) & \square \\ \square & \square \end{bmatrix} = \begin{bmatrix} 11 & \square \\ \square & \square \end{bmatrix}$$

Now, multiply and add to find the 3 missing values:

$$\begin{bmatrix} 1 & 3 & 0 \\ 6 & 2 & 4 \end{bmatrix} \times \begin{bmatrix} 5 & 3 \\ 2 & 1 \\ 4 & 7 \end{bmatrix} =$$

$$\begin{bmatrix} 1 \times 5)+(3 \times 2)+(0 \times 4) & (1 \times 3)+(3 \times 1)+(0 \times 7) \\ (6 \times 5)+(2 \times 2)+(4 \times 4) & (6 \times 3)+(2 \times 1)+(4 \times 7) \end{bmatrix} = \begin{bmatrix} \mathbf{11} & \mathbf{6} \\ \mathbf{50} & \mathbf{48} \end{bmatrix}$$

62. Multiply each value inside the matrix by $6x$.

$$6x \begin{bmatrix} 2 & -3 \\ 6 & 4 \end{bmatrix} = \begin{bmatrix} 6x \times 2 & 6x \times (-3) \\ 6x \times 6 & 6x \times 4 \end{bmatrix} = \begin{bmatrix} \mathbf{12\textit{x}} & \mathbf{-18\textit{x}} \\ \mathbf{36\textit{x}} & \mathbf{24\textit{x}} \end{bmatrix}$$

CHAPTER FOUR
Algebra

Algebraic Expressions

Algebraic expressions and equations include **VARIABLES**, or letters standing in for numbers. These expressions and equations are made up of **TERMS**, which are groups of numbers and variables (e.g., $2xy$). An **EXPRESSION** is simply a set of terms (e.g., $\frac{2x}{3yz} + 2$). When those terms are joined only by addition or subtraction, the expression is called a polynomial (e.g., $2x + 3yz$). When working with expressions, you'll need to use many different mathematical properties and operations, including addition/subtraction, multiplication/division, exponents, roots, distribution, and the order of operations.

EVALUATING ALGEBRAIC EXPRESSIONS

To evaluate an algebraic expression, simply plug the given value(s) in for the appropriate variable(s) in the expression.

EXAMPLE

1. Evaluate $2x + 6y - 3z$ if $x = 2$, $y = 4$, and $z = -3$.

ADDING and SUBTRACTING EXPRESSIONS

Only **LIKE TERMS**, which have the exact same variable(s), can be added or subtracted. **CONSTANTS** are numbers without variables attached, and those can be added and subtracted together as well. When simplifying an expression, like terms should be added or subtracted so that no individual group of variables occurs in more than one term. For example, the expression $5x + 6xy$ is in its simplest form, while $5x + 6xy - 11xy$ is not because the term xy appears more than once.

EXAMPLE

2. Simplify the expression: $5xy + 7y + 2yz + 11xy - 5yz$

MULTIPLYING and DIVIDING EXPRESSIONS

To multiply a single term by another, simply multiply the coefficients and then multiply the variables. Remember that when multiplying variables with exponents, those exponents are added together. For example: $(x^5y)(x^3y^4) = x^8 y^5$.

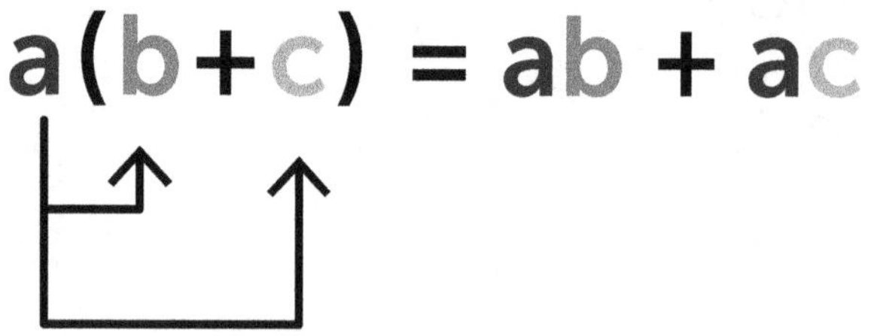

$$a(b+c) = ab + ac$$

Figure 4.1. Distribution

When multiplying a term by a set of terms inside parentheses, you need to distribute to each term inside the parentheses as shown below:

When variables occur in both the numerator and denominator of a fraction, they cancel each other out. So, a fraction with variables in its simplest form will not have the same variable on the top and bottom.

EXAMPLES

3. Simplify the expression $(3x^4 y^2z)(2y^4z^5)$.

4. Simplify the expression: $(2y^2)(y^3 + 2xy^2z + 4z)$

5. Simplify the expression: $(5x + 2)(3x + 3)$

6. Simplify the expression: $\frac{2x^4y^3z}{8x^2z^2}$

FACTORING EXPRESSIONS

Factoring is splitting one expression into the multiplication of two expressions. It requires finding the highest common factor and dividing terms by that number. For example, in the expression $15x + 10$, the highest common factor is 5 because both terms are divisible by 5: $\frac{15x}{5} = 3x$ and $\frac{10}{5} = 2$. When you factor the expression you get $5(3x + 2)$.

Sometimes it is difficult to find the highest common factor. In these cases, consider whether the expression fits a polynomial identity. A polynomial is an expression with more than one term. If you can recognize the common polynomials listed below, you can easily factor the expression.

- ► $a^2 - b^2 = (a + b)(a - b)$
- ► $a^2 + 2ab + b^2 = (a + b)(a + b) = (a + b)^2$
- ► $a^2 - 2ab + b^2 = (a - b)(a - b) = (a - b)^2$
- ► $a^3 + b^3 = (a + b)(a^2 - ab + b^2)$
- ► $a^3 - b^3 = (a - b)(a^2 + ab + b^2)$

7. Factor the expression: $27x^2 - 9x$.

8. Factor the expression: $25x^2 - 16$.

9. Factor the expression: $100x^2 + 60x + 9$.

Linear Equations

An **EQUATION** is a statement saying that two expressions are equal to each other. They always include an equal sign (e.g., $3x + 2xy = 17$). A **LINEAR EQUATION** has only two variables; on a graph, linear equations form a straight line.

SOLVING LINEAR EQUATIONS

To solve an equation, you need to manipulate the terms on each side to isolate the variable, meaning if you want to find x, you have to get the x alone on one side of the equal sign. To do this, you'll need to use many of the tools discussed above: you might need to distribute, divide, add, or subtract like terms, or find common denominators.

Think of each side of the equation as the two sides of a see-saw. As long as the two people on each end weigh the same amount (no matter what it is) the see-saw will be balanced: if you have a 120 pound person on each end, the see-saw is balanced. Giving each of them a 10 pound rock to hold changes the weight on each end, but the see-saw itself stays balanced. Equations work the same way: you can add, subtract, multiply, or divide whatever you want as long as you do the same thing to both sides.

DID YOU KNOW?
If you're stumped, try plugging the answer choices back into the original problem to see which one works.

Most equations you'll see on the SAT can be solved using the same basic steps:

1. distribute to get rid of parentheses
2. use LCD to get rid of fractions
3. add/subtract like terms on either side
4. add/subtract so that constants appear on only one side of the equation
5. multiply/divide to isolate the variable

10. Solve for x: $25x + 12 = 62$

11. Solve the following equation for x: $2x - 4(2x + 3) = 24$.

12. Solve the following equation for x: $\frac{x}{3} + \frac{1}{2} = \frac{x}{6} - \frac{5}{12}$

13. Find the value of x: $2(x + y) - 7x = 14x + 3$

GRAPHING LINEAR EQUATIONS

Linear equations can be plotted as straight lines on a coordinate plane. The **x-AXIS** is always the horizontal axis and the **y-AXIS** is always the vertical axis. The x-axis is positive to the right of the y-axis and negative to the left. The y-axis is positive above the x-axis and negative below. To describe the location of any point on the graph, write the coordinates in the form (x, y). The origin, the point where the x- and y-axes cross, is $(0, 0)$.

The **y-INTERCEPT** is the y coordinate where the line crosses the y-axis. The **SLOPE** is a measure of how steep the line is. Slope is calculated by dividing the change along the y-axis by the change along the x-axis between any two points on the line.

Linear equations are easiest to graph when they are written in **POINT-SLOPE FORM**: $y = mx + b$. The constant m represents slope and the constant b represents the y-intercept. If you know two points along the line (x_1, y_1) and (x_2, y_2), you can calculate slope using the following equation: $m = \frac{y_2 - y_1}{x_2 - x_1}$. If you know the slope and one other point along the line, you can calculate the y-intercept by plugging the number 0 in for x_2 and solving for y_2.

When graphing a linear equation, first plot the y-intercept. Next, plug in values for x to solve for y and plot additional points. Connect the points with a straight line.

EXAMPLES

14. Find the slope of the line: $\frac{3y}{2} + 3 = x$.

15. Plot the linear equation: $2y - 4x = 6$.

SYSTEMS of EQUATIONS

A system of equations is a group of related questions sharing the same variable. The problems you see on the SAT will most likely involve two equations that each have two variables, although you may also solve sets of equations with any number of variables as long as there are a corresponding number of equations (e.g., to solve a system with four variables, you need four equations).

DID YOU KNOW?
The math section will always include a set of questions that require you to understand and manipulate a real-life equation (usually related to physics).

There are two main methods used to solve systems of equations. In **SUBSTITUTION**, solve one equation for a single variable, then substitute the solution for that variable into the second equation to solve for the other variable. Or, you can use **ELIMINATION** by adding equations together to cancel variables and solve for one of them.

16. Solve the following system of equations: $3y - 4 + x = 0$ and $5x + 6y = 11$.

17. Solve the system $2x + 4y = 8$ and $4x + 2y = 10$.

BUILDING EQUATIONS

Word problems describe a situation or a problem without explicitly providing an equation to solve. It is up to you to build an algebraic equation to solve the problem. You must translate the words into mathematical operations. Represent the quantity you do not know with a variable. If there is more than one unknown, you will likely have to write more than one equation, then solve the system of equations by substituting expressions. Make sure you keep your variables straight!

EXAMPLES

18. David, Jesse, and Mark shoveled snow during their snow day and made a total of $100. They agreed to split it based on how much each person worked. David will take $10 more than Jesse, who will take $15 more than Mark. How much money will David get?

19. The sum of three consecutive numbers is 54. What is the middle number?

20. There are 42 people on the varsity football team. This is 8 more than half the number of people on the swim team. There are 6 fewer boys on the swim team than girls. How many girls are on the swim team?

Linear Inequalities

INEQUALITIES look like equations, except that instead of having an equal sign, they have one of the following symbols:

>   greater than: the expression left of the symbol is larger than the expression on the right

<   less than: the expression left of the symbol is smaller than the expression on the right

≥   greater than or equal to: the expression left of the symbol is larger than or equal to the expression on the right

≤   less than or equal to: the expression left of the symbol is less than or equal to the expression on the right

SOLVING LINEAR INEQUALITIES

Inequalities are solved like linear and algebraic equations. The only difference is that the symbol must be reversed when both sides of the equation are multiplied by a negative number.

EXAMPLE

21. Solve for x: $-7x + 2 < 6 - 5x$

GRAPHING LINEAR INEQUALITIES

Graphing a linear inequality is just like graphing a linear equation, except that you shade the area on one side of the line. To graph a linear inequality, first rearrange the inequality expression into $y = mx + b$ form. Then treat the inequality symbol like an equal sign and plot the line. If the inequality symbol is < or >, make a broken line; for ≤ or ≥, make a solid line. Finally, shade the correct side of the graph:

> For $y < mx + b$ or $y ≤ mx + b$, shade **below** the line.
>
> For $y > mx + b$ or $y ≥ mx + b$, shade **above** the line.

EXAMPLE

22. Plot the inequality: $-3 ≥ 4 - y$.

Quadratic Equations

A quadratic equation is any equation in the form $ax^2 + bx + c = 0$. In quadratic equations, x is the variable and a, b, and c are all known numbers. a cannot be 0.

SOLVING QUADRATIC EQUATIONS

There is more than one way to solve a quadratic equation. One way is by **FACTORING**. By rearranging the expression $ax^2 + bx + c$ into one factor multiplied by another factor, you can easily solve for the **ROOTS**, the values of x for which the quadratic expression equals 0. Another way to solve a quadratic equation is by using the **QUADRATIC FORMULA**:

$$x = \frac{-b \pm \sqrt{b^2 - 4ac}}{2a}$$

The expression $b^2 - 4ac$ is called the **DISCRIMINANT**; when it is positive you will get two real numbers for x, when it is negative you will get one real number and one imaginary number for x, and when it is zero you will get one real number for x.

GRAPHING QUADRATIC EQUATIONS

Graphing a quadratic equation forms a **PARABOLA**. A parabola is a symmetrical, horseshoe-shaped curve; a vertical axis passes through its vertex. Each term in the equation $ax^2 + bx + c = 0$ affects the shape of the parabola. A bigger value for a makes the curve narrower, while a smaller value makes the curve wider. A negative value for a flips the parabola upside down. The **AXIS OF SYMMETRY** is the vertical line $x = \frac{-b}{2a}$. To find the y-coordinate for the **VERTEX** (the highest or lowest point on the parabola), plug this value for x into the expression $ax^2 + bx + c$. The easiest way to graph a quadratic equation is to find the axis of symmetry, solve for the vertex, and then create a table of points by plugging in other numbers for x and solving for y. Plot these points and trace the parabola.

Functions

FUNCTIONS describe how an input relates to an output. Linear equations, sine, and cosine are examples of functions. In a function, there must be one and only one output for each input. $\sqrt{x}$ is not a function because there are two outputs for any one input: $\sqrt{4} = 2, -2$.

DESCRIBING FUNCTIONS

Functions are often written in $f(x)$ form: $f(x) = x^2$ means that for input x the output is x^2. In relating functions to linear equations, you can think of $f(x)$ as equivalent to y. The **DOMAIN** of a function is all the possible inputs of that function. The **RANGE** of a function includes the outputs of the inputs. For example, for the function $f(x) = x^2$, if the domain includes all positive and negative integers the range will include 0 and only positive integers. When you graph a function, the domain is plotted on the x-axis and the range is plotted on the y-axis.

EXAMPLES

26. Given $f(x) = 2x - 10$, find $f(9)$.

27. Given $f(x) = \frac{4}{x}$ with a domain of all positive integers except zero, and $g(x) = \frac{4}{x}$ with a domain of all positive and negative integers except zero, which function has a range that includes the number −2?

EXPONENTIAL FUNCTIONS

An **EXPONENTIAL FUNCTION** is in the form $f(x) = a^x$, where $a > 0$. When $a > 1$, $f(x)$ approaches infinity as x increases and zero as x decreases. When $0 < a < 1$, $f(x)$ approaches zero as x increases and infinity as x increases. When $a = 1$, $f(x) = 1$. The graph of an exponential function where $a \neq 1$ will have a horizontal asymptote along the x-axis; the graph will never cross below the x-axis. The graph of an exponential function where $a = 1$ will be a horizontal line at $y = 1$. All graphs of exponential functions include the points $(0, 1)$ and $(1, a)$.

EXAMPLES

28. Graph the function: $f(x) = 3^x$.

29. Given $f(x) = 2^x$, solve for x when $f(x) = 64$.

LOGARITHMIC FUNCTIONS

A **LOGARITHMIC FUNCTION** is the inverse of an exponential function. Remember the definition of a log: if $\log_a x = b$, then $a^b = x$. Logarithmic functions are written in the form $f(x) = \log_a x$, where a is any number greater than 0, except for 1. If a is not shown, it is assumed that $a = 10$. The function $\ln x$ is called a **NATURAL LOG**, equal to $\log_e x$. When $0 < a < 1$, $f(x)$ approaches infinity as x approaches zero and negative infinity as x increases. When $a > 1$, $f(x)$ approaches negative infinity as x approaches zero and infinity as x increases. In either case, the graph of a logarithmic function has a vertical asymptote along the y-axis; the graph will never cross to the left of the y-axis. All graphs of logarithmic functions include the points $(1, 0)$ and $(a, 1)$.

EXAMPLES

30. Graph the function $f(x) = \log 4x$.

31. Given $f(x) = \log_{\frac{1}{3}} x$, solve for $f(81)$.

ARITHMETIC and GEOMETRIC SEQUENCES

SEQUENCES are patterns of numbers. In most questions about sequences you must determine the pattern. In an **ARITHMETIC SEQUENCE**, add or subtract the same number between terms. In a **GEOMETRIC SEQUENCE**, multiply or divide by the same number between terms. For example, 2, 6, 10, 14, 18 and 11, 4, –3, –10, –17 are arithmetic sequences because you add 4 to each term in the first example and you subtract 7 from each term in the second example. The sequence 5, 15, 45, 135 is a geometric sequence because you multiply each term by 3. In arithmetic sequences, the number by which you add or subtract is called the **COMMON DIFFERENCE**. In geometric sequences, the number by which you multiply or divide is called the **COMMON RATIO**.

In an arithmetic sequence, the nth term (a_n) can be found by calculating $a_n = a_1 + (n - 1)d$, where d is the common difference and a_1 is the first term in the sequence. In a geometric sequence, $a_n = a_1(r^n)$, where r is the common ratio.

EXAMPLES

32. Find the common difference and the next term of the following sequence: 5, –1, –7, –13

33. Find the 12th term of the following sequence: 2, 6, 18, 54

34. The fourth term of a sequence is 9. The common difference is 11. What is the 10th term?

Absolute Value

The **ABSOLUTE VALUE** of a number (represented by the symbol $||$) is its distance from zero, not its value. For example, $|3| = 3$, and $|-3| = 3$ because both 3 and –3 are three units from zero. The absolute value of a number is always positive.

Equations with absolute values will have two answers, so you need to set up two equations. The first is simply the equation with the absolute value symbol removed. For the second equation, isolate the absolute value on one side of the equation and multiply the other side of the equation by –1.

EXAMPLES

35. Solve for x: $|2x - 3| = x + 1$

36. Solve for y: $2|y + 4| = 10$

Solving Word Problems

Any of the math concepts discussed here can be turned into a word problem, and you'll likely see word problems in various formats throughout the test. (In fact, you may have noticed that several examples in the ratio and proportion sections were word problems.)

Be sure to read the entire problem before beginning to solve it: a common mistake is to provide an answer to a question that wasn't actually asked. Also, remember that not all of the information provided in a problem is necessarily needed to solve it.

When working multiple-choice word problems like those on the SAT, it's important to check your work. Many of the incorrect answer choices will be answers that result from common mistakes. So even if a solution you calculated is listed as an answer choice, that doesn't necessarily mean you've done the problem correctly—you have to check your own answer to be sure.

Some general steps for word-problem solving are:

1. Read the entire problem and determine what the question is asking.
2. List all of the given data and define the variables.
3. Determine the formula(s) needed or set up equations from the information in the problem.
4. Solve.
5. Check your answer. (Is the amount too large or small? Are the answers in the correct unit of measure?)

Word problems generally contain **KEY WORDS** that can help you determine what math processes may be required in order to solve them.

▶ **Addition:** *added, combined, increased by, in all, total, perimeter, sum,* and *more than*

▶ **Subtraction:** *how much more, less than, fewer than, exceeds, difference,* and *decreased*

▶ **Multiplication:** *of, times, area,* and *product*

▶ **Division:** *distribute, share, average, per, out of, percent,* and *quotient*

▶ **Equals:** *is, was, are, amounts to,* and *were*

BASIC WORD PROBLEMS

A word problem in algebra is just an equation or a set of equations described using words. Your task when solving these problems is to turn the *story* of the problem into mathematical equations. Converting units can often help you avoid operations with fractions when dealing with time.

37. A store owner bought a case of 48 backpacks for $476.00. He sold 17 of the backpacks in his store for $18 each, and the rest were sold to a school for $15 each. What was the store owner's profit?

38. Thirty students in Mr. Joyce's room are working on projects over 2 days. The first day, he gave them $\frac{3}{5}$ hour to work. On the second day, he gave them $\frac{1}{2}$ as much time as the first day. How much time did each student have to work on the project?

DISTANCE WORD PROBLEMS

Distance word problems involve something traveling at a constant or average speed. Whenever you read a problem that involves *how fast*, *how far*, or *for how long*, you should think of the distance equation, where *d* stands for distance, *r* for rate (speed), and *t* for time.

These problems can be solved by setting up a grid with *d*, *r*, and *t* along the top and each moving object on the left. When setting up the grid, make sure the units are consistent. For example, if the distance is in meters and the time is in seconds, the rate should be meters per second.

EXAMPLES

39. Will drove from his home to the airport at an average speed of 30 mph. He then boarded a helicopter and flew to the hospital at an average speed of 60 mph. The entire distance was 150 miles, and the trip took 3 hours. Find the distance from the airport to the hospital.

40. Two riders on horseback start at the same time from opposite ends of a field that is 45 miles long. One horse is moving at 14 mph and the second horse is moving at 16 mph. How long after they begin will they meet?

WORK PROBLEMS

WORK PROBLEMS involve situations where several people or machines are doing work at different rates. Your task is usually to figure out how long it will take these people or machines to complete a task while working together. The trick to doing work problems is to figure out how much of the project each person or machine completes in the same unit of time. For example, you might calculate how much of a wall a person can paint in 1 hour, or how many boxes an assembly line can pack in 1 minute.

DID YOU KNOW?

The SAT will give you most formulas you need to work problems, but they won't give you the formulas for percent change or work problems.

The next step is to set up an equation to solve for the total time. This equation is usually similar to the equation for distance, but here *work = rate × time*.

EXAMPLES

41. Bridget can clean an entire house in 12 hours while her brother Tom takes 8 hours. How long would it take for Bridget and Tom to clean 2 houses together?

42. Farmer Dan needs to water his cornfield. One hose can water a field 1.25 times faster than a second hose. When both hoses are running, they water the field together in 5 hours. How long would it take to water the field if only the slower hose is used?

43. Ben takes 2 hours to pick 500 apples, and Frank takes 3 hours to pick 450 apples. How long will they take, working together, to pick 1000 apples?

Answer Key

1. Plug in each number for the correct variable and simplify:

   $2x + 6y - 3z = 2(2) + 6(4) - 3(-3) =$
   $4 + 24 + 9 = $ **37**

2. Start by grouping together like terms:

   $(5xy + 11xy) + (2yz - 5yz) + 7y$

   Now you can add together each set of like terms:

   $16xy + 7y - 3yz$

3. Multiply the coefficients and variables together:

   $3 \times 2 = 6$

   $y^2 \times y^4 = y^6$

   $z \times z^5 = z^6$

   Now put all the terms back together:

   $6x^4y^6z^6$

4. Multiply each term inside the parentheses by the term $2y^2$:

   $(2y^2)(y^3 + 2xy^2z + 4z) =$

   $(2y^2 \times y^3) + (2y^2 \times 2xy^2z) \times$
   $(2y^2 \times 4z) =$

   $2y^5 + 4xy^4z + 8y^2z$

5. Use the acronym FOIL—first, outer, inner, last—to multiply the terms:

   first: $5x \times 3x = 15x^2$

   outer: $5x \times 3 = 15x$

   inner: $2 \times 3x = 6x$

   last: $2 \times 3 = 6$

   Now combine like terms:

   $15x^2 + 21x + 6$

6. Simplify by looking at each variable and checking for those that appear in the numerator and denominator:

   $\frac{2}{8} = \frac{1}{4}$

   $\frac{x^4}{x^2} = \frac{x^2}{1}$

   $\frac{z}{z^2} = \frac{1}{z}$

   $\frac{2x^4y^3z}{8x^2z^2} = \frac{x^2y^3}{4z}$

7. First, find the highest common factor. Both terms are divisible by 9:

   $\frac{27x^2}{9} = 3x^2$ and $\frac{9x}{9} = x$.

   Now the expression is $9(3x^2 - x)$. But wait, you're not done! Both terms can be divided by x:

   $\frac{3x^2}{x} = 3x$ and $\frac{x}{x} = 1$.

   The final factored expression is **$9x(3x - 1)$**.

8. Since there is no obvious factor by which you can divide terms, you should consider whether this expression fits one of your polynomial identities. This expression is a difference of squares: $a^2 - b^2$, where $a^2 = 25x^2$ and $b^2 = 16$.

   Recall that $a^2 - b^2 = (a + b)(a - b)$. Now solve for a and b:

   $a = 25x^2 = 5x$

   $b = \sqrt{16} = 4$

   $(a + b)(a - b) = $ **$(5x + 4)(5x - 4)$**

   You can check your work by using the FOIL acronym to expand your answer back to the original expression:

   first: $5x \times 5x = 25x^2$

   outer: $5x \times -4 = -20x$

   inner: $4 \times 5x = 20x$

   last: $4 \times -4 = -16$

   $25x^2 - 20x + 20x - 16 = 25x^2 - 16$

9. This is another polynomial identity, $a^2 + 2ab + b^2$. (The more you practice these problems, the faster you will recognize polynomial identities.)

$a^2 = 100x^2$, $2ab = 60x$, and $b^2 = 9$

Recall that $a^2 + 2ab + b^2 = (a + b)^2$. Now solve for a and b:

$a = \sqrt{100x^2} = 10x$

$b = \sqrt{9} = 3$

(Double check your work by confirming that $2ab = 2 \times 10x \times 3 = 60x$)

$(a + b)^2 = \mathbf{(10x + 3)^2}$

10. This equation has no parentheses, fractions, or like terms on the same side, so you can start by subtracting 12 from both sides of the equation:

$25x + 12 = 62$

$(25x + 12) - 12 = 62 - 12$

$25x = 50$

Now, divide by 25 to isolate the variable:

$\frac{25x}{25} = \frac{50}{25}$

$\mathbf{x = 2}$

11. Start by distributing to get rid of the parentheses (don't forget to distribute the negative):

$2x - 4(2x + 3) = 24 \rightarrow$

$2x - 8x - 12 = 24$

There are no fractions, so now you can join like terms:

$2x - 8x - 12 = 24 \rightarrow -6x - 12 = 24$

Now add 12 to both sides and divide by -6.

$-6x - 12 = 24 \rightarrow$

$(-6x - 12) + 12 = 24 + 12 \rightarrow$

$-6x = 36 \rightarrow \frac{-6x}{-6} = \frac{36}{-6}$

$\mathbf{x = -6}$

12. Start by multiplying by the least common denominator to get rid of the fractions:

$\frac{x}{3} + \frac{1}{2} = \frac{x}{6} - \frac{5}{12} \rightarrow$

$12\left(\frac{x}{3} + \frac{1}{2}\right) = 12\left(\frac{x}{6} - \frac{5}{12}\right) \rightarrow$

$4x + 6 = 2x - 5$

Now you can isolate the x:

$(4x + 6) - 6 = (2x - 5) - 6 \rightarrow$

$4x = 2x - 11 \rightarrow$

$(4x) - 2x = (2x - 11) - 2x \rightarrow$

$2x = -11$

$\mathbf{x = -\dfrac{11}{2}}$

13. This equation looks more difficult because it has 2 variables, but you can use the same steps to solve for x. First, distribute to get rid of the parentheses and combine like terms:

$2(x + y) - 7x = 14x + 3 \rightarrow$

$2x + 2y - 7x = 14x + 3 \rightarrow$

$-5x + 2y = 14x + 3$

Now you can move the x terms to one side and everything else to the other, and then divide to isolate x:

$-5x + 2y = 14x + 3 \rightarrow$

$-19x = -2y + 3 \rightarrow$

$\mathbf{x = \dfrac{2y - 3}{19}}$

14. Slope is easiest to find when the equation is in point-slope form: ($y = mx + b$). Rearrange the equation to isolate y:

$\frac{3y}{2} + 3 = x$

$3y + 6 = 2x$

$y + 2 = \frac{2x}{3}$

$y = \frac{2x}{3} - 2$

Finally, identify the term m to find the slope of the line:

$\mathbf{m = \dfrac{2}{3}}$

15. First, rearrange the linear equation to point-slope form

$(y = mx + b)$:

$2y - 4x = 6$

$y = 2x + 3$

Next, identify the y-intercept (b) and the slope (m):

$b = 3, m = 2$

Now, plot the y-intercept $(0,b) = (0,3)$:

Next, plug in values for x and solve for y:

$y = 2(1) + 3 = 5 \rightarrow (1,5)$

$y = 2(-1) + 3 = 1 \rightarrow (-1,1)$

Plot these points on the graph, and connect the points with a straight line:

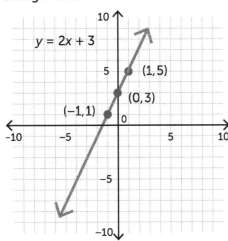

16. To solve this system using substitution, first solve one equation for a single variable:

$3y - 4 + x = 0$

$3y + x = 4$

$x = 4 - 3y$

Next, substitute the expression to the right of the equal sign for x in the second equation:

$5x + 6y = 11$

$5(4 - 3y) + 6y = 11$

$20 - 15y + 6y = 11$

$20 - 9y = 11$

$-9y = -9$

$y = 1$

Finally, plug the value for y back into the first equation to find the value of x:

$3y - 4 + x = 0$

$3(1) - 4 + x = 0$

$-1 + x = 0$

$x = 1$

The solution is **$x = 1$ and $y = 1$**, or the point **(1,1)**.

17. To solve this system using elimination, start by manipulating one equation so that a variable (in this case x) will cancel when the equations are added together:

$2x + 4y = 8$

$-2(2x + 4y = 8)$

$-4x - 8y = -16$

Now you can add the two equations together, and the x variable will drop out:

$-4x - 8y = -16$

$\underline{4x + 2y = 10}$

$-6y = -6$

$y = 1$

Lastly, plug the y value into one of the equations to find the value of x:

$2x + 4y = 8$

$2x + 4(1) = 8$

$2x + 4 = 8$

$2x = 4$

$x = 2$

The solution is **$x = 2$ and $y = 1$**, or the point **(2,1)**.

18. Start by building an equation. David's amount will be d, Jesse's amount will be j, and Mark's amount will be m. All three must add up to $100:

$$d + j + m = 100$$

It may seem like there are three unknowns in this situation, but you can express j and m in terms of d:

Jesse gets $10 less than David, so $j = d - 10$. Mark gets $15 less than Jesse, so $m = j - 15$.

Substitute the previous expression for j to solve for m in terms of d:

$$m = (d - 10) - 15 = d - 25$$

Now back to our original equation, substituting for j and m:

$$d + (d - 10) + (d - 25) = 100$$
$$3d - 35 = 100$$
$$3d = 135$$
$$d = 45$$

David will get **$45.**

19. Start by building an equation. One of the numbers in question will be x. The three numbers are consecutive, so if x is the smallest number then the other two numbers must be $(x + 1)$ and $(x + 2)$. You know that the sum of the three numbers is 54:

$$x + (x + 1) + (x + 2) = 54$$

Now solve for the equation to find x:

$$3x + 3 = 54$$
$$3x = 51$$
$$x = 17$$

The question asks about the middle number $(x + 1)$, so the answer is **18**.

Notice that you could have picked any number to be x. If you picked the middle number as x, your equation would be $(x - 1) + x + (x + 1) = 54$. Solve for x to get 18.

20. This word problem might seem complicated at first, but as long as you keep your variables straight and translate the words into mathematical operations you can easily build an equation. The quantity you want to solve is the number of girls on the swim team, so this will be x.

The number of boys on the swim team will be y. There are 6 fewer boys than girls so $y = x - 6$.

The total number of boys and girls on the swim team is $x + y$.

42 is 8 more than half this number, so $42 = 8 + (x + y) \div 2$

Now substitute for y to solve for x:

$$42 = 8 + (x + x - 6) \div 2$$
$$34 = (2x - 6) \div 2$$
$$68 = 2x - 6$$
$$74 = 2x$$
$$x = 37$$

There are 37 girls on the swim team.

21. Collect like terms on each side as you would for a regular equation:

$$-7x + 2 < 6 - 5x \rightarrow$$
$$-2x < 4$$

When you divide by a negative number, the direction of the sign switches:

$$-2x < 4 = \boldsymbol{x > -2}$$

22. To rearrange the inequality into $y = mx + b$ form, first subtract 4 from both sides:

$$-3x - 4 \geq -y$$

Next divide both sides by -1 to get positive y; remember to switch the direction of the inequality symbol:

$$3x + 4 \leq y$$

Now plot the line $y = 3x + 4$, making a solid line:

Finally, shade the side above the line:

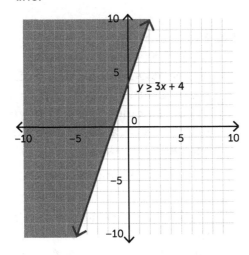

$y \geq 3x + 4$

23. Not every quadratic equation you see will be presented in the standard form. Rearrange terms to set one side equal to 0:

$2x^2 + 14x = 0$

Note that $a = 2$, $b = 14$, and $c = 0$ because there is no third term.

Now divide the expression on the left by the common factor:

$(2x)(x + 7) = 0$

To find the roots, set each of the factors equal to 0:

$2x = 0 \rightarrow x = \textbf{0}$

$x + 7 = 0 \rightarrow x = \textbf{-7}$

24. First rearrange the equation to set one side equal to 0:

$3x^2 - 7x + 2 = 0$

Next identify the terms a, b, and c:

$a = 3$, $b = -7$, $c = 2$

Now plug those terms into the quadratic formula:

$x = \dfrac{-b \pm \sqrt{b^2 - 4ac}}{2a}$

$x = \dfrac{7 \pm \sqrt{(-7)^2 - 4(3)(2)}}{2(3)}$

$x = \dfrac{7 \pm \sqrt{25}}{6}$

$x = \dfrac{7 \pm 5}{6}$

Since the determinant is positive, you can expect two real numbers for x. Solve for the two possible answers:

$x = \dfrac{7 + 5}{6} \rightarrow \textbf{x = 2}$

$x = \dfrac{7 - 5}{6} \rightarrow \textbf{x = }\dfrac{\textbf{1}}{\textbf{3}}$

25. First, find the axis of symmetry. The equation for the line of symmetry is $x = \dfrac{-b}{2a}$.

$x = \dfrac{-4}{2(1)} = -2$

Next, plug in −2 for x to find the y coordinate of the vertex:

$y = (-2)^2 + 4(-2) + 1 = -3$

The vertex is $(-2, -3)$.

Now, make a table of points on either side of the vertex by plugging in numbers for x and solving for y:

x	$y = x^2 + 4x + 1$	(x, y)
−3	$y = (-3)^2 + 4(-3)$ $+ 1 = -2$	(−3,−2)
−1	$y = (-1)^2 + 4(-1)$ $+ 1 = -2$	(−1,−2)
−4	$y = (-4)^2 + 4(-4)$ $+ 1 = 1$	(−4,1)
0	$y = 0^2 + 4(0)$ $+ 1 = 1$	(0,1)

Finally, draw the axis of symmetry, plot the vertex and your table of points, and trace the parabola:

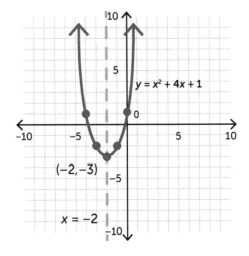

$y = x^2 + 4x + 1$

$(-2,-3)$

$x = -2$

26. Plug in 9 for x:

$f(9) = 2(9) - 10$

$\boldsymbol{f(9) = 8}$

27. The function $f(x)$ has a range of only positive numbers, since x cannot be negative. The function $g(x)$ has a range of positive and negative numbers, since x can be either positive or negative.

The number −2, therefore, must be in the range for $g(x)$ but not for $f(x)$.

28. First, estimate the shape and direction of the graph based on the value of a. Since $a > 1$, you know that $f(x)$ will approach infinity as x increases and there will be a horizontal asymptote along the negative x-axis.

Next, plot the points (0, 1) and (1, a).

Finally, plug in one or two more values for x, plot those points and trace the graph:

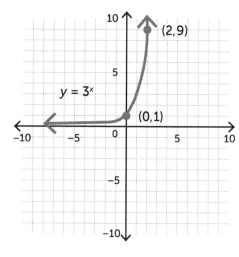

$f(2) = 3^2 = 9 \rightarrow (2, 9)$

29. $64 = 2^x$

The inverse of an exponent is a log. Take the log of both sides to solve for x:

$\log_2 64 = x$

$\boldsymbol{x = 6}$

30. First, estimate the shape and direction of the graph based on the value of a. Since $a > 1$, you know that $f(x)$ will approach infinity as x increases and there will be a vertical asymptote along the negative y-axis.

Next, plot the points (1, 0) and (a, 1).

Finally, it is easier to plug in a value for $f(x)$ and solve for x rather than attempting to solve for $f(x)$. Plug in one or two values for $f(x)$, plot those points and trace the graph:

$2 = \log_4 x$

$4^2 = x$

$16 = x \rightarrow (16, 2)$

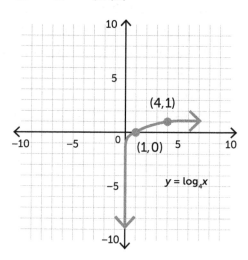

31. Rewrite the function in exponent form:

$x = \frac{1}{3}^{f(x)}$

$81 = \frac{1}{3}^{f(x)}$

The question is asking: to what power must you raise $\frac{1}{3}$ to get 81? Recognize that $3^4 = 81$,

so $\frac{1}{3}^4 = \frac{1}{81}$

Switch the sign of the exponent to flip the numerator and denominator:

$$\frac{1}{3}^{-4} = \frac{81}{1}$$

$$f(81) = -4$$

32. Find the difference between two terms that are next to each other:

$$5 - (-1) = -6$$

The common difference is –6. (It must be negative to show the difference is subtracted, not added.)

Now subtract 6 from the last term to find the next term:

$$-13 - 6 = -19$$

The next term is –19.

33. First, decide whether this is an arithmetic or geometric sequence. Since the numbers are getting farther and farther apart, you know this must be a geometric sequence.

Divide one term by the term before it to find the common ratio:

$$18 \div 6 = 3$$

Next, plug in the common ratio and the first term to the equation $a_n = a_1(r^n)$:

$$a_{12} = 2(3^{12})$$

$$\mathbf{a_{12} = 1{,}062{,}882}$$

Notice that it would have taken a very long time to multiply each term by 3 until you got the 12th term – this is where that equation comes in handy!

34. To answer this question, you can simply add 9 + 11 = 20 to get the 5th term, 20 + 11 = 31 to get the 6th term, and so on until you get the 10th term. Or you can plug the information you know into your equation $a_n = a_1 + (n-1)d$. In this

case, you do not know the first term. If you use the fourth term instead, you must replace $(n - 1)$ with $(n - 4)$:

$$a_{10} = 9 + (10 - 4)11$$

$$\mathbf{a_{10} = 75}$$

35. Set up the first equation by removing the absolute value symbol then solve for x:

$$|2x - 3| = x + 1$$

$$2x - 3 = x + 1$$

$$x = 4$$

For the second equation, remove the absolute value and multiply by –1:

$$|2x - 3| = x + 1 \rightarrow$$

$$2x - 3 = -(x + 1) \rightarrow$$

$$2x - 3 = -x - 1 \rightarrow$$

$$3x = 2$$

$$x = \frac{2}{3}$$

Both answers are correct, so the complete answer is $\mathbf{x = 4}$ **or** $\mathbf{\frac{2}{3}}$.

36. Set up the first equation:

$$2(y + 4) = 10$$

$$y + 4 = 5$$

$$y = 1$$

Set up the second equation. Remember to isolate the absolute value before multiplying by –1:

$$2|y + 4| = 10 \rightarrow$$

$$|y + 4| = 5 \rightarrow$$

$$y + 4 = -5$$

$$y = -9$$

$$\mathbf{y = 1 \text{ or } -9}$$

37. Start by listing all the data and defining the variable:

total number of backpacks = 48

cost of backpacks = \$476.00

backpacks sold in store at price of $18 = 17

backpacks sold to school at a price of $15 = 48 − 17 = 31

total profit = x

Now set up an equation:

income − cost = total profit

(306 + 465) − 476 = 295

The store owner made a profit of **$295**.

38. Start by listing all the data and defining your variables. Note that the number of students, while given in the problem, is not needed to find the answer:

    time on 1st day = $\frac{3}{5}$ hr. = 36 min.

    time on 2nd day = $\frac{1}{2}$(36) = 18 min.

    total time = x

    Now set up the equation and solve:

    total time = time on 1st day + time on 2nd day

    x = 36 + 18 = 54

    The students had **54 minutes** to work on the projects.

39. The first step is to set up a table and fill in a value for each variable:

	d	r	t
driving	d	30	t
flying	150 − d	60	3 − t

    You can now set up equations for driving and flying. The first row gives the equation $d = 30t$ and the second row gives the equation 150 − d = 60(3 − t).

    Next, solve this system of equations. Start by substituting for d in the second equation:

    $d = 30t$

150 − d = 60(3 − t) → 150 − 30t = 60(3 − t)

Now solve for t:

150 − 30t = 180 − 60t

−30 = −30t

1 = t

Although you've solved for t, you're not done yet. Notice that the problem asks for distance. So, you need to solve for d: what the problem asked for. It does not ask for time, but you need to calculate it to solve the problem.

Driving: 30t = 30 miles

Flying: 150 − d = 120 miles

The distance from the airport to the hospital is 120 miles.

40. First, set up the table. The variable for time will be the same for each, because they will have been on the field for the same amount of time when they meet:

	d	r	t
horse #1	d	14	t
horse #2	45 − d	16	t

    Next set up two equations:

    Horse #1: $d = 14t$

    Horse #2: 45 − d = 16t

    Now substitute and solve:

    $d = 14t$

    45 − d = 16t → 45 − 14t = 16t

    45 = 30t

    t = 1.5

    They will meet 1.5 hr. after they begin.

41. Start by figuring out how much of a house each sibling can clean on his or her own. Bridget can clean the house in 12 hours, so she can clean $\frac{1}{12}$ of the house in an hour.

Using the same logic, Tom can clean $\frac{1}{8}$ of a house in an hour.

By adding these values together, you get the fraction of the house they can clean together in an hour:

$\frac{1}{12} + \frac{1}{8} = \frac{5}{24}$

They can do $\frac{5}{24}$ of the job per hour.

Now set up variables and an equation to solve:

t = time spent cleaning (in hours)

h = number of houses cleaned = 2

work = rate × time

$h = \frac{5}{24}t \rightarrow$

$2 = \frac{5}{24}t \rightarrow$

$t = \frac{48}{5} = \mathbf{9\frac{3}{5}}$ **hr.**

42. In this problem you don't know the exact time, but you can still find the hourly rate as a variable:

The first hose completes the job in f hours, so it waters $\frac{1}{f}$ field per hour. The slow hose waters the field in $1.25f$, so it waters the field in $\frac{1}{1.25f}$ hours. Together, they take 5 hours to water the field, so they water $\frac{1}{5}$ of the field per hour.

Now you can set up the equations and solve:

$\frac{1}{f} + \frac{1}{1.25f} = \frac{1}{5} \rightarrow$

$1.25f(\frac{1}{f} + \frac{1}{1.25f}) = 1.25f(\frac{1}{5}) \rightarrow$

$1.25 + 1 = 0.25f$

$2.25 = 0.25f$

$f = 9$

The fast hose takes 9 hours to water the field. The slow hose takes 1.25(9) = **11.25 hours**.

43. Calculate how many apples each person can pick per hour:

Ben: $\frac{500 \text{ apples}}{2 \text{ hr.}} = \frac{250 \text{ appes}}{\text{hr.}}$

Frank: $\frac{450 \text{ aples}}{3 \text{ hr.}} = \frac{150 \text{ appes}}{\text{hr.}}$

Together: $\frac{250 + 150 \text{ aples}}{\text{hr.}} = \frac{400 \text{ apples}}{\text{hr.}}$

Now set up an equation to find the time it takes to pick 1000 apples:

total time = $\frac{1 \text{ hr.}}{400 \text{ apples}} \times 1000$

apples = $\frac{1000}{400 \text{ hr.}} = \mathbf{2.5 \text{ hours}}$

CHAPTER FIVE
Geometry

Properties of Shapes
AREA and PERIMETER

AREA and PERIMETER problems require you to use the equations shown in the table below to find either the area inside a shape or the distance around it (the perimeter). These equations will not be given on the test, so you need to have them memorized on test day.

Table 5.1. Area and Perimeter Equations

SHAPE	AREA	PERIMETER
circle	$A = \pi r^2$	$C = 2\pi r = \pi d$
triangle	$A = \dfrac{b \times h}{2}$	$P = s_1 + s_2 + s_3$
square	$A = s^2$	$P = 4s$
rectangle	$A = l \times w$	$P = 2l + 2w$

EXAMPLES

1. A farmer has purchased 100 meters of fencing to enclose his rectangular garden. If one side of the garden is 20 meters long and the other is 28 meters long, how much fencing will the farmer have left over?

2. Taylor is going to paint a square wall that is 3.5 meters high. How much paint will he need?

VOLUME

Volume is the amount of space taken up by a three-dimensional object. Different formulas are used to find the volumes of different shapes.

Table 5.2. Volume Formulas	
SHAPE	VOLUME
cylinder	$V = \pi r^2 h$
pyramid	$V = \frac{l \times w \times h}{3}$
cone	$V = \frac{\pi r^2 h}{3}$
sphere	$V = \frac{4}{3}\pi r^3$

EXAMPLES

3. Charlotte wants to fill her circular swimming pool with water. The pool has a diameter of 6 meters and is 1 meter deep. How many cubic meters of water will she need to fill the pool?

4. Danny has a fishbowl that is filled to the brim with water, and purchased some spherical glass marbles to line the bottom of it. He dropped in four marbles, and water spilled out of the fishbowl. If the radius of each marble is 1 centimeter, how much water spilled?

CIRCLES

The definition of a circle is the set of points that are equal distance from a center point. The distance from the center to any given point on the circle is the **RADIUS**. If you draw a straight line segment across the circle going through the center, the distance along the line segment from one side of the circle to the other is called the **DIAMETER**. The radius is always equal to half the diameter: $d = 2r$.

DID YOU KNOW?
The equation for a circle on coordinate plane is $(x - h)2 + (y - k)2 = r2$ where (h,k) is the center of the circle and r is the radius.

A **CENTRAL ANGLE** is formed by drawing radii out from the center to two points A and B along the circle. The **INTERCEPTED ARC** is the portion of the circle (the arc length) between points A and B. You can find the intercepted arc length l if you know the central angle θ and vice versa:

$$l = 2\pi r \frac{\theta}{360°}$$

A **CHORD** is a line segment that connects two points on a circle. Unlike the diameter, a chord does not have to go through the center. You can find the chord length if you know either the central angle θ or the radius of the circle r and the distance from the center of the circle to the chord d (d must be at a right angle to the chord):

If you know the central angle, chord length = $2r\sin\frac{\theta}{2}$

If you know the radius and distance, chord length = $2\sqrt{r^2 - d^2}$

A **SECANT** is similar to a chord; it connects two points on a circle. The difference is that a secant is a line, not a line segment, so it extends outside of the circle on either side.

A **TANGENT** is a straight line that touches a circle at only one point.

A **SECTOR** is the area within a circle that is enclosed by a central angle; if a circle is a pie, a sector is the piece of pie cut by two radii. You can find the **AREA OF A SECTOR** if you know either the central angle θ or the arc length s

If you know the central angle, the area of the sector = $\pi r^2 \frac{\theta}{360°}$

If you know the arc length, the area of a sector = $\frac{1}{2}rl$

There are two other types of angles you can create in or around a circle. **INSCRIBED ANGLES** are *inside* the circle: the vertex is a point P on the circle and the rays extend to two other points on the circle (A and B). As long as A and B remain constant, you can move the vertex P anywhere along the circle and the inscribed angle will be the same. **CIRCUMSCRIBED ANGLES** are *outside* of the circle: the rays are formed by two tangent lines that touch the circle at points A and B.

You can find the inscribed angle if you know the radius of the circle r and the arc length l between A and B:

$$\text{inscribed angle} = \frac{90°l}{\pi r}$$

To find the circumscribed angle, find the central angle formed by the same points A and B and subtract that angle from 180°.

EXAMPLES

5. A circle has a diameter of 10 centimeters. What is the intercepted arc length between points A and B if the central angle between those points measures 46°?

6. A chord is formed by line segment $\overline{QP}$. The radius of the circle is 5 cm and the chord length is 6 cm. Find the distance from center C to the chord.

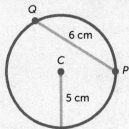

Congruence

CONGRUENCE means having the same size and shape. Two shapes are congruent if you can turn (rotate), flip (reflect), and/or slide (translate) one to fit perfectly on top of the other. Two angles are congruent if they measure the same number of degrees; they do not have to face the same direction nor must they necessarily have rays of equal length. If two triangles have one of the combinations of congruent sides and/or angles listed below, then those triangles are congruent:

▶ **SSS** – side, side, side

▶ **ASA** – angle, side, angle

▶ **SAS** – side, angle, side

▶ **AAS** – angle, angle, side

There are a number of common sets of congruent angles in geometry. An **ISOSCELES TRIANGLE** has two sides of equal length (called the legs) and two congruent angles. If you bisect an isosceles triangle by drawing a line perpendicular to the third side (called the base), you will form two congruent right triangles.

Where two lines cross and form an *X*, the opposite angles are congruent and are called **VERTICAL ANGLES**. **PARALLEL LINES** are lines that never cross; if you cut two parallel lines by a transversal, you will form four pairs of congruent **CORRESPONDING ANGLES**.

A **PARALLELOGRAM** is a quadrilateral in which both pairs of opposite sides are parallel and congruent (of equal length). In a parallelogram, the two pairs of opposite angles are also congruent. If you divide a parallelogram by either of the diagonals, you will form two congruent triangles.

EXAMPLES

7. Kate and Emily set out for a bike ride together from their house. They ride 6 miles north, then Kate turns 30° to the west and Emily turns 30° to the east. They both ride another 8 miles. If Kate rides 12 miles to return home, how far must Emily ride to get home?

8. Angle *A* measures 53°. Find angle *H*.

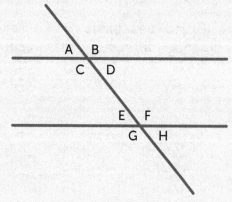

Right Triangles and Trigonometry
PYTHAGOREAN THEOREM

Shapes with 3 sides are known as **TRIANGLES**. In addition to knowing the formulas for their area and perimeter, you should also know the Pythagorean Theorem, which describes the relationship between the three sides (a, b, and c) of a triangle:

$$a^2 + b^2 = c^2$$

EXAMPLE

9. Erica is going to run a race in which she'll run 3 miles due north and 4 miles due east. She'll then run back to the starting line. How far will she run during this race?

TRIGONOMETRY

Using **TRIGONOMETRY**, you can calculate an angle in a right triangle based on the ratio of two sides of that triangle. You can also calculate one of the side lengths using the measure of an angle and another side. **SINE (SIN)**, **COSINE (COS)**, and **TANGENT (TAN)** correspond to the three possible ratios of side lengths. They are defined below:

$$\sin \theta = \frac{opposite}{hypotenuse} \qquad \cos \theta = \frac{adjacent}{hypotenuse} \qquad \tan \theta = \frac{opposite}{adjacent}$$

Opposite is the side opposite from the angle θ, *adjacent* is the side adjacent to the angle θ, and *hypotenuse* is the longest side of the triangle, opposite from the right angle. SOH-CAH-TOA is an acronym to help you remember which ratio goes with which function.

When solving for a side or an angle in a right triangle, first identify which function to use based on the known lengths or angle.

EXAMPLES

10. Phil is hanging holiday lights. To do so safely, he must lean his 20-foot ladder against the outside of his house an angle of 15° or less. How far from the house he can safely place the base of the ladder?

11. Grace is practicing shooting hoops. She is 5 feet 4 inches tall; her basketball hoop is 10 feet high. From 8 feet away, at what angle does she have to look up to see the hoop? Assume that her eyes are 4 inches lower than the top of her head.

Coordinate Geometry

Coordinate geometry is the study of points, lines, and shapes that have been graphed on a set of axes.

POINTS, LINES, and PLANES

In coordinate geometry, points are plotted on a **COORDINATE PLANE**, a two-dimensional plane in which the *x*-**AXIS** indicates horizontal direction and the *y*-**AXIS** indicates vertical direction. The intersection of these two axes is the **ORIGIN**. Points are defined by their location in relation to the horizontal and vertical axes. The coordinates of a point are written **(X, Y)**. The coordinates of the origin are $(0, 0)$. The *x*-coordinates to the right of the origin and the *y*-coordinates above it are positive; the *x*-coordinates to the left of the origin and the *y*-coordinates below it are negative.

A **LINE** is formed by connecting any two points on a coordinate plane; lines are continuous in both directions. Lines can be defined by their **SLOPE**, or steepness, and their *y*-**INTERCEPT**, or the point at which they intersect the *y*-axis. A line is represented by the equation $y = mx + b$. The constant *m* represents slope and the constant *b* represents the *y*-intercept.

EXAMPLES

12. Matt parks his car near a forest where he goes hiking. From his car he hikes 1 mile north, 2 miles east, then 3 miles west. If his car represents the origin, find the coordinates of Matt's current location.

13 A square is drawn on a coordinate plane. The bottom corners are located at (−2,3) and (4,3). What are the coordinates for the top right corner?

THE DISTANCE and MIDPOINT FORMULAS

To determine the distance between the points (x_1, y_1) and (x_2, y_2) from a grid use the formula:

$$d = \sqrt{(x_2 - x_1)^2 + (y_2 - y_1)^2}$$

The midpoint, which is halfway between the 2 points, is the point:

$$\left(\frac{x_1 + x_2}{2}, \frac{y_1 + y_2}{2} \right)$$

EXAMPLES

14. What is the distance between points (3,−6) and (−5,2)?

15. What is the midpoint between points (3,−6) and (−5,2)?

Answer Key

1. The perimeter of a rectangle is equal to twice its length plus twice its width:

   $P = 2(20) + 2(28) = 96$ m

   The farmer has 100 meters of fencing, so he'll have 100 − 96 = **4 meters** left.

2. Each side of the square wall is 3.5 meters:

   $A = 3.5^2 =$ **12.25m²**

3. This question is asking about the volume of Charlotte's pool. The circular pool is actually a cylinder, so use the formula for a cylinder: $V = \pi r^2 h$.

   The diameter is 6 meters. The radius is half the diameter so $r = 6 \div 2 = 3$ meters.

   Now solve for the volume:

   $V = \pi r^2 h$

   $V = \pi (3 \text{ m})^2 (1 \text{ m})$

   $V = 28.3$ m³

   Charlotte will need approximately **28.3 cubic meters** of water to fill her pool.

4. Since the fishbowl was filled to the brim, the volume of the water that spilled out of it is equal to the volume of the marbles that Danny dropped into it. First, find the volume of one marble using the equation for a sphere:

   $V = \frac{4}{3}\pi r^3$

   $V = \frac{4}{3}\pi (1 \text{ cm})^3$

   $V = 4.2$ cm³

   Since Danny dropped in 4 marbles, multiply this volume by 4 to find the total volume:

   $4.2 \text{cm}^3 \times 4 = 16.8$ cm³

Approximately **16.8 cubic centimeters** of water spilled out of the fishbowl.

5. First divide the diameter by two to find the radius:

   $r = 10 \text{ cm} \div 2 = 5 \text{ cm}$

   Now use the formula for intercepted arc length:

   $l = 2\pi r \frac{\theta}{360°}$

   $l = 2\pi (5 \text{ cm}) \frac{46°}{360°}$

   $l = 4.0$ cm

6. Use the formula for chord length:

   chord length $= 2\sqrt{r^2 - d^2}$

   In this example, we are told the chord length and the radius, and we need to solve for d:

   $6 \text{ cm} = 2\sqrt{(5 \text{ cm})^2 - d^2}$

   $3 \text{ cm} = \sqrt{(5 \text{ cm})^2 - d^2}$

   $9 \text{ cm}^2 = 25 \text{ cm}^2 - d^2$

   $d^2 = 16 \text{ cm}^2$

   $d = 4$ cm

   Points A and B are located on a circle. The arc length between A and B is 2 centimeters. The diameter of the circle is 8 centimeters. Find the inscribed angle.

   First, divide the diameter by two to find the radius:

   $r = \frac{1}{2}(8 \text{ cm})$

   $r = 4$ cm

   Now use the formula for an inscribed angle:

   inscribed angle $= \frac{9°l}{\pi r}$

   insribed angle $= \frac{90°(2 \text{ cm})}{\pi(4 \text{ cm})}$

   inscribed angle = 14.3°

7. Draw out Kate's and Emily's trips to see that their routes form two triangles. The triangles have corresponding sides with lengths of 6 miles and 8 miles, and a corresponding angle in between of 120°. This fits the "SAS" rule so the triangles must be congruent. The length Kate has to ride home corresponds to the length Emily has to ride home, so **Emily must ride 12 miles.**

8. For parallel lines cut by a transversal, look for vertical and corresponding angles.

Angles *A* and *D* are vertical angles, so angle *D* must be congruent to angle *A*. Angle *D* = 53°.

Angles *D* and *H* are corresponding angles, so angle *H* must be congruent to angle *D*. **Angle H = 53°.**

9. Start by drawing a picture of Erica's route. You'll see it forms a triangle:

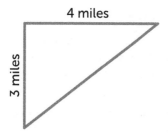

One leg of the triangle is missing, but you can find its length using the Pythagorean Theorem:

$a^2 + b^2 = c^2$

$3^2 + 4^2 = c^2$

$25 = c^2$

$c = 5$

Adding all 3 sides gives the length of the whole race:

$3 + 4 + 5 =$ **12 miles**

10. Draw a triangle with the known length and angle labeled.

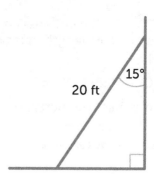

The known side (the length of the ladder) is the hypotenuse of the triangle, and the unknown distance is the side opposite the angle. Therefore, you can use sine:

$\sin\theta = \dfrac{oposite}{hypotenuse}$

$\sin15° = \dfrac{opposite}{20 \text{ feet}}$

Now solve for the opposite side:

$opposite = \sin15°(20 \text{ feet})$

$opposite =$ **5.2 feet**

11. Draw a diagram and notice that the line from Grace's eyes to the hoop of the basket forms the hypotenuse of a right triangle. The side adjacent to the angle of her eyes is the distance from the basket: 8 feet. The side opposite to Grace's eyes is the difference between the height of her eyes and the height of the basket: 10 feet – 5 feet = 5 feet.

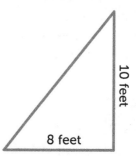

Next, use the formula for tangent to solve for the angle:

$$\tan\theta = \frac{opposite}{adjacent}$$

$$\tan\theta = \frac{5\ ft}{8\ ft}$$

Now take the inverse tangent of both sides to solve for the angle:

$$\theta = \tan^{-1}\frac{5}{8}.$$

$$\theta = 32°$$

12. To find the coordinates, you must find Matt's displacement along the x- and y-axes. Matt hiked 1 mile north and zero miles south, so his displacement along the y-axis is +1 mile. Matt hiked 2 miles east and 3 miles west, so his displacement along the x-axis is + 2 miles − 3 miles = −1 mile.

   Matt's coordinates are (−1,1).

13. Draw the coordinate plane and plot the given points. If you connect these points you will see that the bottom side is 6 units long. Since it is a square, all sides must be 6 units long. Count 6 units up from the point (4,3) to find the top right corner.

   The coordinates for the top right corner are (4,9).

14. Plug the values for $x_1, x_2, y_1,$ and y_2 into the distance formula and simplify:

$$d = \sqrt{(-5-3)^2 + (2-(-6))^2} =$$
$$\sqrt{64+64} = \sqrt{64 \times 2} = \mathbf{8\sqrt{2}}$$

15. Plug the values for $x_1, x_2, y_1,$ and y_2 into the midpoint formula and simplify:

$$midpoint = \left(\frac{3+(-5)}{2}, \frac{(-6)+2}{2}\right)$$
$$= \left(\frac{-2}{2}, \frac{-4}{2}\right) = \mathbf{(-1,-2)}$$

CHAPTER SIX
Statistics and Probability

Describing Sets of Data

STATISTICS is the study of sets of data. The goal of statistics is to take a group of values—numerical answers from a survey, for example—and look for patterns in how that data is distributed.

When looking at a set of data, it's helpful to consider the **MEASURES OF CENTRAL TENDENCY**, a group of values that describe the central or typical data point from the set. The SAT covers three measures of central tendency: mean, median, and mode.

MEAN is the mathematical term for *average*. To find the mean, total all the terms and divide by the number of terms. The **MEDIAN** is the middle number of a given set. To find the median, put the terms in numerical order; the middle number will be the median. In the case of a set of even numbers, the middle two numbers are averaged. **MODE** is the number which occurs most frequently within a given set. If two different numbers both appear with the highest frequency, they are both the mode.

When examining a data set, also consider **MEASURES OF VARIABILITY**, which describe how the data is dispersed around the central data point. The SAT covers two measures of variability: range and standard deviation. **RANGE** is simply the difference between the largest and smallest values in the set. **STANDARD DEVIATION** is a measure of how dispersed the data is, or how far it reaches from the mean.

EXAMPLES

1. Find the mean of 24, 27, and 18.

2. The mean of three numbers is 45. If two of the numbers are 38 and 43, what is the third number?

3. What is the median of 24, 27, and 18?

4. What is the median of 24, 27, 18, and 19?

5. What is the mode of 2, 5, 4, 4, 3, 2, 8, 9, 2, 7, 2, and 2?

6. What is the standard deviation of 62, 63, 61, and 66?

Graphs and Charts

These questions require you to interpret information from graphs and charts; they are pretty straightforward as long as you pay careful attention to detail. There are several different graph and chart types that may appear on the SAT.

BAR GRAPHS

BAR GRAPHS present the numbers of an item that exist in different categories. The categories are shown on the *x*-axis, and the number of items is shown on the *y*-axis. Bar graphs are usually used to easily compare amounts.

EXAMPLES

7. The chart below shows rainfall in inches per month. Which month had the least amount of rainfall? Which had the most?

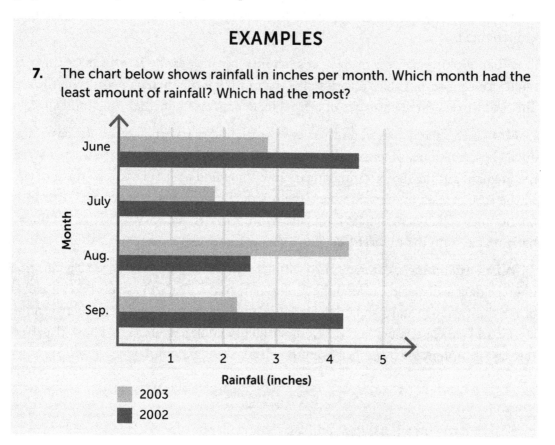

8. Using the chart below, how many more ice cream cones were sold in July than in September?

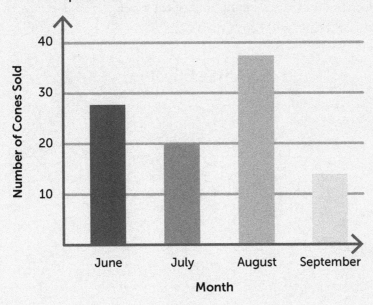

PIE CHARTS

PIE CHARTS present parts of a whole, and are often used with percentages. Together, all the slices of the pie add up to the total number of items, or 100%.

EXAMPLES

9. The pie chart below shows the distribution of birthdays in a class of students. How many students have birthdays in the spring or summer?

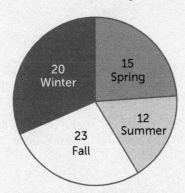

Distribution of Students' Birthdays

10. Using the same graph above, what percentage of students have birthdays in winter?

LINE GRAPHS

LINE GRAPHS show trends over time. The number of each item represented by the graph will be on the *y*-axis, and time will be on the *x*-axis.

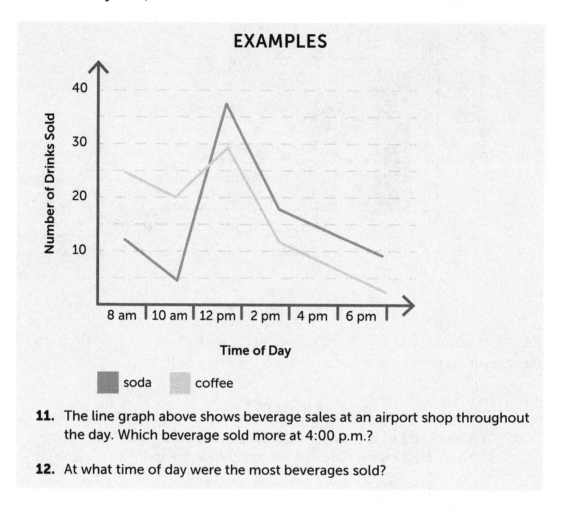

EXAMPLES

11. The line graph above shows beverage sales at an airport shop throughout the day. Which beverage sold more at 4:00 p.m.?

12. At what time of day were the most beverages sold?

HISTOGRAMS

A HISTOGRAM shows a distribution of types within a whole in bar chart form. While they look like bar graphs, they are more similar to pie charts: they show you parts of a whole.

EXAMPLE

13. The chart on the following page shows the number of cars that traveled through a toll plaza throughout the day. How many cars passed through the toll plaza between 8:00 a.m. and 5:00 p.m.?

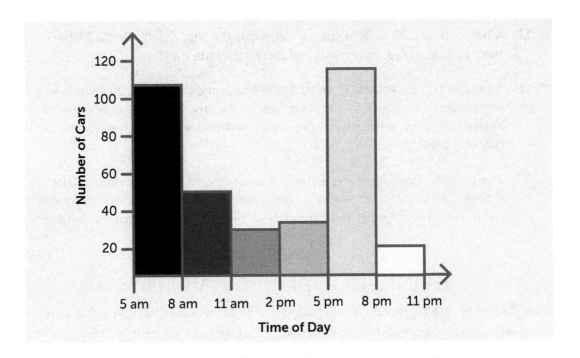

Probability

PROBABILITY is the likelihood that an event will take place. This likelihood is expressed as a value between 0 and 1. The closer the probability is to zero, the less likely the event is to occur; the closer the probability is to 1, the more likely it is to occur.

PROBABILITY of a SINGLE EVENT

The probability of an outcome occurring is found by dividing the number of desired outcomes by the number of total possible outcomes. As with percentages, a probability is the ratio of a part to a whole, with the whole being the total number of possibilities, and the part being the number of desired results. Probabilities can be written using percentages (40%), decimals (0.4), fractions, or in words (the probability of an outcome is 2 in 5).

$$\text{probability} = \frac{\text{desired outcomes}}{\text{total possible outcomes}}$$

EXAMPLES

14. A bag holds 3 blue marbles, 5 green marbles, and 7 red marbles. If you pick one marble from the bag, what is the probability it will be blue?

15. A bag contains 75 balls. If the probability is 0.6 that a ball selected from the bag will be red, how many red balls are in the bag?

16. A theater has 230 seats: 75 seats are in the orchestra area, 100 seats are in the mezzanine, and 55 seats are in the balcony. If a ticket is selected at random, what is the probability that it will be for either a mezzanine or balcony seat?

17. The probability of selecting a student whose name begins with the letter *S* from a school attendance log is 7%. If there are 42 students whose names begin with *S* enrolled at the school, how many students in total attend it?

CONDITIONAL PROBABILITY

CONDITIONAL PROBABILITY refers to the chances of one event occurring, given that another event has already occurred. INDEPENDENT EVENTS are events that have no effect on one another. The classic example is flipping a coin: whether you flip heads or tails one time has no bearing on how you might flip the next time. Your chance of flipping heads is always 50/50. DEPENDENT EVENTS, on the other hand, have an effect on the next event's probability. If you have a bag full of red and blue marbles, removing a red marble the first time will decrease the probability of picking a red marble the second time, since now there are fewer red marbles in the bag. The probability of event *B* occurring, given that event *A* has occurred, is written *P(B|A)*.

The probability of either event *A* or event *B* occurring is called the UNION of events *A* and *B*, written $A \cup B$. The probability of $A \cup B$ is equal to the sum of the probability of *A* occurring and the probability of *B* occurring, minus the probability of both *A* and *B* occurring. The probability of both *A* and *B* occurring is called the INTERSECTION of events *A* and *B*, written $A \cap B$. The probability of $A \cap B$ is equal to the product of the probability of *A* and the probability of *B*, given *A*. Review the equations for the probabilities of unions and intersections below:

$$P(A \cup B) = P(A) + P(B) - P(A \cap B)$$
$$P(A \cap B) = P(A) \times P(B|A)$$

The COMPLEMENT of an event is when the event does not occur. The probability of the complement of event *A*, written *P(A')*, is equal to 1 – *P(A)*.

EXAMPLES

18. A bag contains 5 red marbles and 11 blue marbles. What is the probability of pulling out a blue marble, followed by a red marble?

19. Caroline randomly draws a playing card from a full deck. What is the chance she will select either a queen or a diamond?

Test Your Knowledge

For questions 1 – 10, work the problem and choose the most correct answer.

1. A car rental company charges a daily fee of $48 plus 25% of the daily fee for every hour the car is late. If you rent a car for 2 days and bring it back 2 hours late, what will be the total charge?

   A) $72
   B) $108
   C) $120
   D) $144

2. One-way city bus tickets cost $1.75. The transportation department offers a monthly bus pass for $48. During the week, Jun commutes to work roundtrip on the bus. If Jun bought the monthly pass, how many days would he have to commute per month in order to save money?

   A) 7
   B) 13
   C) 14
   D) 28

3. A bag contains 30 marbles: $\frac{1}{6}$ are red, $\frac{1}{3}$ are blue, $\frac{1}{5}$ are white, and $\frac{3}{10}$ are black. If 2 white marbles and 1 blue marble are removed, what proportion of marbles left in the bag is blue?

   A) $\frac{1}{6}$
   B) $\frac{2}{9}$
   C) $\frac{1}{3}$
   D) $\frac{5}{14}$

4. A sporting goods store is offering an additional 30% off all clearance items. Angie purchases a pair of running shoes on clearance for $65.00. If the shoes originally cost $85.00, what was her total discount?

   A) 22.9%
   B) 39.2%
   C) 46.5%
   D) 53.5%

5. $2(b + 4.8) = 11b - 1.2$

   What is the value of b in the equation above?

   A) 0.6
   B) 1.2
   C) 4.5
   D) 5.4

6. If $f(x) = |x - 28|$, what is the value of $f(-12)$?

   A) −40
   B) −16
   C) 16
   D) 40

7. Melissa is ordering fencing to enclose a square area of 5625 square feet. How many feet of fencing does she need?

   A) 75 feet
   B) 150 feet
   C) 300 feet
   D) 5,625 feet

8. To get to school, Kaitlin bikes 4 blocks north from her house, then turns right and bikes 5 blocks east. How many blocks shorter would her trip be if she could ride her bike in a straight line from her house to school?

A) 2.6

B) 3.2

C) 6.0

D) 6.4

9. A circular swimming pool has a circumference of 49 feet. What is the diameter of the pool in feet?

A) 7.8 feet

B) 12.3 feet

C) 15.6 feet

D) 17.8 feet

10. Three boats are positioned in a lake at points A, B, and C as shown below. Which of the following expressions gives the approximate distance, in meters, between Point A and Point C? (Note: For $\triangle DEF$, where d, e, and f are the lengths of the sides opposite $\angle D$, $\angle E$, and $\angle F$, respectively, $\frac{\sin\theta D}{d} = \frac{\sin\theta E}{e} = \frac{\sin\theta F}{f}$).

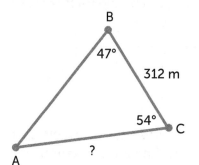

A) $\frac{312\sin47}{\sin79}$

B) $\frac{312\sin54}{\sin79}$

C) $\frac{312\sin79}{\sin47}$

D) $\frac{312\sin47}{\sin54}$

Answer Key
EXAMPLES

1. Add the terms, then divide by the number of terms:

   mean $= \frac{24 + 27 + 8}{3} = $ **23**

2. Set up the equation for mean with x representing the third number, then solve:

   $mean = \frac{38 + 43\ x}{3} = 45$

   $\frac{38 + 43 + x}{3} = 45$

   $38 + 43 + x = 135$

   $x = 54$

3. Place the terms in order, then pick the middle term:

   18, 24, 27

   The median is **24**.

4. Place the terms in order. Because there is an even number of terms, the median will be the average of the middle 2 terms:

   18, 19, 24, 27

   $median = \frac{19 + 4}{2} = $ **21.5**

5. The mode is **2** because it appears the most within the set.

6. To find the standard deviation, first find the mean:

   $mean = \frac{62 + 63 + 61 + 66}{4} = 63$

   Next, find the difference between each term and the mean, and square that number:

   $63 - 62 = 1 \rightarrow 1^2 = 1$

   $63 - 63 = 0 \rightarrow 0^2 = 0$

   $63 - 61 = 2 \rightarrow 2^2 = 4$

   $63 - 66 = -3 \rightarrow (-3)^2 = 9$

   Now, find the mean of the squares:

   mean $= \frac{1 + 0 + 4 + 9}{4} = 3.5$

   Finally, find the square root of the mean:

   $\sqrt{3.5} = 1.87$

   The standard deviation is **1.87**.

7. The shortest bar will be the month that had the least rain, and the longest bar will correspond to the month with the greatest amount: **July 2003 had the least**, and **June 2002 had the most**.

8. Tracing from the top of each bar to the scale on the left shows that sales in July were 20 and September sales were 15. So, **5 more cones were sold in July**.

9. 15 students have birthdays in the spring and 12 in winter, so there are **27 students** with birthdays in spring or summer.

10. Use the equation for percent:

    percent $= \frac{part}{whole} = \frac{winter\ birthdays}{total\ birthdays} \rightarrow$

    $\frac{20}{20 + 15 + 23 + 12} = \frac{20}{70} = \frac{2}{7} = .286$

    or **28.6%**

11. At 4:00 p.m., approximately 12 sodas and 5 coffees were sold, so more **soda** was sold.

12. This question is asking for the time of day with the most sales of coffee and soda combined. It is not necessary to add up sales at each time of day to find the answer. Just from looking at the graph, you can see that sales for both beverages were highest at

noon, so the answer must be **12:00 p.m.**

13. To find the total number, we need to add the number of cars for each relevant time period (note that all number are approximations):

    8:00 a.m. − 11:00 a.m.: 50 cars

    11:00 a.m. − 2:00 p.m.: 30 cars

    2:00 p.m. − 5:00 p.m.: 35 cars

    50 + 30 + 35 = **115 cars**

14. Because there are 15 marbles in the bag (3 + 5 + 7), the total number of possible outcomes is 15. Of those outcomes, 3 would be blue marbles, which is the desired outcome. Using that information, you can set up an equation:

    $probability = \frac{desired\ outcomes}{total\ possible\ outcomes}$
    $= \frac{3}{15} = \frac{1}{5}$

    The probability is **1 in 5 or 0.2** that a blue marble is picked.

15. Because you're solving for desired outcomes (the number of red balls), first you need to rearrange the equation:

    $probability = \frac{desired\ outcomes}{total\ possible\ outcomes}$
    $desired\ outcomes = probability \times total\ possible\ outcomes$

    Here, choosing a red ball is the desired outcome; the total possible outcomes are represented by the 75 total balls.

    There are **45 red balls** in the bag.

16. In this problem, the desired outcome is a seat in either the mezzanine or balcony area, and the total possible outcomes are represented by the 230 total seats. So you can write this equation:

    $probability = \frac{desired\ outcomes}{total\ possible\ outcomes}$

$= 100 + \frac{55}{230} = \mathbf{0.67}$

17. Because you're solving for total possible outcomes (total number of students), first you need to rearrange the equation:

    total possible outcomes
    $= \frac{desired\ outcomes}{probability}$

    In this problem, you are given a probability (7% or 0.07) and the number of desired outcomes (42). Plug these numbers into the equation to solve:

    total possible outcomes $= \frac{42}{0.07} =$ **600 students**

18. This question is asking about an intersection of events. The equation for an intersection of events is

    $P(A \cap B) = P(A) \times P(B|A)$.

    The first event, event A, is picking out a blue marble. Find $P(A)$:

    $P(A) = \frac{11\ blue\ marbles}{16\ total\ marbles} = \frac{11}{16}$

    The second event, event B, is picking out a red marble, now that there are 15 marbles left. Find $P(B|A)$:

    $P(B|A) = \frac{5\ red\ marbles}{15\ total\ marbles} = \frac{5}{15} = \frac{1}{3}$

    $P(A \cap B) = P(A) \times P(B|A)$
    $= \frac{11}{16} \times \frac{1}{3} = \frac{11}{48}$

19. This question is asking about a union of events. The equation for a union of events is

    $P(A \cup B) = P(A) + P(B) - P(A \cap B)$.

    The first event, event A, is selecting a queen. Find $P(A)$:

    $P(A) = \frac{4\ queens}{52\ total\ cards} = \frac{4}{52}$

    The second event, event B, is selecting a diamond. Find $P(B)$:

    $P(B) = \frac{13\ diamonds}{52\ total\ cards} = \frac{13}{52}$

Now, find the probability of selecting a queen that is also a diamond:

$$P(A \cap B) = \frac{1 \text{ diamondqueen}}{52 \text{ total cards}} = \frac{1}{52}$$

$$P(A \cup B) = P(A) + P(B) - P(A \cap B)$$
$$= \frac{4}{52} + \frac{13}{52} - \frac{1}{52} = \frac{16}{52} = \mathbf{\frac{4}{13}}$$

TEST YOUR KNOWLEDGE

1. C) is correct.

2. C) is correct.

3. C) is correct.

4. C) is correct.

5. B) is correct.

6. D) is correct.

7. C) is correct.

8. A) is correct.

9. C) is correct.

10. A) is correct.

PART III
The Essay

1 prompt ¦ 50 minutes

On the Essay section of the SAT, you'll be required to read a short passage and write an essay analyzing the author's argument. The passage will address an issue from science, art, or civics and provide different viewpoints and a range of supporting evidence. Your job will be to describe how the author presented his or her argument. Your essay should include a discussion of the following:

▶ the author's main argument

▶ the structure of the passage

▶ the evidence the author uses to support his or her claim

▶ the rhetorical elements (e.g., metaphors, word choice, or appeals to emotion and authority) used by the author

You should not discuss your own opinion or reactions to the passage in your essay. Your only task is to objectively analyze the author's argument, not to discuss how you personally feel about either the topic or the effectiveness of the passage.

CHAPTER SEVEN

Writing the Essay

Structuring the Essay

There are a few different ways to organize an essay, but some basics apply no matter what the style.

Essays may differ in how they present an idea, but they all have the same basic parts—introduction, body, and conclusion. The most common essay types are persuasive essays and expository essays. A persuasive essay takes a position on an issue and attempts to show the reader why it is correct. An expository essay explains different aspects of an issue without necessarily taking a side.

INTRODUCTIONS

Present your argument or idea in the introduction. Usually, the introductory paragraph ends with a thesis statement, which clearly sets forth the position or point the essay will prove. The introduction is a good place to bring up complexities, counterarguments, and context, all of which will help the reader understand the reasoning behind your position on the issue at hand. Later, revisit those issues and wrap all of them up in the conclusion.

EXAMPLE

Below is an example of an introduction. Note that it provides some context for the argument, acknowledges an opposing perspective, and gives the reader a good idea of the issue's complexities. Pay attention to the thesis statement in the last few lines, which clearly states the author's position.

Technology has changed immensely in recent years, but today's generation barely notices—high school students are already experienced with the internet, computers, apps, cameras, cell phones, and more. Teenagers must learn to use these tools safely and responsibly. Opponents of 1:1 technology programs might argue that students will be distracted or misuse the technology, but that is exactly why schools must teach them to use it. By providing technology to students, schools can help them apply it positively by creating projects with other students, communicating with teachers and classmates, and conducting research for class projects. In a world where technology is improving and changing at a phenomenal rate, schools have a responsibility to teach students how to navigate that technology safely and effectively; providing each student with a laptop or tablet is one way to help them do that.

THE BODY PARAGRAPHS

The body of an essay consists of a series of structured paragraphs. You may organize the body of your essay by creating paragraphs that describe or explain each reason you give in your thesis; addressing the issue as a problem and offering a solution in a separate paragraph; telling a story that demonstrates your point (make sure to break it into paragraphs around related ideas); or comparing and contrasting the merits of two opposing sides of the issue (make sure to draw a conclusion about which is better at the end).

Make sure that each paragraph is structurally consistent, beginning with a topic sentence to introduce the main idea, followed by supporting ideas and examples. No extra ideas unrelated to the paragraph's focus should appear. Use transition words and phrases to connect body paragraphs and improve the flow and readability of your essay.

In the *Providing Supporting Evidence* section you will find an example of a paragraph that is internally consistent and explains one of the main reasons given in the example introduction that you just read. Your essay should have one or more paragraphs like this to form the main body.

CONCLUSIONS

In order to end your essay smoothly, write a conclusion that reminds the reader why you were talking about these topics in the first place. Go back to the ideas in the introduction and thesis statement, but be careful not to simply restate your ideas; rather, reinforce your argument.

EXAMPLE

Below is a sample conclusion paragraph that could go with the introduction above. Notice that this conclusion talks about the same topics as the introduction (changing technology and the responsibility of schools), but it does not simply rewrite the thesis.

As technology continues to change, teens will need to adapt to it. Schools already teach young people myriad academic and life skills, so it makes sense that they would teach students how to use technology appropriately, too.

Providing students with their own devices is one part of that important task, and schools should be supporting it.

Writing a Thesis Statement

The THESIS, or THESIS STATEMENT, is central to the structure and meaning of an essay. It presents the writer's argument, or position on an issue; in other words, it tells readers specifically what you think and what you will discuss. A strong, direct thesis statement is key to the organization of any essay. The thesis statement is typically located at the end of the introductory paragraph.

Writing a good thesis statement is as simple as stating your idea and why you think it is true or correct.

EXAMPLE

The Prompt

Many high schools have begun to adopt 1:1 technology programs, meaning that each school provides every student with a computing device such as a laptop or tablet. Educators who support these initiatives say that the technology allows for more dynamic collaboration and that students need to learn technology skills to compete in the job market. On the other hand, opponents cite increased distraction and the dangers of cyber-bullying or unsupervised internet use as reasons not to provide students with such devices.

In your essay, take a position on this question. You may write about either one of the two points of view given, or you may present a different point of view on this question. Use specific reasons and examples to support your position.

Possible thesis statements:

Providing technology to every student is good for education because it allows students to learn important skills such as typing, web design, and video editing; it also gives students more opportunities to work cooperatively with their classmates and teachers.

I disagree with the idea that schools should provide technology to students because most students will simply be distracted by the free access to games and websites when they should be studying or doing homework.

In a world where technology is improving and changing at a phenomenal rate, schools have a responsibility to teach students how to navigate that technology safely and effectively; providing each student with a laptop or tablet is one way to help them do that.

Providing Supporting Evidence

Your essay requires not only structured, organized paragraphs; it must also provide specific evidence supporting your arguments. Whenever you make a general statement, follow it with specific examples that will help to convince the reader that your argument has merit. These specific examples do not bring new ideas to the paragraph; rather, they explain or defend the general ideas that have already been stated.

The following are some examples of general statements and specific statements that provide more detailed support:

GENERAL: Students may get distracted online or access harmful websites.

SPECIFIC: Some students spend too much time using chat features or social media, or they get caught up in online games. Others spend time reading websites that have nothing to do with an assignment.

SPECIFIC: Teens often think they are hidden behind their computer screens. If teenagers give out personal information such as age or location on a website, it can lead to dangerous strangers seeking them out.

GENERAL: Schools can teach students how to use technology appropriately and expose them to new tools.

SPECIFIC: Schools can help students learn to use technology to work on class projects, communicate with classmates and teachers, and carry out research for classwork.

SPECIFIC: Providing students with laptops or tablets will allow them to get lots of practice using technology and programs at home, and only school districts can ensure that these tools are distributed widely, especially to students who may not have them at home.

EXAMPLE

Below is an example of a structured paragraph that uses specific supporting ideas. This paragraph supports the thesis introduced above (see Introductions).

Providing students with their own laptop or tablet will allow them to explore new programs and software in class with teachers and classmates and to practice using it at home. In schools without laptops for students, classes have to visit computer labs where they share old computers that are often missing keys or that run so slowly they are hardly powered on before class ends. When a teacher tries to show students how to use a new tool or website, students must scramble to follow along and have no time to explore the new feature. If they can take laptops home instead, students can do things like practice editing video clips or photographs until they are perfect. They can email classmates or use shared files to collaborate even after school. If schools expect students to learn these skills, it is the schools' responsibility to provide students with enough opportunities to practice them.

This paragraph has some general statements:

> ... their own laptop or tablet will allow them to explore new programs and software... and to practice...

> ...it is the schools' responsibility to provide... enough opportunities...

It also has some specific examples to back them up:

> ...computers... run so slowly they are hardly powered on... students must scramble to follow along and have no time to explore...

> They can email classmates or use shared files to collaborate...

Writing Well
TRANSITIONS

Transitions are words, phrases, and ideas that help connect ideas throughout a text. You should use them between sentences and between paragraphs. Some common transitions include *then, next, in other words, as well, in addition to*. Be creative with your transitions, and make sure you understand what the transition you are using shows about the relationship between the ideas. For instance, the transition *although* implies that there is some contradiction between the first idea and the second.

SYNTAX

The way you write sentences is important to maintaining the reader's interest. Try to begin sentences differently. Make some sentences long and some sentences short. Write simple sentences. Write complex sentences that have complex ideas in them. Readers appreciate variety.

There are four basic types of sentences: simple, compound, complex, and compound-complex. Try to use some of each type. Be sure that your sentences make sense, though—it is better to have clear and simple writing that a reader can understand than to have complex, confusing syntax that does not clearly express the idea.

WORD CHOICE and TONE

The words you choose influence the impression you make on readers. Use words that are specific, direct, and appropriate to the task. For instance, a formal text may benefit from complex sentences and impressive vocabulary, while it may be more appropriate to use simple vocabulary and sentences in writing intended for a young audience. Make use of strong vocabulary; avoid using vague, general words such as *good*, *bad*, *very*, or *a lot*. However, make sure that you are comfortable with the vocabulary you choose; if you are unsure about the word's meaning or its use in the context of your essay, don't use it at all.

EDITING, REVISING, and PROOFREADING

When writing a timed essay, you will not have very much time for these steps; spend any time you have left after writing the essay looking over it and checking for spelling and grammar mistakes that may interfere with a reader's understanding. Common mistakes to look out for include: subject/verb disagreement, pronoun/antecedent disagreement, comma splices and run-ons, and sentence fragments (phrases or dependent clauses unconnected to an independent clause).

Test Your Knowledge

Read the passage from John F. Kennedy's 1963 Commencement Address, and then write an essay based on the prompt.

As you read the passage below, consider how John F. Kennedy uses:

▶ evidence, such as facts or examples, to support claims

▶ reasoning to develop ideas and to connect claims and evidence

▶ stylistic or persuasive elements, such as word choice or appeals to emotion, to add power to the ideas expressed

ADAPTED FROM THE COMMENCEMENT ADDRESS GIVEN BY JOHN F. KENNEDY AT AMERICAN UNIVERSITY ON JUNE 10, 1963.

I have, therefore, chosen this time and place to discuss a topic on which ignorance too often abounds and the truth is too rarely perceived. And that is the most important topic on Earth: peace. What kind of peace do I mean and what kind of a peace do we seek? Not a Pax Americana enforced on the world by American weapons of war. Not the peace of the grave or the security of the slave. I am talking about genuine peace, the kind of peace that makes life on Earth worth living, and the kind that enables men and nations to grow, and to hope, and build a better life for their children; not merely peace for Americans but peace for all men and women, not merely peace in our time but peace in all time.

I speak of peace because of the new face of war. Total war makes no sense in an age where great powers can maintain large and relatively invulnerable nuclear forces and refuse to surrender without resort to those forces. It makes no sense in an age where a single nuclear weapon contains almost ten times the explosive force delivered by all the allied air forces in the Second World War.

It makes no sense in an age when the deadly poisons produced by a nuclear exchange would be carried by wind and water and soil and seed to the far corners of the globe and to generations yet unborn.

Today the expenditure of billions of dollars every year on weapons acquired for the purpose of making sure we never need them is essential to the keeping of peace. But surely the acquisition of such idle stockpiles which can only destroy and never create is not the only, much less the most efficient, means of assuring peace. I speak of peace, therefore, as the necessary, rational end of rational men. I realize the pursuit of peace is not as dramatic as the pursuit of war, and frequently the words of the pursuers fall on deaf ears. But we have no more urgent task.

Some say that it is useless to speak of peace or world law or world disarmament, and that it will be useless until the leaders of the Soviet Union adopt a more enlightened attitude. I hope they do. I believe we can help them do it. But I also believe that we must reexamine our own attitudes, as individuals and as a Nation, for our attitude is as essential as theirs.

And every graduate of this school, every thoughtful citizen who despairs of war and wishes to bring peace, should begin by looking inward, by examining his own attitude towards the possibilities of peace, towards the Soviet Union, towards the course of the Cold War and towards freedom and peace here at home.

First examine our attitude towards peace itself. Too many of us think it is impossible. Too many think it is unreal. But that is a dangerous, defeatist belief. It leads to the conclusion that war is inevitable, that mankind is doomed, that we are gripped by forces we cannot control. We need not accept that view. Our problems are manmade; therefore, they can be solved by man. And man can be as big as he wants.

No problem of human destiny is beyond human beings. Man's reason and spirit have often solved the seemingly unsolvable, and we believe they can do it again. I am not referring to the absolute, infinite concept of universal peace and good will of which some fantasies and fanatics dream. I do not deny the value of hopes and dreams but we merely invite discouragement and incredulity by making that our only and immediate goal.

Let us focus instead on a more practical, more attainable peace, based not on a sudden revolution in human nature but on a gradual evolution in human institutions, on a series of concrete actions and effective agreements which are in the interest of all concerned. There is no single, simple key to this peace; no grand or magic formula to be adopted by one or two powers. Genuine peace must be the product of many nations, the sum of many acts. It must be dynamic, not static, changing to meet the challenge of each new generation. For peace is a process, a way of solving problems.

PROMPT

Write an essay explaining how John F. Kennedy builds his argument to convince his audience that peace between the United States and Soviet Union will come about not through a "Pax Americana" obtained in an American victory in a nuclear war, but through a fundamental shift in the human attitude towards peace. In your essay, explain how he uses the techniques and elements listed above to strengthen his argument; be sure to focus on the most relevant ones. Remember not to discuss whether you agree with Kennedy or not; analyze his argument and explain it to your audience instead.

PART IV
Test Your Knowledge

154 multiple choice questions; 1 essay ¦ 3 hours and 50 minutes

CHAPTER EIGHT
Practice Test One

Reading

There are several passages in this test and each passage is accompanied by several questions. After reading a passage, choose the best answer to each question and fill in the corresponding oval on your answer document. You may refer to the passages as often as necessary.

Questions 1 – 10 are based on the following passage, adapted from Nathaniel Hawthorne's short story "The Artist of the Beautiful," originally published in 1844. Owen Warland is a young watchmaker, who studied his trade as an apprentice under retired watchmaker Peter Hovenden.

From the time that his little fingers could grasp a penknife, Owen had been remarkable for a delicate ingenuity, which sometimes produced pretty shapes in wood, principally figures of flowers and birds, and sometimes seemed to aim at the hidden mysteries of mechanism. But it was always for purposes of grace, and never with any mockery of
(5) the useful. He did not, like the crowd of school-boy artisans, construct little windmills on the angle of a barn or watermills across the neighboring brook. Those who discovered such peculiarity in the boy as to think it worth their while to observe him closely, sometimes saw reason to suppose that he was attempting to imitate the beautiful movements of Nature as exemplified in the flight of birds or the activity of little animals.
(10) It seemed, in fact, a new development of the love of the beautiful, such as might have made him a poet, a painter, or a sculptor, and which was as completely refined from all utilitarian coarseness as it could have been in either of the fine arts. He looked with singular distaste at the stiff and regular processes of ordinary machinery. Being once carried to see a steam-engine, in the expectation that his intuitive comprehension of
(15) mechanical principles would be gratified, he turned pale and grew sick, as if something monstrous and unnatural had been presented to him. This horror was partly owing to

the size and terrible energy of the iron laborer; for the character of Owen's mind was microscopic, and tended naturally to the minute, in accordance with his diminutive frame and the marvelous smallness and delicate power of his fingers. Not that his sense
(20) of beauty was thereby diminished into a sense of prettiness. The beautiful idea has no relation to size, and may be as perfectly developed in a space too minute for any but microscopic investigation as within the ample verge that is measured by the arc of the rainbow. But, at all events, this characteristic minuteness in his objects and accomplishments made the world even more incapable than it might otherwise have been
(25) of appreciating Owen Warland's genius. The boy's relatives saw nothing better to be done—as perhaps there was not—than to bind him apprentice to a watchmaker, hoping that his strange ingenuity might thus be regulated and put to utilitarian purposes.

Peter Hovenden's opinion of his apprentice has already been expressed. He could make nothing of the lad. Owen's apprehension of the professional mysteries, it is true,
(30) was inconceivably quick; but he altogether forgot or despised the grand object of a watchmaker's business, and cared no more for the measurement of time than if it had been merged into eternity. So long, however, as he remained under his old master's care, Owen's lack of sturdiness made it possible, by strict injunctions and sharp oversight, to restrain his creative eccentricity within bounds; but when his apprenticeship was served
(35) out, and he had taken the little shop which Peter Hovenden's failing eyesight compelled him to relinquish, then did people recognize how unfit a person was Owen Warland to lead old blind Father Time along his daily course. One of his most rational projects was to connect a musical operation with the machinery of his watches, so that all the harsh dissonances of life might be rendered tuneful, and each flitting moment fall
(40) into the abyss of the past in golden drops of harmony. If a family clock was entrusted to him for repair,—one of those tall, ancient clocks that have grown nearly allied to human nature by measuring out the lifetime of many generations,—he would take upon himself to arrange a dance or funeral procession of figures across its venerable face, representing twelve mirthful or melancholy hours. Several freaks of this kind quite
(45) destroyed the young watchmaker's credit with that steady and matter-of-fact class of people who hold the opinion that time is not to be trifled with, whether considered as the medium of advancement and prosperity in this world or preparation for the next. His custom rapidly diminished—a misfortune, however, that was probably reckoned among his better accidents by Owen Warland, who was becoming more and more
(50) absorbed in a secret occupation which drew all his science and manual dexterity into itself, and likewise gave full employment to the characteristic tendencies of his genius.

1. The main purpose of the first paragraph is—
   A) to characterize Owen as an unconventional genius
   B) to explain how Owen came to be apprenticed at the watch shop
   C) to recall a significant event in Owen's life
   D) to describe Owen's most recent project

2. The narrator implies that Owen is—
   A) incompetent as a watchmaker
   B) overwhelmed by the details of life
   C) an outsider in his community
   D) a highly rational thinker

3. In line 12, *utilitarian* most nearly means—
   A) noble
   B) creative
   C) practical
   D) artistic

4. The description of Owen's response to the train in lines 13 through 16 primarily serves to—
   A) describe a significant, formative event in Owen's life
   B) illustrate Owen's interest in mechanical systems
   C) define Owen's unique definition of beauty
   D) further characterize Owen's peculiar affinity for the minute

5. Which choice provides the best evidence for the answer to the previous question?
   A) *But, at all events, this characteristic minuteness in his objects and accomplishments made the world even more incapable than it might otherwise have been of appreciating Owen Warland's genius.*
   B) *Peter Hovenden's opinion of his apprentice has already been expressed. He could make nothing of the lad.*
   C) *So long, however, as he remained under his old master's care, Owen's lack of sturdiness made it possible, by strict injunctions and sharp oversight, to restrain his creative eccentricity within bounds.*
   D) *One of his most rational projects was to connect a musical operation with the machinery of his watches, so that all the harsh dissonances of life might be rendered tuneful, and each flitting moment fall into the abyss of the past in golden drops of harmony.*

6. Which statement best characterizes the relationship between Owen Warland and Peter Hovenden?
   A) Owen is disinterested in Peter Hovenden's artistic endeavors.
   B) Owen is flattered to apprentice under such an accomplished watchmaker as Peter Hovenden.
   C) Peter Hovenden is perplexed by Owen's unique brilliance.
   D) Peter Hovenden resents Owen for the negative attention he has received from the community.

7. Which choice provides the best evidence for the answer to the previous question?

   A) *But, at all events, this characteristic minuteness in his objects and accomplishments made the world even more incapable than it might otherwise have been of appreciating Owen Warland's genius.*

   B) *Peter Hovenden's opinion of his apprentice has already been expressed. He could make nothing of the lad.*

   C) *So long, however, as he remained under his old master's care, Owen's lack of sturdiness made it possible, by strict injunctions and sharp oversight, to restrain his creative eccentricity within bounds.*

   D) *One of his most rational projects was to connect a musical operation with the machinery of his watches, so that all the harsh dissonances of life might be rendered tuneful, and each flitting moment fall into the abyss of the past in golden drops of harmony.*

8. As used in line 34, *eccentricity* most nearly means—

   A) brilliance.
   B) peculiarity.
   C) energy.
   D) fickleness.

9. According to the passage, Peter Hovenden turned his shop over to Owen Warland because—

   A) Failing eyesight prevented him from continuing the work himself.
   B) Owen had become an accomplished watchmaker and no longer needed Peter.
   C) He did not understand Owen and no longer felt they could work together.
   D) He was embarrassed by the reputation Owen had earned in the community.

10. The description of *the steady and matter-of-fact class of people* in lines 40 through 42 primarily serves to—

   A) illustrate the open-mindedness of the community in which Owen lives
   B) characterize Owen's community as responsible and reliable
   C) distinguish between those who value time and those who do not
   D) draw a contrast between Owen and the other members of the community

Questions 11 – 21 are based on the following passages, which address the topic of America's involvement in foreign affairs. Passage 1 is adapted from George Washington's farewell address, published in American newspapers in 1796 at the end of the president's third term. In his letter, Washington offers his advice on America's future involvement with foreign nations. Passage 2 is adapted from an address given by Harry S. Truman, the 33rd American president, before a joint session of Congress in 1947. In his speech, Truman urges Congress to provide assistance to countries at risk of Communist takeover.

PASSAGE 1

The great rule of conduct for us, in regard to foreign nations, is, in extending our commercial relations, to have with them as little political connection as possible. So far as we have already formed engagements, let them be fulfilled with perfect good faith. Here let us stop.

(5)   Europe has a set of primary interests, which to us have none, or a very remote relation. Hence she must be engaged in frequent controversies, the causes of which are essentially foreign to our concerns. Hence, therefore, it must be unwise in us to implicate ourselves, by artificial ties, in the ordinary vicissitudes of her politics, or the ordinary combinations and collisions of her friendships or enmities.

(10)   Our detached and distant situation invites and enables us to pursue a different course. If we remain one people, under an efficient government, the period is not far off, when we may defy material injury from external annoyance; when we may take such an attitude as will cause the neutrality, we may at any time resolve upon, to be scrupulously respected; when belligerent nations, under the impossibility of making

(15) acquisitions upon us, will not lightly hazard the giving us provocation; when we may choose peace or war, as our interest, guided by justice, shall counsel.

Why forego the advantages of so peculiar a situation? Why quit our own to stand upon foreign ground? Why, by interweaving our destiny with that of any part of Europe, entangle our peace and prosperity in the toils of European ambition, rivalship, interest,

(20) humor, or caprice?

It is our true policy to steer clear of permanent alliances with any portion of the foreign world; so far, I mean, as we are now at liberty to do it; for let me not be understood as capable of patronizing infidelity to existing engagements. I hold the maxim no less applicable to public than to private affairs, that honesty is always the best policy. I

(25) repeat it, therefore, let those engagements be observed in their genuine sense. But, in my opinion, it is unnecessary and would be unwise to extend them.

PASSAGE 2

One of the primary objectives of the foreign policy of the United States is the creation of conditions in which we and other nations will be able to work out a way of life free from coercion. This was a fundamental issue in the war with Germany and Japan. Our

(30) victory was won over countries which sought to impose their will, and their way of life, upon other nations.

To ensure the peaceful development of nations, free from coercion, the United States has taken a leading part in establishing the United Nations. The United Nations is designed to make possible lasting freedom and independence for all its members.

(35) We shall not realize our objectives, however, unless we are willing to help free peoples

to maintain their free institutions and their national integrity against aggressive movements that seek to impose upon them totalitarian regimes. This is no more than a frank recognition that totalitarian regimes imposed on free peoples, by direct or indirect aggression, undermine the foundations of international peace and hence the (40) security of the United States.

The peoples of a number of countries of the world have recently had totalitarian regimes forced upon them against their will. The Government of the United States has made frequent protests against coercion and intimidation, in violation of the Yalta agreement, in Poland, Romania, and Bulgaria. I must also state that in a number of (45) other countries there have been similar developments.

At the present moment in world history nearly every nation must choose between alternative ways of life. The choice is too often not a free one.

One way of life is based upon the will of the majority, and is distinguished by free institutions, representative government, free elections, guarantees of individual liberty, (50) freedom of speech and religion, and freedom from political oppression.

The second way of life is based upon the will of a minority forcibly imposed upon the majority. It relies upon terror and oppression, a controlled press and radio; fixed elections, and the suppression of personal freedoms.

I believe that it must be the policy of the United States to support free peoples who (55) are resisting attempted subjugation by armed minorities or by outside pressures.

I believe that we must assist free peoples to work out their own destinies in their own way.

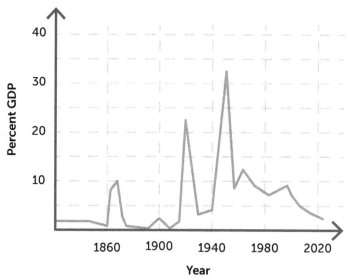

11. As used in line 8, *vicissitudes* most nearly means—

   A) fluctuations
   B) ideals
   C) mutations
   D) stagnation

12. Washington's central argument in Passage 1 is that—

    A) America should back out of the alliances it has made with other countries.

    B) America should increase its involvement with foreign nations.

    C) America should attempt to intervene in European conflicts whenever international safety is a concern.

    D) America should avoid foreign entanglements whenever it is able to do so.

13. Which choice provides the best evidence for the answer to the previous question?

    A) *It is our true policy to steer clear of permanent alliances with any portion of the foreign world; so far, I mean, as we are now at liberty to do it...*

    B) *So far as we have already formed engagements, let them be fulfilled with perfect good faith.*

    C) *Europe has a set of primary interests, which to us have none, or a very remote relation.*

    D) *If we remain one people, under an efficient government, the period is not far off, when we may defy material injury from external annoyance...*

14. Washington most likely employs a series of questions in the fourth paragraph in order to—

    A) challenge the reader to consider his own entanglements with others

    B) question the assumption that neutrality is the best course of action

    C) emphasize the absurdity of giving up a position of safe, passive neutrality

    D) minimize the impact of his opponent's counterargument

15. As used in line 43, *coercion* most nearly means—

    A) intimidation

    B) brutality

    C) cruelty

    D) authority

16. Which choice provides the best evidence for the answer to the previous question?

    A) *This was a fundamental issue in the war with Germany and Japan.*

    B) *The United Nations is designed to make possible lasting freedom and independence for all its members.*

    C) *We shall not realize our objectives, however, unless we are willing to help free peoples to maintain their free institutions and their national integrity against aggressive movements that seek to impose upon them totalitarian regimes.*

    D) *At the present moment in world history nearly every nation must choose between alternative ways of life.*

17. In Passage 2, President Truman most likely references *the war with Germany and Japan* in order to—

A) remind Americans of the nation's stance on foreign intervention

B) reassure Americans that they can win another war

C) suggest a comparison between the current situation and the one that led to the war

D) distinguish between the current situation and the one that led to America's intervention in the war

18. In lines 39 through 44, Truman most likely contrasts two ways of life in order to _____

A) illustrate some of the benefits of a democratic government

B) challenge the tyrannical leaders of oppressed nations to reconsider their approach to government

C) describe the reasons that America might consider intervening in a foreign nation

D) suggest that free people have a responsibility to fight on behalf of those who are not free

19. Which statement best describes the relationship between the passages?

A) The two presidents take similar perspectives on foreign intervention.

B) The two presidents take opposing perspectives on foreign intervention.

C) The two presidents agree on most items related to foreign intervention but disagree on some key point.

D) The two presidents agree on a few items related to foreign intervention but disagree of most key points.

20. President Truman (Passage 2) would most likely respond to Washington's claim in lines 6 through 14 by asserting that—

A) *Our victory [in the war with Germany and Japan] was won over countries which sought to impose their will, and their way of life, upon other nations.*

B) *To ensure the peaceful development of nations, free from coercion, the United States has taken a leading part in establishing the United Nations.*

C) *...totalitarian regimes imposed on free peoples, by direct or indirect aggression, undermine the foundations of international peace and hence the security of the United States.*

D) *The peoples of a number of countries of the world have recently had totalitarian regimes forced upon them against their will.*

21. Based on the passages and the graph, what conclusion can be drawn about the relationship between foreign policy and government spending in the 20th century?

A) Government spending on national defense significantly decreased as a result of the new foreign policy approach.

B) There was a correlation between the new foreign policy approach and increased government spending on defense.

C) Government spending on national defense remained stagnate despite the new approach to foreign policy.

D) The was no recognizable correlation between the new foreign policy approach and government spending on defense.

Questions 22 – 31 are based on the following passage, which provides an overview of the purpose and applications of social psychology. Information was drawn from Dr. Eliot Aronson's acclaimed book The Social Animal.

In his treatise *Politics*, Aristotle wrote, "Man is by nature a social animal; an individual who is unsocial naturally and not accidentally is either beneath our notice or more than human. Society is something in nature that precedes the individual. Anyone who either cannot lead the common life or is so self-sufficient as not to need to, and therefore does

(5) not partake of society, is either a beast or a god." For centuries, philosophers have been examining the relationship between man and his social world. It is no wonder, then, that a field of study has arisen to examine just that; the field is referred to as social psychology.

Social psychologists have been studying the effect of societal influences on human

(10) behavior for decades, and a number of fascinating findings have been the result. Together, these discoveries have shed light on one clear truth—that human behavior cannot be understood in a vacuum; that is, our daily behaviors are inextricably linked with the social context in which they occur.

Why is this important? According to social psychologist Eliot Aronson, it's

(15) important because it helps us to understand that the behaviors we witness in others may be as much a result of social influence as they are of the individual's disposition. For example, if you have ever been cut off in the middle of bad city traffic, you may have immediately assumed that the offender was inconsiderate or incompetent. While this may be true, it may be equally likely that the person is dealing with an emergency

(20) situation or that they simply did not see you. According to Aronson, this tendency to attribute behaviors, especially negative behaviors, to disposition is risky and can ultimately be detrimental to us and to the other person.

Take, for example, Philip Zimbardo's famous prison experiment, conducted at Stanford University in 1971. At the beginning of the experiment, the participants, all

(25) healthy, stable, intelligent male Stanford University students, were classified as either guards or prisoners and told they would be acting their parts in a simulated prison environment for two weeks. However, after just six days, Zimbardo had to terminate

the experiment because of the extreme behaviors he was witnessing in both groups: prisoners had become entirely submissive to and resentful of the guards, while the
(30) guards had become cruel and unrelenting in their treatment of the prisoners. The otherwise healthy, well-adjusted students had experienced dramatic transformations as a result of their assigned roles. Zimbardo's conclusion? Even giving individuals temporary power over others was enough to completely alter the way they viewed and behaved toward each other; indeed, the behaviors he witnessed in each of the groups
(35) were not a result of the dispositions of the participants but of the situation in which they had been placed.

Today, social psychologists study the effect of social influence on a number of different behaviors: conformity, obedience, aggression, prejudice, and even attraction and love. The insights these researchers have gained have laid the foundation for further
(40) examination of human social behavior and, ultimately, for a refined approach to legal and social policy.

22. The author most likely uses the Aristotle quote in lines 1 through 5 in order to—
   A) illustrate the seriousness with which social psychology should be treated
   B) support his/her claim that curiosity about man's relationship with the social world is not a quality unique to modern thinking
   C) encourage introverts to build stronger relationships with those around them
   D) compare the social environment of beasts with the social environment of man

23. Which choice provides the best evidence for the answer to the previous question?
   A) *For centuries, philosophers have been examining the relationship between man and his social world.*
   B) *Social psychologists have been studying the effect of societal influences on human behavior for decades, and a number of fascinating findings have been the result.*
   C) *According to social psychologist Eliot Aronson, it's important because it helps us to understand that the behaviors we witness in others may be as much a result of social influence as they are of the individual's disposition.*
   D) *The insights these researchers have gained have laid the foundation for further examination of human social behavior and, ultimately, for a refined approach to legal and social policy.*

24. As used in line 12, the phrase *in a vacuum* most nearly means—
   A) without evidence of intention
   B) in conjunction with other behaviors
   C) without consideration of the individual's needs
   D) in isolation

25. The author indicates that making assumptions about people based on isolated actions is—

- **A)** a prudent way to draw conclusions about one's social world
- **B)** recommended when no other information is available
- **C)** the most accurate way to assess various personality strengths
- **D)** unwise and potentially harmful to all involved

26. In lines 24 and 25, the author most likely includes the description of the Stanford students in order to—

- **A)** provide a contrast between their normal dispositions and the behavior they displayed during the experiment
- **B)** engage the reader through characterization
- **C)** illustrate the importance of quality education
- **D)** shed light on the characteristics that made them susceptible to social influence

27. The author most likely includes the example of the Stanford Prison Experiment in order to—

- **A)** encourage the reader to participate in social psychology studies
- **B)** challenge the reader to question how he or she would behave in the same situation
- **C)** illustrate the extent to which social context can influence behavior
- **D)** undermine the reader's assumption that the quality of one's education can influence his or her behavior

28. As used in line 30, the term *unrelenting* most nearly means—

- **A)** insistent
- **B)** forgetful
- **C)** remorseless
- **D)** persistent

29. Which choice provides the best evidence for the answer to the previous question?

- **A)** *According to Aronson, this tendency to attribute behaviors, especially negative behaviors, to disposition is risky and can ultimately be detrimental to us and to the other person.*
- **B)** *At the beginning of the experiment, the participants, all healthy, stable, intelligent male Stanford University students, were classified as either guards or prisoners and told they would be acting their parts in a simulated prison environment for two weeks.*
- **C)** *Even giving individuals temporary power over others was enough to completely alter the way they viewed and behaved toward each other...*
- **D)** *Today, social psychologists study the effect of social influence on a number of different behaviors: conformity, obedience, aggression, prejudice, and even attraction and love.*

30. The author most likely includes *attraction and love* in the list in lines 38 and 39 in order to—

A) suggest that individuals who are struggling with relationship issues should contact a social psychologist

B) discount the assumption that social psychologists are only interested in negative human behaviors

C) illustrate the diversity of topics that social psychologists study

D) dispel any doubts about the qualifications of social psychologists to study human behavior

31. The author most likely includes the statement in lines 40 and 41 about legal and social policy in order to—

A) mention one possible application for the findings of social psychologists.

B) advocate for prison reform.

C) criticize the work of social psychologists.

D) dispel doubts regarding the reliability of the research of social psychologists.

Questions 32 – 41 are based on the following passage, which is adapted from an article entitled "NASA Finds Good News on Forests and Carbon Dioxide," published online by the National Aeronautics and Space Administration in December 2014.

A new NASA-led study shows that tropical forests may be absorbing far more carbon dioxide than many scientists thought, in response to rising atmospheric levels of the greenhouse gas. The study estimates that tropical forests absorb 1.4 billion metric tons of carbon dioxide out of a total global absorption of 2.5 billion—more than is absorbed
(5) by forests in Canada, Siberia and other northern regions, called boreal forests.

"This is good news, because uptake in boreal forests is already slowing, while tropical forests may continue to take up carbon for many years," said David Schimel of NASA's Jet Propulsion Laboratory, Pasadena, California. Schimel is lead author of a paper on the new research, appearing online today in the *Proceedings of National Academy of*
(10) *Sciences.*

Forests and other land vegetation currently remove up to 30 percent of human carbon dioxide emissions from the atmosphere during photosynthesis. If the rate of absorption were to slow down, the rate of global warming would speed up in return.

The new study is the first to devise a way to make apples-to-apples comparisons of
(15) carbon dioxide estimates from many sources at different scales: computer models of ecosystem processes, atmospheric models run backward in time to deduce the sources of today's concentrations (called inverse models), satellite images, data from experimental forest plots and more. The researchers reconciled all types of analyses and assessed the accuracy of the results based on how well they reproduced independent, ground-based
(20) measurements. They obtained their new estimate of the tropical carbon absorption from the models they determined to be the most trusted and verified.

"Until our analysis, no one had successfully completed a global reconciliation of information about carbon dioxide effects from the atmospheric, forestry and modeling communities," said co-author Joshua Fisher of JPL. "It is incredible that all these (25) different types of independent data sources start to converge on an answer."

The question of which type of forest is the bigger carbon absorber "is not just an accounting curiosity," said co-author Britton Stephens of the National Center for Atmospheric Research, Boulder, Colorado. "It has big implications for our understanding of whether global terrestrial ecosystems might continue to offset our carbon dioxide (30) emissions or might begin to exacerbate climate change."

As human-caused emissions add more carbon dioxide to the atmosphere, forests worldwide are using it to grow faster, reducing the amount that stays airborne. This effect is called carbon fertilization. "All else being equal, the effect is stronger at higher temperatures, meaning it will be higher in the tropics than in the boreal forests," (35) Schimel said.

But climate change also decreases water availability in some regions and makes Earth warmer, leading to more frequent and larger wildfires. In the tropics, humans compound the problem by burning wood during deforestation. Fires don't just stop carbon absorption by killing trees, they also spew huge amounts of carbon into the atmosphere as the (40) wood burns.

For about 25 years, most computer climate models have been showing that mid-latitude forests in the Northern Hemisphere absorb more carbon than tropical forests. That result was initially based on the then-current understanding of global air flows and limited data suggesting that deforestation was causing tropical forests to release (45) more carbon dioxide than they were absorbing.

In the mid-2000s, Stephens used measurements of carbon dioxide made from aircraft to show that many climate models were not correctly representing flows of carbon above ground level. Models that matched the aircraft measurements better showed more carbon absorption in the tropical forests. However, there were still not (50) enough global data sets to validate the idea of a large tropical-forest absorption. Schimel said that their new study took advantage of a great deal of work other scientists have done since Stephens' paper to pull together national and regional data of various kinds into robust, global data sets.

Schimel noted that their paper reconciles results at every scale from the pores of a (55) single leaf, where photosynthesis takes place, to the whole Earth, as air moves carbon dioxide around the globe. "What we've had up till this paper was a theory of carbon dioxide fertilization based on phenomena at the microscopic scale and observations at the global scale that appeared to contradict those phenomena. Here, at least, is a hypothesis that provides a consistent explanation that includes both how we know (60) photosynthesis works and what's happening at the planetary scale."

32. As it is used in line 18, the term *reconciled* most nearly means—

A) forgave.

B) studied.

C) integrated.

D) gathered.

33. Which choice provides the best evidence for the answer to the previous question?

A) *They obtained their new estimate of the tropical carbon absorption from the models they determined to be the most trusted and verified.*

B) *"It is incredible that all these different types of independent data sources start to converge on an answer."*

C) *That result was initially based on the then-current understanding of global air flows and limited data suggesting that deforestation was causing tropical forests to release more carbon dioxide than they were absorbing.*

D) *Models that matched the aircraft measurements better showed more carbon absorption in the tropical forests. However, there were still not enough global data sets to validate the idea of a large tropical-forest absorption.*

34. According to the passage, what is the relationship between photosynthesis and global warming?

A) Photosynthesis allows carbon dioxide gas to be released into the atmosphere, exacerbating the issue of global warming.

B) Carbon dioxide prevents trees from flourishing, thus increasing the amount of greenhouse gas and exacerbating the issue of global warming.

C) Trees absorb carbon dioxide during photosynthesis, removing much of the carbon dioxide from the atmosphere and slowing the effects of global warming.

D) Greenhouse gases like carbon dioxide slow the effects of global warming by prevent trees from completing the cycle of photosynthesis.

35. The passage indicates that research into carbon dioxide absorption is significant because—

A) It challenges us to question our own opinions on global warming and climate change.

B) It forces us to recognize that global warming poses a significant threat to our vegetation.

C) It encourages us to consider whether forests are effective alternatives to carbon dioxide emissions.

D) It allows us to understand the impact of the earth's forests on climate change.

36. The passage indicates that wildfires—
   A) both result from and contribute to climate change
   B) are the most significant contributor to climate change
   C) occur when temperature and humidity are both high
   D) have little to no effect on carbon dioxide emissions

37. According to the passage, increased carbon dioxide emissions may result in—
   A) increased water availability.
   B) smaller, less frequent wildfires.
   C) faster-growing forests.
   D) decreased oxygen availability.

38. A student claims that preserving the earth's forests is an essential step in slowing climate change. Which of the following statements from the passage supports this student's claim?
   A) *This is good news, because uptake in boreal forests is already slowing, while tropical forests may continue to take up carbon for many years," said David Schimel of NASA's Jet Propulsion Laboratory, Pasadena, California.*
   B) *If the rate of absorption [of carbon dioxide] were to slow down, the rate of global warming would speed up in return.*
   C) *But climate change also decreases water availability in some regions and makes Earth warmer, leading to more frequent and larger wildfires.*
   D) *That result was initially based on the then-current understanding of global air flows and limited data suggesting that deforestation was causing tropical forests to release more carbon dioxide than they were absorbing.*

39. As used in line 53, the term *robust* most nearly means—
   A) round
   B) comprehensive
   C) sturdy
   D) prosperous

40. The author mostly likely mentions the Stephens study in lines 46 through 49 in order to—
   A) criticize the work of environmental scientists before Stephens
   B) demonstrate the effect that a limited data set can have on the results of an experiment
   C) question that findings of Stephens and his colleagues
   D) emphasize the need for thorough data sets in drawing conclusions about climate change

41. According to the final paragraph (lines 54 through 60), NASA's recent study into carbon dioxide absorption was significant because—

A) it provided insight into the absorption speeds of two different kinds of forests.

B) it offered a hypothesis on how to predict and prevent wildfires.

C) it demonstrated the power of collaborative research methods.

D) it resulted in a theory of climate change that accommodated both large and small-scale considerations.

Questions 42 – 52 are based on the following passage, which is adapted from an article entitled "NASA Contributes to First Global Review of Arctic Marine Mammals," published online by the National Aeronautics and Space Administration in April 2015. The accompanying graphic was initially published to NASA's Cryosphere Science Research Portal, alongside an article entitled "Current State of the Sea Ice Cover."

Many human communities want answers about the current status and future of Arctic marine mammals, including scientists who dedicate their lives to studying them and indigenous people whose traditional ways of subsistence are intertwined with the fate of species such as ice seals, narwhals, walruses and polar bears.

(5)   But there are many unknowns about the current status of eleven species of marine mammals who depend on Arctic sea ice to live, feed and breed, and about how their fragile habitat will evolve in a warming world.

A recently published multinational study attempted to gauge the population trends of Arctic marine mammals and changes in their habitat, identify missing scientific
(10)   information, and provide recommendations for the conservation of Arctic marine mammals over the next decades.

The Arctic sea ice cover, made of frozen seawater floating on top of the Arctic Ocean and its neighboring seas, naturally grows in the fall and winter and melts during the spring and summer every year. But over the past decades, the melt season has grown
(15)   longer and the average extent of Arctic sea ice has diminished, changing the game for many Arctic marine mammals – namely beluga, narwhal and bowhead whales; ringed, bearded, spotted, ribbon, harp and hooded seals; walruses; and polar bears.

"This research would not have been possible without support from NASA," said Kristin Laidre, lead author of the new study and a polar scientist with University of
(20)   Washington in Seattle. "NASA backed us on research related to the biodiversity and ecology of Arctic marine mammals, as well as the development of metrics for the loss of sea ice, their habitat."

Laidre's team used the Arctic sea ice record derived from microwave measurements taken by NASA and Department of Defense satellites. This record began in late 1978, (25) is uninterrupted, and relies on NASA-developed methods for processing the microwave data.

"It's really our best global view of the Arctic sea ice," said Harry Stern, author of the paper with Laidre and a mathematician specializing in sea ice and climate at University of Washington.

(30) Stern divided the Arctic Ocean into twelve regions. Using daily sea ice concentration data from the satellite record, he calculated changes in the dates of the beginning of the melt season in spring and the start of the fall freeze-up from 1979 to 2013. He found that, in all regions but one, the melt season had grown longer (mostly by five to ten weeks, and by twenty weeks in one region).

(35) "Sea ice is critical for Arctic marine mammals because events such as feeding, giving birth, molting, and resting are closely timed with the availability of their ice platform," Laidre said. "It is especially critical for the ice-dependent species—seals and polar bears. Ice seals use the sea ice platform to give birth and nurse pups during very specific weeks of the spring, and polar bears use sea ice for feeding, starting in late winter and (40) continuing until the ice breaks up."

Pacific walrus use the floating pack ice both as a platform on which to rest between feeding bouts and as a passive transport around their habitat.

"Loss of sea ice has resulted in walrus hauling out on land in Alaska and Russia in massive numbers—these land haul outs result in trampling of their young," Laidre (45) said. "Also, now walrus must travel a longer way to reach their feeding areas, which is energetically costly."

In the case of Arctic whales, the changes in sea ice might benefit their populations, at least in the short term: the loss and earlier retreat of sea ice opens up new habitats and, in some areas of the Arctic, has also led to an increase in food production and the (50) length of their feeding season.

In the future, Stern said higher-resolution satellite microwave data might come in handy when studying the interactions of Arctic marine mammals with their icy habitat.

"For example, we know that narwhals congregate in specific areas of the Arctic in the wintertime, so maybe a higher spatial resolution in these areas might help us better (55) understand their relationship with the ice," Stern said. "But mainly, just continuing daily coverage is what's important for the long-term monitoring of habitat changes ."

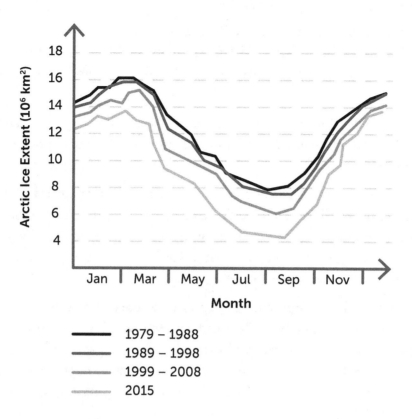

42. In the first paragraph, the author includes a detail about indigenous people of the Arctic in order to—

A) provide readers with a relatable story to consider as they read the article

B) emphasize the importance of protecting the habitats of Arctic marine mammals

C) challenge readers to make Arctic preservation efforts their top priority

D) illustrate a contrast between the indigenous people and the scientists mentioned in the first part of the sentence

43. In lines 12 through 17, the author indicates that while fluctuation in sea ice extent is expected throughout the year—

A) variability from year to year is a recent phenomenon.

B) the fluctuation is usually minute.

C) daily changes in sea ice extent are becoming more typical.

D) changes in the populations of Arctic mammals are not.

44. The author most likely includes the list of Arctic marine mammals in lines 16 through 17 in order to—

A) illustrate a discrepancy between the number of Arctic species and the number of species that depend on sea ice for survival

B) challenge the assertion that the recession of sea ice is significant

C) articulate a general truth about life in the Arctic

D) highlight the number of species that depend on sea ice for their survival

45. The passage indicates that when it comes to research about sea ice and the animals who rely on it—

   A) Scientists know everything they need to know.

   B) Data collection is rarely a simple process.

   C) Very few answers currently exist.

   D) Vigilant observation is an essential tool in gaining insight.

46. As used in line 7, the term *fragile* most nearly means—

   A) brittle

   B) flimsy

   C) breakable

   D) unstable

47. Which choice provides the best evidence for the answer to the previous question?

   A) *Using daily sea ice concentration data from the satellite record, he calculated changes in the dates of the beginning of the melt season in spring and the start of the fall freeze-up from 1979 to 2013.*

   B) *"Sea ice is critical for Arctic marine mammals because events such as feeding, giving birth, molting, and resting are closely timed with the availability of their ice platform[.]"*

   C) *The Arctic sea ice cover, made of frozen seawater floating on top of the Arctic Ocean and its neighboring seas, naturally grows in the fall and winter and melts during the spring and summer every year.*

   D) *But over the past decades, the melt season has grown longer and the average extent of Arctic sea ice has diminished, changing the game for many Arctic marine mammals...*

48. The passage indicates that in a little over three decades, the length of the melt seasons in most regions of the Arctic—

   A) decreased by more than two months

   B) increased by more than two months

   C) decreased by more than a month

   D) increased by more than a month

49. In lines 32 through 46, the author indicates that—

   A) Most, but not all, animals struggle when the availability of sea ice decreases.

   B) Many animals will continue to thrive despite the change in climate.

   C) All Arctic mammals use sea ice for the same reason.

   D) All Arctic mammals struggle when the availability of sea ice decreases.

50. As it is used in line 48, the term *retreat* most nearly means—

A)   surrender

B)   refuge

C)   recession

D)   departure

51. Which choice provides the best evidence for the answer to the previous question?

A)   *But there are many unknowns about the current status of 11 species of marine mammals who depend on Arctic sea ice to live, feed and breed, and about how their fragile habitat will evolve in a warming world.*

B)   *Using daily sea ice concentration data from the satellite record, he calculated changes in the dates of the beginning of the melt season in spring and the start of the fall freeze-up from 1979 to 2013.*

C)   *In the future, Stern said higher-resolution satellite microwave data might come in handy when studying the interactions of Arctic marine mammals with their icy habitat.*

D)   *"But mainly, just continuing daily coverage is what's important for the long-term monitoring of habitat changes."*

52. Which claim about Arctic ice extent is supported by the graph?

A)   Arctic ice extent has remained steady over the last three decades.

B)   Patterns of formation and recession are largely unpredictable.

C)   Arctic ice extent during late summer is significantly lower today than it was in 1979.

D)   Sea ice extent during winter was significantly lower in 1979 than it is today.

Writing and Language

In the following passages, there are numbered and underlined words and phrases that correspond with the questions. You are to choose the answer that best completes the statement grammatically, stylistically, and/or logically. If you think the original version is best, select "NO CHANGE."

POLICE WORK

Some (1)careers, especially those in the public eye, lend themselves to controversy and caricatures. In the 21st century, police work

lands squarely in this category: (2)crooked cops and detectives with donuts are commonplace in the worlds of media and entertainment. Still, officers of the law and public investigators play an essential role in our criminal justice system, a role that comes with a great deal of responsibility.

1. **A)** NO CHANGE
    B) careers—especially those in the public eye
    C) careers, especially those in the public eye—
    D) careers, especially those in the public eye

2. Which of the following best supports the claim made earlier in the sentence?
    A) NO CHANGE
    B) however, it is an extremely challenging profession, and its significance should not be underestimated.
    C) the work itself is challenging, but the perks that come along with it are substantial.
    D) most people admire and respect officers of the law.

Go On

(3)

They must first be strong communicators, as they must be able to gather information and effectively communicate that information in written reports. In order to evaluate and respond to situations quickly and appropriately, they must also be highly perceptive and must possess good judgment. In addition, physical strength and stamina are a necessity for officers of the law, as the job can be strenuous and demanding. Finally, they must be empathetic, as they must be able to relate to and treat the people

of their community (4)with sincere care and unwavering equity.

To become a police officer, one must complete a rigorous series of hiring

requirements, (5)which begin with providing proof of their citizenship, age, education, and criminal history. After meeting these basic requirements, each candidate must pass a

series of (6)evaluations, which are intended

3. Which of the following provides the most effective introduction to the material in the next paragraph?

A) Police officers should not be worried if they do not fit the stereotypes.

B) The amount of responsibility that comes with being a police officer can be overwhelming.

C) Police officers must possess a number of varied characteristics in order to be successful as representatives of the law.

D) The question of whether someone should pursue police work can be answered knowing oneself.

4. Which of the following choices suggests that officers of the law must possess strong moral character?

A) NO CHANGE

B) as innocent until they are proven guilty

C) as though they are their closest friends

D) without regard for the concerns of others

5. **A)** NO CHANGE

B) which begins

C) that begin

D) that begins

6. **A)** NO CHANGE

B) evaluations, they are intended

C) evaluations, being intended

D) evaluations—these are intended

to determine (7)their suitability for police work. First, the candidate must pass a series of challenging physical tests and written exams, which are intended to evaluate the candidate based on his or her physical and mental fitness. Then, each candidate must pass a series of challenging interviews, during which he or she may be asked to complete lie detector and drug tests. Finally, an applicant who meets all of these requirements must gain acceptance into (8)his or her agency's academy to begin training.

Academy training is extensive for officers of the law. In addition to physical training in

(9)self-defense firearms, emergency response and first aid, candidates must also complete a series of classes in constitutional law, state and local law, civil rights, and ethics. Federal agents or officers with specialized responsibilities must complete even more training.

An officer who is successful in his or her initial role as patrolman or first responder may find him– or herself in the position of receiving a promotion. Often, this first promotion elevates them to the role of detective or special investigator. Detectives and special investigators are responsible for (10)investigating reported crimes, to gather and protecting evidence, conducting interviews, and for solving crimes in specialized areas such as homicide, vice, or special victims.

7. **A)** NO CHANGE
   B) its
   C) his or her
   D) the

8. **A)** NO CHANGE
   B) his or her agencies
   C) their agencies
   D) their agency's

9. **A)** NO CHANGE
   B) self-defense, firearms, emergency, response and first aid,
   C) self-defense, firearms energy response and first aid,
   D) self-defense, firearms, emergency response, and first aid,

10. **A)** NO CHANGE
    B) investigate reported crimes, gather and protecting evidence, conduct interviews, and solve crimes
    C) investigating reported crimes, gathering and protecting evidence, conducting interviews, and solving crimes
    D) investigation reported crimes, to gather and protect evidence, to conduct interview, and solving crimes

<u>(11)</u>

11. At this point, the writer is considering adding the following sentence:

According to the United States Bureau of Labor Statistics, this promotion is a valuable one: in 2012, the median pay for detectives was nearly $20,000 more than the median pay for uniformed officers of the law.

Should he/she make this addition?

A) Yes, because it provides more information about the work of detectives and their motivation for doing it.

B) Yes, because it provides more information about the difference between uniformed officers and detectives.

C) No, because it distracts the reader from the main point of the passage.

D) No, because the reader does not know how much uniformed police officers usually make.

SCIENTIFIC EVIDENCE

For many centuries, scientists like Galileo and Charles Darwin have defended their hypotheses in the face of stark opposition. (12)Even today in an era of rapidly advancing technology and better-than-ever research facilities; public opinion on science's most pressing issues is consistently divided. Science, it seems, should have the right answers, so why do we so often reject scientific evidence when it is presented to us? According to a National Geographic article by Joel Achenbach, our individual perspectives and biases may be to blame.

(13)

One factor that may be at the center of scientific debate is the significant effect that deeply held beliefs have on our ability to make judgments. (14)Recent studies have showed that many individuals are hesitant to answer difficult scientific questions, even when they are advanced in their knowledge and even when

12.
- **A)** NO CHANGE
- **B)** Even today—in an era of rapidly advancing technology, and better-than-even research facilities,
- **C)** Even today, in an era of rapidly advancing technology and better-than-ever research facilities,
- **D)** Even today, in an era of rapidly advancing technologies and better-than-ever research facilities—

13. Which of the following most effectively establishes the central claim of this passage?
- **A)** NO CHANGE
- **B)** According to a National Geographic article by Joel Achenbach, it may be because we are not familiar enough with scientific terminology and law.
- **C)** Sometimes we simply do not want to believe what we hear.
- **D)** Most likely, this tendency is related to our desire for consistency.

14.
- **A)** NO CHANGE
- **B)** Recent studies will show
- **C)** Recent studies shown
- **D)** Recent studies have shown

(15)it is largely unanimous about the topic at hand. According to Achenbach, this tendency, to hold fast to our deeply held beliefs and assumptions, remains with us despite any new information we may (16)gain—we try to explain the novel data through the context of our belief, rather than changing our opinion to better reflect the new information.

(17)Sometimes it is easier for us to believe our friends and family than it is for us to believe scientific evidence. For example, if an individual's brother or father is diagnosed with breast cancer, he or she may incorrectly assume that breast cancer in men is much more common than it actually is. Alternatively, an individual may assume a particular disease is

(18)uncommon simply because he or she does not have any personal acquaintance with the disease.

15. A) NO CHANGE
    B) the scientific community is
    C) science is
    D) they are

16. A) NO CHANGE
    B) gain, we
    C) gain: we
    D) gain, but

17. Which of the following provides the most effective transition between the previous paragraph and this one?
    A) NO CHANGE
    B) Occasionally, we have an experience that changes our perspective on the world.
    C) Though it is not always easy, we must fight the urge to believe our personal experience is reflective of the world at large.
    D) In addition to leaning on deeply held beliefs, we tend also to rely on personal experience and anecdotal, rather than statistical, evidence to understand the world.

18. A) NO CHANGE
    B) lawful
    C) certain
    D) natural

(19)As social animals, we are understandably reliant on our social world to reveal information to us: however, to draw legitimate conclusions from evidence, we must also be aware of how our social world can skew our perspective.

19. At this point, the writer is considering deleting the underlined sentence. Should he/she make this deletion?

A) Yes, because it distracts the reader from the main point of the argument.

B) Yes, because it is a repetition of the information that has already been given.

C) No, because it provides a concise and effective conclusion to the argument made in the paragraph.

D) No, because it is important for the reader's understanding of the scientific community.

(20)

Most importantly, according to Achenbach, we tend to view science in a

20. The best placement for the preceding paragraph is—

A) where it is now.

B) before the first paragraph.

C) after the first paragraph.

D) at the end of the essay.

(21)deceptively misleading light: specifically,

21. **A)** NO CHANGE

B) misleading

C) misleading and deceptive

D) misleading, deceptive, and confusing

(22)we thought of science as a set of information rather than a process of evaluation. As children, most of us learn as fact that our earth, and the other planets in our solar system, revolve around our sun. But students of science in the early modern age would have drawn no such conclusion. It is important, then, that we recognize that science is not a fixed, inarguable set of facts: rather, it is a process that allows us to continually reevaluate our hypotheses, examine

22. **A)** NO CHANGE

B) we think of science

C) we would think of science

D) we will think

new evidence, and draw new conclusions about our complex world.

BIOLUMINESCENCE

(23)Adaptations, features that develop over centuries of natural selection, allow the animals to function more effectively in their environments and can be found in many species. Sometimes these adaptations are physical: the giraffe's long neck allows it to reach food in the highest trees, and the camel's hump allows it to survive for days in an arid environment. Other adaptations, like bioluminescence, are chemical.

Bioluminescence, the ability to create light, is an adaptation that is most present in animals that live in primarily dark environments like the ocean. It is caused by a chemical reaction in the animal's body, which allows the animal to fulfill a particular need. Like other types of adaptations, bioluminescence serves a different function in each species that displays the ability; however, for the most part, these functions can be divided into three categories:

(24)protection, hunting, and reproduction.

For many ocean-dwelling, bioluminescent creatures, the ability to create light serves a defensive function. The vampire squid, for example, uses the light to stun and confuse its predators.

23. **A)** NO CHANGE
    B) Many species display adaptations, which allow the animals to function more effectively in their environments, and are features that develop over centuries of natural selection.
    C) Adaptations are features that develop over centuries of natural selection, which allow the animals to function more effectively in their environments, and can be found in many species.
    D) Many species display adaptations, features that develop over centuries of natural selection, which allow the animals to function more effectively in their environments.

24. **A)** NO CHANGE
    B) for protection, to hunt, and reproduction.
    C) protecting, to hunt, and reproducing.
    D) for protection, hunting, and to reproduce.

Unlike other squid, which may emit a dark liquid to confuse predators, the vampire squid has adapted to a deep ocean environment—where light is limited and darkliquid has no effect. As a result, the vampire squid instead emits (25)a glowing goo, which

25. Which of the following is most appropriate considering the tone and purpose of the passage?

A) a bright, nasty gunk

B) a secretion of organic, bioluminescent matter

C) a glowing goo

D) this slime

(26)surprises their predators and distracts them while the squid escapes capture.

26. A) NO CHANGE

B) surprises its predators and distracts it

C) surprise their predators and distracts them

D) surprises its predator and distracts it

Bioluminescence serves other defensive purposes as well. Some species, like the hatchet fish, use their own light to create a sort of camouflage: (27)when a predator is swimming, below, a lit underbelly allows the prey to swim along unnoticed blending in with the light from above. Misdirection is also a common application of bioluminescence. Some animals, like the brittle star, can detach lit body parts and leave

27. A) NO CHANGE

B) when a predator is swimming below, a lit underbelly allows the prey to swim along unnoticed, blending in with the light from above.

C) when a predator is swimming below a lit underbelly allows the prey to swim along unnoticed, blending in, with the light from above.

D) when a predator is swimming below, a lit underbelly, allows the prey to swim along unnoticed, blending in, with the light from above.

(28)them behind in order to draw predators away from themselves.

28. A) NO CHANGE

B) it behind in order to draw predators away from itself.

C) them behind in order to draw predators away from itself.

D) it behind in order to draw predators away from themselves.

(29)Other animals use their bioluminescent abilities differently. On the head of an anglerfish, for example, is a long barb that lights up at the tip. The fish uses this light to lure smaller fish directly into its mouth.

29. Which choice provides the most effective transition between the previous paragraph and this one?

A) NO CHANGE

B) There are myriad reasons that an animal might use bioluminescence, and protection is just one of them.

C) While many creatures create light for defensive purposes, not all do: some animals, instead, use bioluminescence to find and capture prey.

D) If an animal is hungry, it might use bioluminescence to find its food.

(30)

30. At this point, the writer wants to add an additional detail about animals that use bioluminescence to hunt. Considering the tone and purpose of the passage, which of the following choices is most effective?

    A) Even some sharks light up to attract prey.

    B) If you ever have an opportunity to go deep-sea diving, you should take advantage of it and hope that you get to see an anglerfish in action.

    C) The anglerfish may look scary, but it won't eat anything as large as a human.

    D) These creatures are fascinating to watch in action.

(31)In addition, bioluminescent animals may use their natural spotlight to seek out prey in dark places; still others use their light to surprise, disorient, and capture their meals.

Finally, some animals, like the firefly and some types of underwater crustaceans, use bioluminescence in their mating practices. Female syllid fireworms, for example, luminesce while swimming in circles in order to attract males of their species.

31. The best placement for the underlined sentence is—

    A) where it is now.

    B) at the beginning of this paragraph.

    C) at the end of the second paragraph.

    D) after the first sentence of the fourth paragraph.

Go On

<u>(32)</u>

32. At this point the writer wants to add a concluding sentence. Considering the tone and purpose of the passage, which choice is most appropriate?

A) Despite its initial intrigue, bioluminescence is far more common and less interesting than one might assume.

B) In conclusion, bioluminescence is an essential adaptation for many animals species, and we would be irresponsible to ignore it.

C) Bioluminescent species are some of the most fascinating animals on our planet, so it is essential that we consider committing time and resources to preserving their natural habitats.

D) With its commonality among species and its variety of applications, bioluminescence is a fascinating topic that can enliven our senses and spark our curiosities about the natural world.

<u>(33)</u>

Species and Function		
SPECIES	APPLICATION	FUNCTION
vampire squid	protection	distraction
green bomber worms	protection	misdirection
flashlight fish	reproduction	gender distinction
syllid fireworms	reproduction	sexual attraction

33. What type of information should the author consider adding to the table in order to make it better align with the passage as a whole?

A) Details about the diets of each of the species

B) Descriptions of the appearance of each species

C) Information about species that use bioluminescence for hunting

D) Material about where each species can be found

LEONARDO?

Dr. Martin Kemp sat at his computer (34) examining emails.

34.
A) NO CHANGE
B) sifting through
C) scrutinizing
D) straining

(35)Some he responded to quickly, while marking others for later, still others he deleted immediately. Then he came across an email from someone named Peter. The subject read: *Leonardo?*

35.
A) NO CHANGE
B) Some he responded to quickly, others he marked for later, and still others he deleted immediately.
C) Some he would respond to quickly, and others he marked for later, still others he would delete.
D) Some he is responding to quickly, others he would mark for later, still others he deletes immediately.

Another loonie, Kemp thought. (36) He scoffed a little but clicking to open the message anyway. He received these emails fairly regularly, two or three times a week most weeks, and he had yet to come across an inquiry that even gave him pause.

36.
A) NO CHANGE
B) He scoffed a little and clicking to open the message anyway.
C) He scoffed a little but clicked to open the message anyway.
D) He scoffs a little but clicking to open the message anyway.

Go On

(37)As Professor Emeritus of Art History at Oxford University, Kemp was a DaVinci expert, and he regularly received notes from people thinking they have come across a lost work of the great artist.

(38)

Then he opened the image.

A feeling of utter astonishment fell over Kemp. He put down his coffee, stopped shuffling papers, and stared at the high-resolution image on his screen. He moved his

chair (39)closer to his desk, and attempting to get a better look at the striking portrait. He looked at it in its full form for a number of minutes before zooming in to get a better view. The detail work was magnificent, and the portrait seemed to have a life about it.

37. Which choice provides the most relevant detail about Dr. Kemp?

A) NO CHANGE

B) As a lover of Leonardo DaVinci's work, Dr. Kemp was shocked by how often people sent him emails claiming to have found an undiscovered work by the great artist.

C) Dr. Kemp had viewed a number of DaVinci's works at museums around the world, and he found them to be every bit as magnificent as the artist's reputation would suggest.

D) Dr. Kemp is a professor and a lover of DaVinci's works.

38. The writer wants to add the following sentence about Dr. Kemp's skepticism toward the contents of the email:

He had no reason to believe this one was any different.

For the sake of logic and coherence, this sentence should be placed—

A) at the beginning of the paragraph

B) after the first sentence

C) after the second sentence

D) after the third sentence

39. A) NO CHANGE

B) closer to his desk but attempted

C) closer to his desk as though

D) closer to his desk, attempting

(40)*Uncanny*, Kemp thought. He decided to respond to the inquiry: he would travel to Zurich, at no fee to the owner of the piece,

to (41)eyeball the work in person.

Outside of his vault in Zurich, Peter Silverman slowly pulled the mysterious portrait out of its protective envelope. He could not believe he was finally here. When he first lost the auction of the portrait almost a decade before, he thought he would never see it again. Now, he held it in his gloved hands, discussing its potential origins with one of the world's leading experts. He laid the portrait down carefully in front of Martin Kemp and waited for the (42)connoisseur's expert opinion.

Kemp stared silently down at the piece. A rush of energy rolled over him, a feeling he would later have trouble describing in words. He only knew that this portrait was special, unlike any of the works he had evaluated before.

40. Which choice best expresses Dr. Kemp's cautious interest in the image?

A) NO CHANGE

B) That's weird

C) It must be a DaVinci

D) Stellar

41. A) NO CHANGE

B) inspect

C) display

D) contemplate

42. A) NO CHANGE

B) connoisseur's opinion

C) educated connoisseur's opinion

D) educated connoisseur's expert opinion

Go On

(43)The subject of the portrait, a young woman, appeared composed and thoughtful, as one who was living in a world that required her to act, by today's standards, well beyond her age. Her eyes had been drawn to show her vitality, and her hair seemed to respond naturally to the pressure of the headdress that hugged her head. *These details*…Kemp trailed off.

43. **A)** NO CHANGE

B) A young women, the subject of the portrait, appearing composed and thoughtful, as one living in a world, by today's standards, that required her to act well beyond her age.

C) The subject of the portrait, a young woman who was living, by today's standards, in a world that required her to act well beyond her age, appeared composed and thoughtful.

D) Composed and thoughtful, a young woman, the subject of the portrait, appearing composed and thoughtful, was living in a world that required her to act well beyond her age by today's standards.

44. To conclude, the writer wants to add a sentence that will make the reader want to do further research about Kemp's discovery. Which choice accomplishes this goal?

A) In that moment, Dr. Kent decided that the work was, indeed, a work of the great artist Leonardo DaVinci.

B) He was impressed by the level of sophistication, but he was sure that this was not, after all, a work of the great artist Leonardo DaVinci.

C) He concluded in that moment that only a highly sophisticated forger could produce such a convincing piece of work.

D) He could not know by that time, of course, whether the portrait was actually the work of the great DaVinci, but he knew he wanted to investigate further.

Mathematics

For questions 1 – 15, work the problem and choose the most correct answer. For questions 16 – 20, work the problem and write in the correct answer in the space provided.

FORMULA CHART

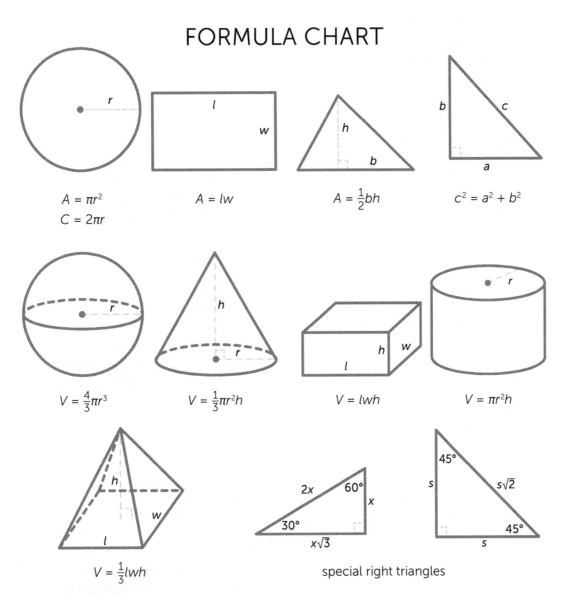

$A = \pi r^2$

$C = 2\pi r$

$A = lw$

$A = \frac{1}{2}bh$

$c^2 = a^2 + b^2$

$V = \frac{4}{3}\pi r^3$

$V = \frac{1}{3}\pi r^2 h$

$V = lwh$

$V = \pi r^2 h$

$V = \frac{1}{3}lwh$

special right triangles

▶ The number of degrees of arc in a circle is 360.

▶ The number of radians of arc in a circle is 2π.

▶ The sum of the measures in degrees of the angles of a triangle is 180.

1. Jane earns $15 per hour babysitting. If she starts out with $275 in her bank account, which of the following equations represents how many hours she will have to babysit for her account to reach $400?

A) $275 = 15h + 400$

B) $400 = 15h$

C) $400 = \frac{1}{h} + 275$

D) $400 = 15h + 275$

2. A bag contains twice as many red marbles as blue marbles, and the number of blue marbles is 88% of the number of green marbles. If g represents the number of green marbles, which of the following expressions represents the total number of marbles in the bag?

A) $2.32g$

B) $2.64g$

C) $3.64g$

D) $3.88g$

3. $3a + 4 = 2a$

What is the value of a in the equation above?

A) -4

B) $\frac{-4}{5}$

C) $\frac{4}{5}$

D) 4

4. If $z = \frac{x^2 - 2y}{y}$, what the value of z when $x = 20$ and $y = \frac{x}{2}$?

A) 0

B) 19

C) 36

D) 38

5. $3x^3 + 4x - (2x + 5y) + y$

Which of the following is equivalent to the expression above?

A) $11x - 4y$

B) $29x - 4y$

C) $3x^3 + 2x - 4y$

D) $3x^3 + 2x + y$

6. Point A is x distance north of point B. Point C is east of point B, and is twice as far from point B as point A is. What is the distance from point A to point C?

A) $\sqrt{3}x$

B) $2x$

C) $\sqrt{5}x$

D) $5x$

7. The slope of a straight line is -3 and its y-intercept is -2. Where does the line cross the x-axis?

A) $x = -3$

B) $x = -2$

C) $x = -\frac{2}{3}$

D) $x = 1\frac{1}{2}$

8. $\frac{4xy^3}{x^5y}$

Which of the following is equivalent to the expression above?

A) $\frac{12}{x^4}$

B) $12x^2y^2$

C) $64x^2y^2$

D) $\frac{4y^2}{x^4}$

9. $9x^2 + 42xy + 49y^2$

Which of the following is equivalent to the expression above?

A) $(3x - 7y)^2$

B) $(3x + 7y)^2$

C) $(3x + 7)(x + y)$

D) $(3x + 7y)(x + 7y)$

10. $m = 5^{-a}$ $m = 4^{-b}$

$m = 3^{-c}$ $m = 2^{-d}$

The variables a, b, c, and d each represent positive real numbers between 0 and 1. If m is a constant, which of the following has the highest value?

A) a

B) b

C) c

D) d

11. If $4x - 3 = 21$, what is the value of $6x - 2$?

A) 6

B) 21

C) 25

D) 34

12. Rebecca, Emily, and Kate all live on the same straight road. Rebecca lives 1.4 miles from Kate and 0.8 miles from Emily. What is the minimum distance Emily could live from Kate?

A) 0.6 miles

B) 0.8 miles

C) 1.1 miles

D) 2.2 miles

13. Adam owns 4 times as many shirts as he has pairs of pants, and he has 5 pairs of pants for every 2 pairs of shoes. What is the ratio of Adam's shirts to Adam's shoes?

A) 10 shirts : 1 pair shoes

B) 15 shirts : 2 pairs shoes

C) 20 shirts : 1 pair shoes

D) 25 shirts : 1 pair shoes

14. Which of the following mathematical expressions is equivalent to $\frac{2(x + y)}{z}$?

A) $\frac{1}{z}(2x + y)$

B) $\frac{2}{z} + \frac{x + y}{z}$

C) $z(2x + 2y)$

D) $\frac{2}{z}(x + y)$

15. $3a^2 - 11a + 10 = 0$

What is the sum of all the values of a that satisfy the equation above?

A) $3\frac{2}{3}$

B) 7

C) 15

D) 30

16. A car dealership has sedans, SUVs, and minivans in a ratio of 6:3:1, respectively. In total there are 200 of these vehicles on the lot. What proportion of those vehicles are sedans?

17. The lines l_1 and l_2 are parallel. If the slope of l_1 is equal to $\frac{3+x}{2}$ and the slope of l_2 is equal to $\frac{2+x}{4}$, what is the value of x?

18. There are 3 red, 4 blue, and 6 black marbles in a bag. When Carlos reaches into the bag and selects a marble without looking, what are the chances that he will select a black marble?

19. $21x + 4.5 = 3y$

$18x - 3 = 2y$

What is the value of x in the system of equations above?

20. In the right triangle $\triangle ABC$, $\angle A$ measures 90°. What is $\sin(B + C)$?

CALCULATOR
Multiple Choice

For questions 1 – 30, work the problem and choose the most correct answer. For questions 31 – 38, work the problem and write in the correct answer in the space provided.

1. Gerardo is riding his bicycle at a speed of 12 miles per hour. At 4:30 p.m. he is 54 miles from his house. If he continues riding toward his house at the same speed, how many miles will he be from his house at 6:00 p.m.?

   A) 18
   B) 36
   C) 40
   D) 48

2. Evaluate the expression $|3x - y| + |2y - x|$ if $x = -4$ and $y = -1$.

   A) -13
   B) -11
   C) 11
   D) 13

3. 1 mile = 5280 feet

   1 foot = 0.3048 meters

   Ashley ran a 10 kilometer race at an average pace of 8 minutes and 15 seconds per mile. Based on the information given above, how long did it take her to complete the race?

   A) 50 minutes, 53 seconds
   B) 51 minutes, 16 seconds
   C) 51 minutes, 23 seconds
   D) 82 minutes, 42 seconds

4. Which of the following is the solution to the inequality $6x + 5 \geq -15 + 8x$?

   A) $x \leq -5$
   B) $x \leq 5$
   C) $x \leq 10$
   D) $x \leq 20$

5. The graph below shows the cumulative distance covered by a car during a road trip. What is the average driving speed during the 5th hour of driving?

   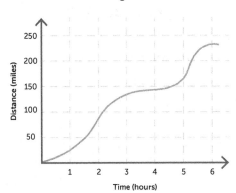

   A) 40 miles per hour
   B) 45 miles per hour
   C) 50 miles per hour
   D) 200 miles per hour

6. For which of the following functions does $f(x) = |f(x)|$ for every value of x?

   A) $f(x) = 3 - x$
   B) $f(x) = 2x + x^2$
   C) $f(x) = x^3 + 1$
   D) $f(x) = x^2 + 2$

7.

Test Scores

CLASS A	CLASS B
63	75
82	85
72	76
95	63
74	63
68	80
81	76
76	69
72	63

The table above shows test scores for students in 2 classes. Which of the following would be most affected by removing the score of 95 from the data set?

A) mean

B) median

C) mode

D) minimum

10. Ed is going to fill his swimming pool with a garden hose. His neighbor, a volunteer firefighter, wants to use a fire hose attached to the hydrant in the front yard to make the job go faster. The fire hose sprays 13.5 times as much water per minute as the garden hose. If the garden hose and the fire hose together can fill the pool in 107 minutes, how long would it have taken to fill the pool with the garden hose alone?

A) 7 hours, 37.9 min

B) 7 hours, 55.6 min

C) 1 day, 1 hour, 4.5 min

D) 1 day, 1 hour, 51.5 min

8. A data set contains n points with a mean of μ. If a new data point with the value x is included in the data set, which of the following expressions is equal to the new mean?

A) $\dfrac{\mu + x}{n}$

B) $\dfrac{\mu n + x}{n + 1}$

C) $\dfrac{\mu n + x}{n}$

D) $\dfrac{(\mu + x)n}{n + 1}$

9. 11, 7, 3, −1, ...

If 11 is defined as the first term in the sequence given above, which of the following functions describes the sequence?

A) $f(n) = 11 + 4(n - 1)$

B) $f(n) = 11(4)^{(n-1)}$

C) $f(n) = 11 - 4n$

D) $f(n) = 15 - 4n$

11. Which of the following is the equation of a circle with a center at (0, 0) that passes through the point (5, 12) on the standard x, y-coordinate plane?

A) $x^2 + y^2 = 169$

B) $x^2 - y^2 = 169$

C) $x + y = 169$

D) $x^2 + y^2 = 13$

12. Which of the following is an x-intercept of the graph $y = |x^2 - 7x + 12$?

A) −4

B) 0

C) 3

D) 7

13. Solve for x: $16x^2 + 8x + 1 = 0$

A) $x = -\frac{1}{4}$

B) $x = -\frac{1}{4}, \frac{1}{4}$

C) $x = -4, 4$

D) $x = 1, 4$

14. A diner's bill comes to $48.30. If she adds a 20% tip, what will she pay in total?

A) $9.66

B) $38.64

C) $68.30

D) $57.96

15. A parabola has a vertex at $(1, -4)$ and passes through the point $(-1, 8)$. Find the equation of the function.

A) $f(x) = 4(x - 3)^2 + 1$

B) $f(x) = 3x^2 - 4x + 1$

C) $f(x) = (x + 4)^2 - 1$

D) $f(x) = 3(x - 1)^2 - 4$

16. The number of college applicants increased in 2014 by 7%. This is 15% larger than the increase in 2013. What was the percentage increase in college applicants in 2013?

A) 2%

B) 4%

C) 6%

D) 8%

17. If $8(x + 5) = -3x - 48$, what is the value of $2x + 4$?

A) −12

B) 5.25

C) 20.00

D) 29.60

18. Which of the following describes the inequality shown in the graph below?

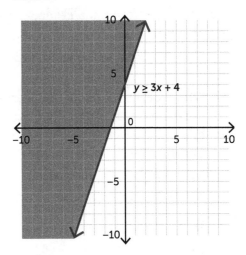

A) $y \leq 3x$

B) $y \geq 3x + 1$

C) $y \geq 3x + 2$

D) $y < 6x + 2$

19. Two congruent circles, A and B, are drawn next to each other with their sides just touching as shown in the figure below. Both circles are enclosed in a rectangle whose sides are tangent to the circles. If the distance between the radii of the two circles is 4 centimeters, what is the area of the rectangle in square centimeters?

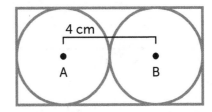

A) 8 cm²

B) 16 cm²

C) 24 cm²

D) 32 cm²

Questions 20 and 21 refer to the following information.

$$C = \varepsilon_0 \frac{A}{d}$$

The capacitance of a parallel-plate capacitor is function of the area of the plates, A, and the distance between them, d, as shown in the equation above. The permittivity of free space, ε_0, is a constant equal to 8.85×10^{-12}.

20. Which of the following expresses the distance between the plates in terms of capacitance and the area of the plates?

A) $d = \dfrac{A}{\varepsilon_0 C}$

B) $d = \varepsilon_0 (AC)$

C) $d = \varepsilon_0 \left(\dfrac{C}{A}\right)$

D) $d = \varepsilon_0 \left(\dfrac{A}{C}\right)$

21. Parallel-plate capacitors X and Y are made with plates of the same area. If the distance between the plates in capacitor X is twice the distance between the plates in capacitor Y, what is the ratio of the capacitance of X relative to Y?

A) 1 : 2

B) 1 : 4

C) 2 : 1

D) 4 : 1

22. If $\measuredangle A$ measures 57°, find $\measuredangle G$.

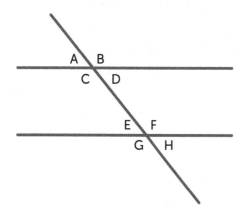

A) 33°

B) 57°

C) 123°

D) 147°

23. Which of the following expressions is equivalent to $(4 + i)(6 - i)$? (Note: $i = \sqrt{-1}$)

A) $24 - i^2$

B) $24 + i$

C) $25 - i$

D) $25 + 2i$

24. The hourglass shown below is made from 2 cones. The diameter of the base of each cone is 3 centimeters, and the height of the 2 cones combined is 12 centimeters. If the hourglass holds 4 milliliters of sand, how much empty space remains inside the hourglass?

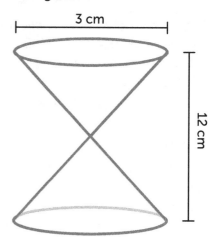

A) 0.5 cm³

B) 4.5 cm³

C) 5 cm³

D) 24.3 cm³

25. If $f(x) = 3^x - 2$, what is the value of $f(5)$?

A) 13

B) 27

C) 241

D) 243

26. A cylindrical canister is 9 inches high and has a diameter of 5 inches. What is the maximum volume this canister can hold?

A) 45 in²

B) 141.4 in²

C) 176.7 in²

D) 706.9 in²

28. A hotel has 200 rooms. Some of them have 2 full beds, and the rest have 1 queen bed. If the probability of getting a room with 2 full beds is 65%, how many rooms have 1 queen bed?

A) 50 rooms

B) 70 rooms

C) 130 rooms

D) 135 rooms

27. The cone-shaped tent shown in the figure below is 8 feet tall and has a slant height of 10 feet. What is the area of the ground covered by the tent in square feet?

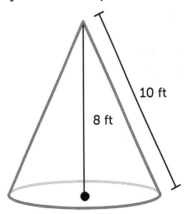

A) 36π

B) 64π

C) 100π

D) 128π

Questions 29 and 30 refer to the following information.

	Number of Participants			
Event	Year			
	2011	2012	2013	2014
Kids 5 km	73	121	212	250
Adult 5 km	243	355	502	656
Kids half marathon	12	25	100	105
Adults half marathon	1063	1506	1997	2510
Adults marathon	352	357	412	503

The data in the table above shows the number of runners who participated in each of 5 races for the years 2011–2014.

29. If the number of participants in the Adult 5 km continues to grow at the same rate as it did from 2012–2014, which of the following is the best approximation of how many people will participate in the Adult 5 km in 2015?

A) 700

B) 750

C) 800

D) 850

30. If a random participant is selected from all the runners who raced in 2012, what is the probability that the participant ran in either the Kids 5 km or the Kids Half-Marathon?

A) $\frac{5}{121}$

B) $\frac{73}{1182}$

C) $\frac{146}{2364}$

D) $\frac{1109}{1182}$

GRID-IN
Calculator

31. A plane makes a trip of 246 miles. For some amount of time, the plane's speed is 115 miles per hour. For the remainder of the trip, the plane's speed is 250 miles per hour. If the total trip time is 72 minutes, for how many minutes did the plane fly at 115 miles per hour?

32. There are 450 students in the 10th grade; of these, 46% are boys. If 21% of the girls have already turned 16, how many girls in the 10th grade are 16?

33. Power is a measure of energy expenditure over time. Watts, a measure of power, are equal to energy in joules over time in seconds. If a 40 watt light bulb is left on for 4.5 hours, how many kilojoules of energy are consumed?

34. A chemical experiment requires that a solute be diluted with 4 parts (by mass) water for every 1 part (by mass) solute. If the desired mass for the solution is 90 grams, how many grams of solute should be used?

$x^2 - 9 < 0$

35. Give a possible value of x given the inequality above.

36. What will be the 10th term in the following sequence: 20, 8, −4, −16, ...

37. Winning a raffle depends on how many raffle tickets an individual buys, and how many tickets are bought in total. If someone who buys two tickets has a 0.004 chance of winning, how many tickets were bought in total?

38. A pizza has a diameter of 10 inches. If you cut a slice with a central angle of 40 degrees, what will be the surface area of the pizza slice in square inches?

Essay

As you read the passage below, consider how Hillary Clinton uses evidence, such as facts or examples, to support claims; reasoning to develop ideas and to connect claims and evidence; and stylistic or persuasive elements, such as word choice or appeals to emotion, to add power to the ideas expressed

ADAPTED FROM HILLARY CLINTON'S SPEECH AT THE UNITED NATION'S 4TH WORLD CONFERENCE ON WOMEN, 1995.

What we are learning around the world is that if women are healthy and educated, their families will flourish. If women are free from violence, their families will flourish. If women have a chance to work and earn as full and equal partners in society, their families will flourish. And when families flourish, communities and nations do as well. That is why every woman, every man, every child, every family, and every nation on this planet does have a stake in the discussion that takes place here...

The great challenge of this conference is to give voice to women everywhere whose experiences go unnoticed, whose words go unheard. Women comprise more than half the world's population, 70% of the world's poor, and two-thirds of those who are not taught to read and write. We are the primary caretakers for most of the world's children and elderly. Yet much of the work we do is not valued—not by economists, not by historians, not by popular culture, not by government leaders...

Those of us who have the opportunity to be here have the responsibility to speak for those who could not. As an American, I want to speak for those women in my own country, women who are raising children on the minimum wage, women who can't afford health care or child care, women whose lives are threatened by violence, including violence in their own homes.

Our goals for this conference, to strengthen families and societies by empowering women to take greater control over their own destinies, cannot be fully achieved unless all governments—here and around the world—accept their responsibility to protect and promote internationally recognized human rights...

Tragically, women are most often the ones whose human rights are violated...I believe that now, on the eve of a new millennium, it is time to break the silence...

These abuses have continued because, for too long, the history of women has been a history of silence. Even today, there are those who are trying to silence our words. But the voices of this conference and of the women at Huairou must be heard loudly and clearly:

It is a violation of human rights when babies are denied food, or drowned, or suffocated, or their spines broken, simply because they are born girls.

It is a violation of human rights when women and girls are sold into the slavery of prostitution for human greed—and the kinds of reasons that are used to justify this practice should no longer be tolerated.

It is a violation of human rights when women are doused with gasoline, set on fire, and burned to death because their marriage dowries are deemed too small.

It is a violation of human rights when individual women are raped in their own communities and when thousands of women are subjected to rape as a tactic or prize of war.

It is a violation of human rights when a leading cause of death worldwide among women ages 14 to 44 is the violence they are subjected to in their own homes by their own relatives.

It is a violation of human rights when young girls are brutalized by the painful and degrading practice of genital mutilation.

It is a violation of human rights when women are denied the right to plan their own families, and that includes being forced to have abortions or being sterilized against their will.

If there is one message that echoes forth from this conference, let it be that human rights are women's rights and women's rights are human rights once and for all. Let us not forget that among those rights are the right to speak freely—and the right to be heard…

Let me be clear. Freedom means the right of people to assemble, organize, and debate openly. It means respecting the views of those who may disagree with the views of their governments. It means not taking citizens away from their loved ones and jailing them, mistreating them, or denying them their freedom or dignity because of the peaceful expression of their ideas and opinions…

Now it is the time to act on behalf of women everywhere. If we take bold steps to better the lives of women, we will be taking bold steps to better the lives of children and families too…

As long as discrimination and inequities remain so commonplace everywhere in the world, as long as girls and women are valued less, fed less, fed last, overworked, underpaid, not schooled, subjected to violence in and outside their homes—the potential of the human family to create a peaceful, prosperous world will not be realized…

PROMPT
Write an essay in which you explain how Hillary Clinton builds an argument to persuade her audience that women's rights should be a global priority. In your essay, analyze how Clinton uses one or more of the features listed above (or features of your own choice) to strengthen the logic and persuasiveness of her argument. Be sure that your analysis focuses on the most relevant features of the passage.

Your essay should not explain whether you agree with Clinton's claims, but rather explain how she builds an argument to persuade her audience.

Practice Test One Answer Key
READING

1. A)	14. C)	27. C)	40. D)
2. C)	15. C)	28. C)	41. D)
3. C)	16. A)	29. C)	42. B)
4. D)	17. C)	30. C)	43. A)
5. A)	18. D)	31. A)	44. D)
6. C)	19. B)	32. C)	45. D)
7. B)	20. C)	33. B)	46. D)
8. B)	21. B)	34. C)	47. D)
9. A)	22. B)	35. D)	48. D)
10. D)	23. A)	36. A)	49. A)
11. A)	24. D)	37. C)	50. C)
12. D)	25. D)	38. B)	51. D)
13. A)	26. A)	39. B)	52. C)

WRITING and LANGUAGE

1. A)	8. A)	15. B)	22. B)
2. A)	9. D)	16. C)	23. D)
3. C)	10. C)	17. D)	24. A)
4. A)	11. C)	18. A)	25. C)
5. B)	12. C)	19. C)	26. D)
6. A)	13. A)	20. A)	27. B)
7. C)	14. D)	21. B)	28. A)

29. C)	33. C)	37. A)	41. B)
30. A)	34. B)	38. D)	42. B)
31. A)	35. B)	39. D)	43. A)
32. D)	36. C)	40. A)	44. D)

MATHEMATICS
No Calculator

1. D)	6. C)	11. D)	16. $\frac{3}{5}$ or 0.6
2. C)	7. C)	12. A)	17. −4
3. A)	8. D)	13. A)	18. 0.46
4. D)	9. B)	14. D)	19. 1.5
5. C)	10. D)	15. B)	20. 1

MATHEMATICS
Calculator

1. B)	11. A)	21. A)	31. 24
2. D)	12. C)	22. C)	32. 51
3. B)	13. A)	23. C)	33. 648
4. C)	14. D)	24. D)	34. 18
5. C)	15. D)	25. C)	35. $-3 < x < 3$
6. D)	16. C)	26. C)	36. −88
7. A)	17. A)	27. A)	37. 500
8. B)	18. C)	28. B)	38. 8.7
9. D)	19. D)	29. C)	
10. D)	20. D)	30. D)	

CHAPTER NINE
Practice Test Two

Reading

There are several passages in this test and each passage is accompanied by several questions. After reading a passage, choose the best answer to each question and fill in the corresponding oval on your answer document. You may refer to the passages as often as necessary.

Questions 1 – 10 are based on the following passage, which is adapted from Charlotte Perkins Gilman's short story "The Yellow Wallpaper," originally published in 1892. The narrator, who is writing in her journal, has been diagnosed by her husband John as having a nervous disorder and, as a result, is confined to the nursery of the old house where they are living for the summer.

I suppose John never was nervous in his life. He laughs at me so about this wall-paper!

At first he meant to repaper the room, but afterwards he said that I was letting it get the better of me, and that nothing was worse for a nervous patient than to give way to such fancies.

(5)   He said that after the wall-paper was changed it would be the heavy bedstead, and then the barred windows, and then that gate at the head of the stairs, and so on.

"You know the place is doing you good," he said, "and really, dear, I don't care to renovate the house just for a three months' rental."

"Then do let us go downstairs," I said, "there are such pretty rooms there."

(10)   Then he took me in his arms and called me a blessed little goose, and said he would go down to the cellar, if I wished, and have it whitewashed into the bargain.

But he is right enough about the beds and windows and things.

It is an airy and comfortable room as any one need wish, and, of course, I would not be so silly as to make him uncomfortable just for a whim.

(15)   I'm really getting quite fond of the big room, all but that horrid paper.

Out of one window I can see the garden, those mysterious deepshaded arbors, the riotous old-fashioned flowers, and bushes and gnarly trees.

Out of another I get a lovely view of the bay and a little private wharf belonging to the estate. There is a beautiful shaded lane that runs down there from the house. I

(20)   always fancy I see people walking in these numerous paths and arbors, but John has cautioned me not to give way to fancy in the least. He says that with my imaginative power and habit of story-making, a nervous weakness like mine is sure to lead to all manner of excited fancies, and that I ought to use my will and good sense to check the tendency. So I try.

(25)   [...]

I wish I could get well faster.

But I must not think about that. This paper looks to me as if it KNEW what a vicious influence it had!

There is a recurrent spot where the pattern lolls like a broken neck and two bulbous

(30)   eyes stare at you upside down.

I get positively angry with the impertinence of it and the everlastingness. Up and down and sideways they crawl, and those absurd, unblinking eyes are everywhere. There is one place where two breadths didn't match, and the eyes go all up and down the line, one a little higher than the other.

(35)   I never saw so much expression in an inanimate thing before, and we all know how much expression they have! I used to lie awake as a child and get more entertainment and terror out of blank walls and plain furniture than most children could find in a toy store.

I remember what a kindly wink the knobs of our big, old bureau used to have, and

(40)   there was one chair that always seemed like a strong friend.

I used to feel that if any of the other things looked too fierce I could always hop into that chair and be safe.

The furniture in this room is no worse than inharmonious, however, for we had to bring it all from downstairs. I suppose when this was used as a playroom they had to

(45)   take the nursery things out, and no wonder! I never saw such ravages as the children have made here.

The wall-paper, as I said before, is torn off in spots, and it sticketh closer than a brother—they must have had perseverance as well as hatred.

Then the floor is scratched and gouged and splintered, the plaster itself is dug out

(50)   here and there, and this great heavy bed which is all we found in the room, looks as if it had been through the wars.

But I don't mind it a bit—only the paper.

1. Which choice best summarizes what is happening in the passage?

   A) The narrator is adjusting to a new residence and is making plans to renovate her bedroom.

   B) The narrator is plotting to escape imprisonment by her own husband.

   C) The narrator is being driven slowly insane by her confinement.

   D) The narrator is questioning her relationship with her husband.

2. The narrator indicates that her husband, John, decides not to repaper the room because—

   A) He does not truly care for her.

   B) He thinks she would benefit more from spending time outside.

   C) He does not want to give in to her anxious whims.

   D) He thinks she is incapable of appreciating the hard work that would be required.

3. As it is used in line 4, the term *fancies* most nearly means—

   A) luxuries

   B) illusions

   C) inconsistencies

   D) fantasies

4. In the third paragraph, the author most likely includes details about the narrator's surroundings in order to—

   A) create a clearer picture of the room in the reader's mind

   B) suggest that she is being held in a state of imprisonment

   C) illustrate her concerns about the previous tenants

   D) foreshadow an arrest

5. As it is used in line 45, the term *ravages* most nearly means—

   A) artwork

   B) damages

   C) mistakes

   D) consequences

6. The narrator indicates that she suppresses her desire to daydream because—

   A) Her husband tells her it will make her anxious condition worse.

   B) It is not beneficial for her growth as a writer.

   C) It distracts her from the task of watching the people in the garden.

   D) Her husband warns her that she may begin to forget how good she truly is.

7. Which choice provides the best evidence for the answer to the previous question?

A) *Then he took me in his arms and called me a blessed little goose, and said he would go down to the cellar, if I wished, and have it whitewashed into the bargain.*

B) *Out of one window I can see the garden, those mysterious deepshaded arbors, the riotous old-fashioned flowers, and bushes and gnarly trees.*

C) *He says that with my imaginative power and habit of story-making, a nervous weakness like mine is sure to lead to all manner of excited fancies, and that I ought to use my will and good sense to check the tendency.*

D) *I never saw so much expression in an inanimate thing before, and we all know how much expression they have!*

8. The narrator assumes that the tattered condition of the wallpaper in her room is a result of—

A) the children's hatred of the décor

B) a game that the children played

C) the restlessness of the children who lived there before

D) a previous tenant whose tastes were questionable

9. Which of the following statements best describes the relationship between the narrator and her husband?

A) The narrator distrusts her husband, whose suspicious behaviors have caused her great distress.

B) The narrator is submissive to her husband, who claims to be doing what is best for her.

C) The narrator resents her husband, who does everything for her.

D) The narrator has genuine affection for her husband, who returns her feelings of love and care.

10. Which choice provides the best evidence for the answer to the previous question?

A) *I suppose John never was nervous in his life. He laughs at me so about this wall-paper!*

B) *Then he took me in his arms and called me a blessed little goose, and said he would go down to the cellar, if I wished, and have it whitewashed into the bargain.*

C) *But he is right enough about the beds and windows and things. It is an airy and comfortable room as any one need wish, and, of course, I would not be so silly as to make him uncomfortable just for a whim.*

D) *I always fancy I see people walking in these numerous paths and arbors, but John has cautioned me not to give way to fancy in the least.*

Questions 11 – 21 are based on the following passage, which is adapted from the United States Declaration of Independence, written in 1776 by Thomas Jefferson.

When in the Course of human events, it becomes necessary for one people to dissolve the political bands which have connected them with another, and to assume among the powers of the earth, the separate and equal station to which the Laws of Nature and of Nature's God entitle them, a decent respect to the opinions of mankind requires that
(5)   they should declare the causes which impel them to the separation.

We hold these truths to be self-evident, that all men are created equal, that they are endowed by their Creator with certain unalienable Rights, that among these are Life, Liberty and the pursuit of Happiness.—That to secure these rights, Governments are instituted among Men, deriving their just powers from the consent of the governed,
(10)   —That whenever any Form of Government becomes destructive of these ends, it is the Right of the People to alter or to abolish it, and to institute new Government, laying its foundation on such principles and organizing its powers in such form, as to them shall seem most likely to affect their Safety and Happiness. Prudence, indeed, will dictate that Governments long established should not be changed for light and transient causes;
(15)   and accordingly all experience hath shewn, that mankind are more disposed to suffer, while evils are sufferable, than to right themselves by abolishing the forms to which they are accustomed. But when a long train of abuses and usurpations, pursuing invariably the same Object evinces a design to reduce them under absolute Despotism, it is their right, it is their duty, to throw off such Government, and to provide new Guards for
(20)   their future security.—Such has been the patient sufferance of these Colonies; and such is now the necessity which constrains them to alter their former Systems of Government. The history of the present King of Great Britain is a history of repeated injuries and usurpations, all having in direct object the establishment of an absolute Tyranny over these States. To prove this, let Facts be submitted to a candid world.

(25)   [...]

In every stage of these Oppressions We have Petitioned for Redress in the most humble terms: Our repeated Petitions have been answered only by repeated injury. A Prince whose character is thus marked by every act which may define a Tyrant, is unfit to be the ruler of a free people.

(30)   Nor have We been wanting in attentions to our British brethren. We have warned them from time to time of attempts by their legislature to extend an unwarrantable jurisdiction over us. We have reminded them of the circumstances of our emigration and settlement here. We have appealed to their native justice and magnanimity, and we have conjured them by the ties of our common kindred to disavow these usurpations,
(35)   which, would inevitably interrupt our connections and correspondence. They too have been deaf to the voice of justice and of consanguinity. We must, therefore, acquiesce in the necessity, which denounces our Separation, and hold them, as we hold the rest of mankind, Enemies in War, in Peace Friends.

We, therefore, the Representatives of the united States of America, in General
(40) Congress, Assembled, appealing to the Supreme Judge of the world for the rectitude of
our intentions, do, in the Name, and by Authority of the good People of these Colonies,
solemnly publish and declare, That these United Colonies are, and of Right ought to be
Free and Independent States; that they are Absolved from all Allegiance to the British
Crown, and that all political connection between them and the State of Great Britain,
(45) is and ought to be totally dissolved; and that as Free and Independent States, they have
full Power to levy War, conclude Peace, contract Alliances, establish Commerce, and
to do all other Acts and Things which Independent States may of right do. And for the
support of this Declaration, with a firm reliance on the protection of divine Providence,
we mutually pledge to each other our Lives, our Fortunes and our sacred Honor.

11. The main purpose of the passage is to—
    A) declare war on Great Britain
    B) detail the grievances that colonists had against their monarch
    C) solidify the commitment that colonists made to each other regarding life in the colonies
    D) proclaim the independence of a new nation

12. Thomas Jefferson indicates that he includes a list of America's grievances—
    A) in order to highlight the severe treatment the colonists suffered at the hands of the king
    B) as a way to make a formal complaint about him as their leader
    C) in case there is need for further action
    D) out of respectful obligation to the rest of the world

13. The central claim of the passage is that—
    A) The king is an unfit ruler, as his actions have proven him to be tyrannical and unresponsive to the colony's concerns.
    B) America's decision to declare independence from Britain is within the rights of the people and necessitated by the king's actions.
    C) The people of Great Britain should have done more to alleviate the concerns of the colonists.
    D) A people who intend to overthrow their government should be respectful of the rights of the rest of the world to understand their reasons.

14. As it is used in line 13, the term *prudence* most nearly means—
    A) judiciousness
    B) innocence
    C) protocol
    D) intelligence

15. Which choice provides the best evidence for the answer to the previous question?

A) *We hold these truths to be self-evident, that all men are created equal, that they are endowed by their Creator with certain unalienable Rights, that among these are Life, Liberty and the pursuit of Happiness.*

B) *Prudence, indeed, will dictate that Governments long established should not be changed for light and transient causes.*

C) *That whenever any Form of Government becomes destructive of these ends, it is the Right of the People to alter or to abolish it, and to institute new Government...*

D) *We must, therefore, acquiesce in the necessity, which denounces our Separation, and hold them, as we hold the rest of mankind, Enemies in War, in Peace Friends.*

16. Jefferson indicates that the American colonists feel compelled to separate from Britain because—

A) The British populous has altogether deserted them.

B) The relationship is no longer profitable for all involved.

C) Their grievances have been repeatedly ignored by the king.

D) Their needs are not considered when new British laws are made.

17. Which choice provides the best evidence for the answer to the previous question?

A) *We hold these truths to be self-evident, that all men are created equal, that they are endowed by their Creator with certain unalienable Rights, that among these are Life, Liberty and the pursuit of Happiness.*

B) *In every stage of these Oppressions We have Petitioned for Redress in the most humble terms: Our repeated Petitions have been answered only by repeated injury.*

C) *We have appealed to their native justice and magnanimity, and we have conjured them by the ties of our common kindred to disavow these usurpations, which, would inevitably interrupt our connections and correspondence.*

D) *And for the support of this Declaration, with a firm reliance on the protection of divine Providence, we mutually pledge to each other our Lives, our Fortunes and our sacred Honor.*

18. In the third paragraph, Jefferson draws a distinction in order to—

A) challenge the king's claim to the throne of Great Britain

B) encourage residents of Great Britain to rise up against their monarch

C) contract the American colonists with the British citizenry

D) characterize American colonial ideals as incompatible with the ruling style of the British monarch

19. As it is used in line 45, the term *dissolved* most nearly means—

A) terminated

B) melted

C) crumbled

D) dispersed

20. Jefferson most likely includes the third and fourth paragraphs in order to—

A) illustrate the fact that the colonists' call for independence is not unjustified

B) describe the nature of the relationship between the colonists and the British monarch

C) highlight the injustice of being governed from a distance

D) emphasize the failure of the king to provide the colonists with supplies and support

21. In the fourth paragraph, Jefferson most likely refers to *the rest of mankind* in order to—

A) compare the American colonists to the people in the rest of the known world

B) indicate the nature of the new, detached relationship between the American colonies and the British people

C) challenge the British populous to change its perspective of the American colonists

D) dispel any misunderstandings about the colonists' perspective on getting involved with other countries

Questions 22 – 31 are based on the following passage, which provides an overview of the history and development of the field of positive psychology. Information was drawn from Dr. Martin E. P. Seligman's landmark book Flourish: A Visionary New Understanding of Happiness and Well-being. *The accompanying graphic was adapted from data collected during a study entitled "Beyond Money: Toward an Economy of Well-being," published in 2004 by Dr. Seligman and his colleague, Dr. Ed Diener.*

Throughout the history of psychology, researchers have sought to relieve human suffering. From the earliest forms of psychotherapy to the cognitive-behavioral therapies of recent decades, nearly all efforts in the study of psychology have been aimed at helping individuals overcome or learn to manage mental illness and extreme emotional

(5) distress. In the early 21st century, however, a new perspective on psychology emerged when Dr. Martin E. P. Seligman received funding to begin research into an idea that he

referred to as positive psychology, a field that would be concerned with understanding the factors that contribute not to psychological distress but to an individual's ability to live a happy, fulfilling, productive life.

(10) According to Seligman's 2011 book *Flourish: A Visionary New Understanding of Happiness and Well-being*, positive psychology began as an inquiry into the experiences that contribute to life satisfaction. Through his theory of authentic happiness, Seligman posited that human happiness could be understood in terms of three elements, all of which we pursue for their inherent value—positive emotions (like joy, amusement,

(15) and gratitude), engagement (the tendency to lose oneself in activity), and meaning (the extent to which one believes his or her life has purpose). These elements together could be evaluated through an individual's assessment of his or her life satisfaction.

More than a decade after the publication of his first theory, however, Seligman views positive psychology somewhat differently. He argues that there are a number of

(20) flaws with his initial theory, especially in its intense focus on the topic of happiness. The term happiness, by today's usage, is inadequate for describing all that contributes to a fulfilling life: the term does not typically refer to the elements of engagement and meaning at all, and "feeling cheerful or merry," writes Seligman, "is a far cry from what Thomas Jefferson declared that we have the right to pursue[.]" In addition, life

(25) satisfaction measures are too dependent on mood to be considered useful in evaluating an individual's overall welfare, and the three elements of happiness as initially defined are too limited.

As a result of these insufficiencies, Seligman has published a new theory that he hopes will drive positive psychology in a different direction: well-being theory. Unlike

(30) authentic happiness theory, well-being theory addresses not only life satisfaction but also the extent to which one flourishes in his or her life: the term well-being refers not to a specific thing that can be evaluated (like life satisfaction) but to a composition of elements that ultimately shape one's overall sense of fulfillment. According to this theory, an individual's well-being is determined by—in addition to subjective expe-

(35) riences like positive emotions, engagement, and meaning—external factors like constructive relationships and personal achievement.

Though positive psychology is a relatively young field within the social sciences, it has already made great strides in attracting attention from researchers and practitioners in the field. Further, it has already begun to gain popular attention, proving that it is on its way to meeting the goal that Dr. Seligman initially set out to accomplish—to

(40) have a positive impact on the lives of everyday people who might otherwise have no motivation to seek therapy.

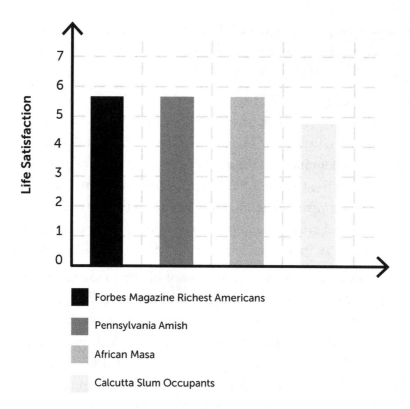

Life Satisfaction

- Forbes Magazine Richest Americans
- Pennsylvania Amish
- African Masa
- Calcutta Slum Occupants

22. In the first paragraph, the author indicates that positive psychology was distinct from other psychological perspectives in that it—

A) did not necessitate psychotherapeutic or cognitive-behavioral treatments

B) is one of the oldest perspectives of psychology still in use today

C) would be focused on understanding and increasing positive experiences rather than minimizing the effects of negative experiences

D) required the practitioner to focus only on the challenges, rather than the strengths, of his or her clients

23. As it is used in line 14, the term *inherent* most nearly means—

A) genetic

B) instinctive

C) intrinsic

D) integral

24. According to the passage, authentic happiness theory was inadequate as a tool in positive psychology because—

A) it does not adhere to the definition that is described in the Declaration of Independence.

B) it did not allow practitioners to understand the subjective experience of their clients.

C) happiness cannot be observed quantitatively.

D) it was overly reliant on fluctuating, subjective measures and failed to take into account the general welfare of the individual.

25. According to authentic happiness theory, life satisfaction could be understood in terms of—

   A) subjective measures of enjoyment, engagement, and fulfillment

   B) positive feelings of joy, amusement, and gratitude and negative feelings of sadness and anger

   C) the number of times per week that the client experienced complete engagement

   D) one's perception of his or her life's purpose

26. Which choice provides the best evidence for the answer to the previous question?

   A) *The term happiness, by today's usage, is inadequate for describing all that contributes to a fulfilling life...*

   B) *Unlike authentic happiness theory, well-being theory addresses not only life satisfaction but also the extent to which one flourishes in his or her life...*

   C) *In addition, life satisfaction measures are too dependent on mood to be considered useful in evaluating an individual's overall welfare, and the three elements of happiness as initially defined are too limited.*

   D) *According to [well-being] theory, an individual's well-being is determined by—in addition to subjective experiences like positive emotions, engagement, and meaning—external factors like constructive relationships and personal achievement.*

27. As it is used in line 32, the term *composition* most nearly means—

   A) combination

   B) configuration

   C) alignment

   D) masterpiece

28. The major difference between authentic happiness and well-being theories is that—

   A) Authentic happiness theory focuses primarily on the impact of positive emotions on an individual's overall life satisfaction.

   B) Well-being theory attempts to understand welfare more holistically by taking into account external measures of prosperity.

   C) Well-being theory does not take into account the impact of positive emotions, engagement, or fulfillment.

   D) Authentic happiness theory seeks to explain the correlation between happiness and financial prosperity.

29. Which choice provides the best evidence for the answer to the previous question?

- **A)** *The term happiness, by today's usage, is inadequate for describing all that contributes to a fulfilling life...*
- **B)** *Through his theory of authentic happiness, Seligman posited that human happiness could be understood in terms of three elements, all of which we pursue for their inherent value...*
- **C)** *In addition, life satisfaction measures are too dependent on mood to be considered useful in evaluating an individual's overall welfare, and the three elements of happiness as initially defined are too limited.*
- **D)** *According to [well-being] theory, an individual's well-being is determined—in addition to subjective experiences like positive emotions, engagement, and meaning—by external factors like constructive relationships and personal achievement.*

30. In the final paragraph, the author indicates that—

- **A)** Individuals who do not seek therapy in response to their life challenges should consider doing so.
- **B)** The popularity of positive psychology discounts it in the eyes of many professionals.
- **C)** Positive psychology is intended for a broad audience both within and outside the field of psychology.
- **D)** There is no reason for individuals who are already in therapy to take an interest in positive psychology.

31. How does the information in the graph relate to the author's claim that life satisfaction is an inadequate measure of overall well-being?

- **A)** Life-satisfaction across groups was fairly steady, suggesting that happiness is a consistent measure by which to evaluate well-being.
- **B)** Life-satisfaction across groups was fairly steady, suggesting that happiness is relative to an individual's experience and not contingent upon objective measures of welfare.
- **C)** Life-satisfaction across groups was fairly steady, suggesting that the definition of happiness fluctuates based on the culture in which it is being explored.
- **D)** Life-satisfaction across groups was fairly steady, suggesting that well-being is an accurate, objective measure, completely unrelated to happiness.

Questions 32 – 42 are based on the following passages, which discuss the topic of pain diagnosis and management in animals. Passage 1 provides a summary of information drawn from Dr. Debbie Grant's book Pain Management in Small Animals. *Passage 2 summarized the findings of a study conducted by Dr. Giorgia della Rocca and colleagues entitled "Diagnosis of Pain in Small Companion Animals."*

PASSAGE 1

In recent decades, scientific inquiry and urbanization have given birth to a new perspective on the human relationship with animal species. Studies into the common biology and ancestral origins of humans and animals, coupled with the increasing popularity of companion animals over working animals, have led scientists and laymen (5) alike to wonder about the mental and emotional lives of other species. Concerns about animal suffering, for example, have led to major changes in a variety of industries from entertainment to food production. In the field of veterinary medicine, this new line of inquiry—into whether animals experience pain and suffering the same way humans do—is especially clear when explored in the context of pain management.

(10)   Though many advancements have been made in research sciences, and though pain management is widely accepted as a necessary job of practitioners, a number of myths about animal pain still plague the field of veterinary medicine and prevent practitioners from making pain management a priority. According to veterinarian and writer Debbie Grant, three myths are especially detrimental to the cause. The first of these is the myth (15) that animals do not feel pain at all or that they feel it less intensely than humans; in fact, according to Grant, the biological mechanisms by which we experience pain are the very same mechanisms by which animals experience pain. Even the emotional reaction to a painful experience (like being afraid to return to the dentist after an unpleasant visit) is mirrored in animals.

(20)   The second myth that prevents the advancement of pain management practices is the myth that pain is a necessary part of an animal's recovery. While some veterinarians believe that pain may prevent a healing dog, for example, from playing too vigorously, Grant says this is simply not the case. In fact, restlessness and discomfort may even lead to unusually high levels of agitation and may consequently slow the recovery process (25) even further.

Finally, contrary to the third myth, animals do not necessarily tolerate pain any better than humans do, though they may handle their pain differently. Grant emphasizes that veterinarians must be aware that a lack of obvious signs does not necessarily suggest that pain is not present: in fact, many animals, especially those that are prey (30) animals in the wild, are likely to conceal their pain out of an instinct to hide weaknesses that may make them easy targets for predators.

PASSAGE 2

Veterinarians have a unique challenge when it comes to diagnosing their patients. Unlike doctors, who typically have the benefit of discussing their patients' concerns, veterinarians cannot ask their patients whether and where they are experiencing dis-(35) comfort. Additionally, veterinarians must be aware of the survival instinct of many animals to mask pain in response to stressful experiences or foreign environments. For these reasons, diagnostic tools and strategies are instrumental in the effective practice of veterinary medicine.

In 2014, researchers of veterinary medicine at the University of Perugia in Italy (40) completed a review of the diagnostic tools and strategies available to today's practitioners and found a number of them to be effective. Presumptive diagnosis, the first of these strategies, involves making a prediction about the animal's pain based on the observable damage to the body or body part. As with human pain, greater damage or disfigurement likely suggests more significant pain. In addition to presumptive diagnosis, veterinarians (45) can use close observation to assess changes in the animal's behavior. Unusual postures, activity levels, and movements are especially useful in determining the presence of pain, but even mood, facial expression, and appetite can be indicators.

In addition to these strategies, a number of useful tools are available to help veterinarians in pain diagnosis. The most common of these is the clinical exam. A clinical (50) session may involve a physical exam, in which the practitioner notes any external signs of injury, and laboratory testing, which could allow the practitioner to pinpoint irregularities in the animal's organic functions. Finally, a veterinarian might make use of an objective pain scale, by which he or she could assess the animal's condition according to a number of criteria. This tool is especially useful throughout the course of treatment, as (55) it provides the practitioner with a quantitative measure for evaluating the effectiveness of various treatment options.

32. As it is used in line 14, the term *detrimental* most nearly means—
- **A)** mischievous
- **B)** damaging
- **C)** disturbing
- **D)** advantageous

33. The author of Passage 1 most likely includes the example of the unpleasant dentist visit in order to—
- **A)** provide a relatable example of how pain can influence a person's emotions
- **B)** challenge the reader to overcome his or her natural, emotional response to painful experiences
- **C)** question a popular perception about the experience of going to the dentist
- **D)** highlight a similarity in the way humans and animals respond to pain

34. As it is used in line 36, the term *foreign* most nearly means—
- **A)** unfamiliar
- **B)** inaccessible
- **C)** distant
- **D)** exotic

35. The author of Passage 1 indicates that despite advancements in veterinary sciences—

A) Many veterinarians do not see the value in pain management practices for their patients.

B) Many veterinarians still employ outdated methods of pain management.

C) Many veterinarians still believe that pain management is a responsibility of the pet owner.

D) Many veterinarians still have misguided beliefs and practices related to pain management in animals.

36. The author of Passage 2 indicates that veterinarians can improve their pain management practices by—

A) attempting to communicate with their patients about the pain they are experiencing

B) employing the best diagnostic practices in their field

C) encouraging pet owners to keep careful watch over their animals

D) inventing novel ways to assess and treat pain in animals

37. Which choice provides the best evidence for the answer to the previous question?

A) *Unlike doctors, who typically have the benefit of discussing their patients' concerns, veterinarians cannot ask their patients whether and where they are experiencing discomfort.*

B) *Additionally, veterinarians must be aware of the survival instinct of many animals to mask pain in response to stressful experiences or foreign environments.*

C) *For these reasons, diagnostic tools and strategies are instrumental in the effective practice of veterinary medicine.*

D) *In 2014, researchers of veterinary medicine at the University of Perugia in Italy completed a review of the diagnostic tools and strategies available to today's practitioners and found a number of them to be effective.*

38. The author of Passage 2 indicates that objective pain measures are useful because—

A) They allow the veterinarian to compare an animal's pain level to the pain levels of other animals.

B) They challenge the veterinarian to devise a treatment plan as quickly as possible.

C) They discount the assumption that pain cannot be measured on an objective scale.

D) They provide the veterinarian with an quantitative method for tracking pain levels over the course of an animal's treatment.

39. The author of Passage 1 would most likely respond to the claim made in lines 41 through 45 of Passage 2 by—

A) asserting that substantial physical damage to an animal's form does not necessarily suggest the presence of pain

B) asserting that presumptive diagnosis is more effective for diagnosing humans and should not be used for diagnosing animals

C) asserting that similarities in methods of pain diagnosis for humans and animals are effective because of the biological similarities between them

D) asserting that veterinarians should not make use of presumptive diagnosis in evaluating and treating patients

40. Which choice provides the best evidence for the answer to the previous question?

A) *Though many advancements have been made in research sciences, and though pain management is widely accepted as a necessary job of practitioners, a number of myths about animal pain still plague the field of veterinary medicine and prevent practitioners from making pain management a priority.*

B) *...in fact, according to Grant, the biological mechanisms by which we experience pain are the very same mechanisms by which animals experience pain.*

C) *Even the emotional reaction to a painful experience (like being afraid to return to the dentist after an unpleasant visit) is mirrored in animals.*

D) *[M]any animals, especially those that are prey animals in the wild, are likely to conceal their pain out of an instinct to hide weaknesses that may make them easy targets for predators.*

41. Which of the following best describes the relationship between the two passages?

A) The first passage makes the claim that pain management should be a priority for veterinarians, while the second passage rejects this claim.

B) The first passage emphasizes the veterinarian's responsibility to prioritize pain management in animals, while the second passage explores the tools by which veterinarians can execute this responsibility.

C) The first passage seeks to dispel myths about pain management in animals, while the second passage denies that they are myths.

D) The first passage sheds light on the shortcomings of veterinary sciences as they currently exist, while the second passage provides insight into how these shortcomings might be overcome.

42. Both authors indicate that veterinarians—

    A) must be aware that a lack of obvious symptoms does not necessarily suggest an absence of pain.

    B) should make pain management for their patients a priority.

    C) ought to be familiar with the misguided assumptions that exist in their field.

    D) need to conduct a thorough examination before releasing an animal back to its owner.

Questions 43 – 52 are based on the following passage and graphic, which were adapted from an article entitled "The Solar System and Beyond Is Awash with Water," published online by the National Aeronautics and Space Administration in April 2015.

As NASA missions explore our solar system and search for new worlds, they are finding water in surprising places. Water is but one piece of our search for habitable planets and life beyond Earth, yet it links many seemingly unrelated worlds in surprising ways.

(5)   "NASA science activities have provided a wave of amazing findings related to water in recent years that inspire us to continue investigating our origins and the fascinating possibilities for other worlds, and life, in the universe," said Ellen Stofan, chief scientist for the agency. "In our lifetime, we may very well finally answer whether we are alone in the solar system and beyond."

The chemical elements in water, hydrogen and oxygen, are some of the most abundant
(10)   elements in the universe. Astronomers see the signature of water in giant molecular clouds between the stars, in disks of material that represent newborn planetary systems, and in the atmospheres of giant planets orbiting other stars.

There are several worlds thought to possess liquid water beneath their surfaces, and many more that have water in the form of ice or vapor. Water is found in primitive
(15)   bodies like comets and asteroids, and dwarf planets like Ceres. The atmospheres and interiors of the four giant planets—Jupiter, Saturn, Uranus and Neptune—are thought to contain enormous quantities of the wet stuff, and their moons and rings have substantial water ice.

Perhaps the most surprising water worlds are the five icy moons of Jupiter and Saturn
(20)   that show strong evidence of oceans beneath their surfaces: Ganymede, Europa and Callisto at Jupiter, and Enceladus and Titan at Saturn.

Scientists using NASA's Hubble Space Telescope recently provided powerful evidence that Ganymede has a saltwater, sub-surface ocean, likely sandwiched between two layers of ice.

(25)   Europa and Enceladus are thought to have an ocean of liquid water beneath their surface in contact with mineral-rich rock, and may have the three ingredients needed for life as we know it: liquid water, essential chemical elements for biological processes, and sources of energy that could be used by living things.

Understanding the distribution of water in our solar system tells us a great deal
(30) about how the planets, moons, comets and other bodies formed 4.5 billion years ago
from the disk of gas and dust that surrounded our sun. The space closer to the sun was
hotter and drier than the space farther from the sun, which was cold enough for water
to condense. The dividing line, called the "frost line," sat around Jupiter's present-day
orbit. Even today, this is the approximate distance from the sun at which the ice on
(35) most comets begins to melt and become "active." Their brilliant spray releases water
ice, vapor, dust and other chemicals, which are thought to form the bedrock of most
worlds of the frigid outer solar system.

Scientists think it was too hot in the solar system's early days for water to condense
into liquid or ice on the inner planets, so it had to be delivered—possibly by comets and
(40) water-bearing asteroids. NASA's Dawn mission is currently studying Ceres, which is
the largest body in the asteroid belt between Mars and Jupiter. Researchers think Ceres
might have a water-rich composition similar to some of the bodies that brought water
to the three rocky, inner planets, including Earth.

The amount of water in the giant planet Jupiter holds a critical missing piece to the
(45) puzzle of our solar system's formation. Jupiter was likely the first planet to form, and it
contains most of the material that wasn't incorporated into the sun. The leading theories
about its formation rest on the amount of water the planet soaked up.

It's easy to forget that the story of Earth's water, from gentle rains to raging rivers,
is intimately connected to the larger story of our solar system and beyond. But our
(50) water came from somewhere—every world in our solar system got its water from the
same shared source. So it's worth considering that the next glass of water you drink
could easily have been part of a comet, or an ocean moon, or a long-vanished sea on
the surface of Mars. And note that the night sky may be full of exoplanets formed by
similar processes to our home world, where gentle waves wash against the shores of
(55) alien seas.

Moons of Jupiter and Saturn		
NAME (DESCRIPTION)	DISTANCE FROM SUN (IN ASTRONOMICAL UNITS)	OCEAN WORLD STATUS
Europa (moon of Jupiter)	5.2 AU	Active
Ganymede (moon of Jupiter)	5.2 AU	Locked (under ice)
Callisto (moon of Jupiter)	5.2 AU	Locked (under ice)
Enceladus (moon of Saturn)	9.5 AU	Active
Titan (moon of Saturn)	9.5 AU	Locked (under ice)

43. In the third paragraph, the author provides details in order to—
    A) pique the reader's curiosity about celestial bodies and events
    B) discount the assertion that the elements found in water are plentiful within our solar system
    C) remind the reader of the relative size of Earth in comparison to the rest of our solar system
    D) illustrate the widespread availability of hydrogen and oxygen in space

44. The passages indicate that water—
    A) can be found across our solar system in various forms
    B) is the most precious resource within our solar system
    C) is only available on our planet and the planets nearest to us
    D) is not a renewable resource

45. Which choice provides the best evidence for the answer to the previous question?
    A) *The chemical elements in water, hydrogen and oxygen, are some of the most abundant elements in the universe.*
    B) *There are several worlds thought to possess liquid water beneath their surfaces, and many more that have water in the form of ice or vapor.*
    C) *Scientists think it was too hot in the solar system's early days for water to condense into liquid or ice on the inner planets, so it had to be delivered—possibly by comets and water-bearing asteroids.*
    D) *So it's worth considering that the next glass of water you drink could easily have been part of a comet, or an ocean moon, or a long-vanished sea on the surface of Mars.*

46. According to the passage, water distribution in our solar system provides—
    A) an efficient system for recycling the precious resource
    B) an important clue about the formation of celestial bodies
    C) proof that life cannot survive outside the "frost line"
    D) plentiful opportunities for transporting the substance across great distances

47. The author indicates that, in addition to liquid water, terrestrial forms of life also require—
    A) certain chemical elements and useable energy sources in order to survive
    B) substantial amounts of hydrogen and oxygen in order to survive
    C) at least some sunlight in order to survive
    D) frozen water in order to survive

48. The author indicates that the frost line is—

   A) a dividing line outside of which planets cannot sustain life

   B) the only location in our solar system where liquid water and frozen water can exist simultaneously

   C) the location at which most new bodies in our solar system form

   D) the distance from the sun at which liquid water begins to freeze

49. As it is used in line 32, the term *bedrock* most nearly means—

   A) pedestal

   B) heart

   C) anchor

   D) foundation

50. Which choice provides the best evidence for the answer to the previous question?

   A) *There are several worlds thought to possess liquid water beneath their surfaces, and many more that have water in the form of ice or vapor.*

   B) *Europa and Enceladus are thought to have...the three ingredients needed for life as we know it: liquid water, essential chemical elements for biological processes, and sources of energy that could be used by living things.*

   C) *Their brilliant spray releases water ice, vapor, dust and other chemicals, which are thought to form the bedrock of most worlds of the frigid outer solar system.*

   D) *Scientists think it was too hot in the solar system's early days for water to condense into liquid or ice on the inner planets, so it had to be delivered—possibly by comets and water-bearing asteroids.*

51. The passage indicates that Earth's liquid water was most likely—

   A) recycled from other planets

   B) transported here by traveling, water-rich bodies like comets

   C) found on Jupiter before it was carried across the solar system by comets

   D) in the form of vapor until it reached our atmosphere

52. Which conclusion is supported by both the passage and the table?

   A) Celestial bodies that exist outside of the frost line are not likely to contain water in any form.

   B) Jupiter's distance from the sun prevents it from hosting liquid water.

   C) Evidence of water in some form has been found on a number of celestial bodies as far from the sun as Saturn.

   D) Water is a rare and valuable substance in our solar system.

Writing and Language

In the following passages, there are numbered and underlined words and phrases that correspond with the questions in the right-hand column. You are to choose the answer that best completes the statement grammatically, stylistically, and/or logically. If you think the original version is best, select "NO CHANGE."

AEROSPACE ENGINEERING

In the 21st century, the growing population and the public interest in space exploration will undoubtedly call for increased investment in air and space travel. (1)Therefore, individuals who excel at maths and sciences and are interested in a full-time career with high salaries and job security ought to consider a career in aerospace engineering.

1. Which of the following choices most effectively frames the main argument of the passage?
   A) NO CHANGE
   B) As such, individuals who enjoy a good challenge ought to consider a career in aerospace engineering.
   C) Accordingly, individuals who want to start a career should consider pursuing aerospace engineering.
   D) Consequently, individuals who like space should consider starting a career in aerospace engineering.

Aerospace engineers typically get to choose from one of two (2)concentrations such as aeronautical engineering or astronautical engineering—and as a result are able to focus their efforts in the field that most interests them. Aeronautical engineers work on designing and constructing aircraft for travel within the earth's

2. A) NO CHANGE
   B) concentrations, aeronautical engineering
   C) concentrations—aeronautical engineering
   D) concentrations. Aeronautical engineering

Go On

(3)atmosphere, astronautical engineers, on the other hand, build spacecraft for use both inside and outside of earth's atmosphere. Though the two specialties have their own

(4)unique challenges and demands, both require a strong grasp of physics and higher-level mathematics, so individuals who excel at logical reasoning are well-suited for these fields.

Aerospace engineers typically work full time schedules and, when in leadership positions, may work as much as fifty or sixty hours per week. The bulk of those hours occurs in an office setting, where these engineers use advanced software programs to design models and run simulations. Most of these individuals work for firms that are contracted out to the federal government; they may contribute to the design and construction of aircraft, missiles, or systems for national defense. As a result, many aerospace engineering jobs require advanced security clearance. Citizenship in the U.S. may even be a requirement for many positions.

Like other kinds of engineers, aerospace engineers must have a bachelor's degree in their field. While in school, (5)they studied advanced calculus, trigonometry, general engineering, and physics (including propulsion, mechanics, structures, and aerodynamics). As a result, the degree is typically more rigorous than degrees in other areas of engineering.

3. **A)** NO CHANGE
   B) atmosphere and astronautical engineers
   C) atmosphere, however, astronautical engineers
   D) atmosphere; astronautical engineers

4. **A)** NO CHANGE
   B) challenging demands
   C) challenges
   D) demand that are challenging

5. **A)** NO CHANGE
   B) they must study
   C) they would study
   D) they will study

(6)However, aerospace engineers usually see a much bigger payoff in terms of salary than do other engineers: the median salary for aerospace engineers is quite a bit larger than the median salary for other engineering professions.

(7)

6. Which of the following completes this sentence with accurate information from the graph at the conclusion of the passage?

A) NO CHANGE

B) the median salary for aerospace engineers is almost twenty thousand dollars more than the median salary for other engineering professions.

C) the median salary for aerospace engineers is almost fifty thousand dollars more than the median salary for other engineering professions.

D) the median salary for aerospace engineers is about the same as the median salary for other engineering professions.

7. For the sake of logical coherence, the preceding sentence should be placed—

A) where it is now

B) at the beginning of the paragraph

C) after the first sentence

D) after the second sentence

Go On

(8) In 2012, the United States Bureau of Labor Statistics projected that the profession of aerospace engineering would expand by seven percent before 2022, creating over six thousand new jobs over the next decade. Further, opportunities for advancement

8. Which of the following provides the most effective transition from the previous paragraph to this one?
   A) The Bureau of Labor Statistics researches various professions to gather information about the changing job market.
   B) The field of aerospace engineering is not shrinking.
   C) In addition to earning a high salary, aerospace engineers can expect a high level of job security.
   D) Aerospace engineering is clearly a great option for those entering the workforce.

(9)is plentiful. Aerospace engineers

9. A) NO CHANGE
   B) are
   C) were
   D) was

(10)which excel in their field can work their way toward careers as technical specialists, supervisors, or even engineering or program

10. A) NO CHANGE
    B) whom
    C) that
    D) who

managers. (11)

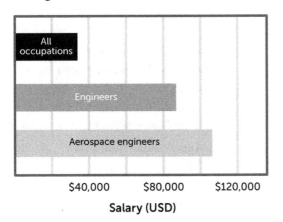

Salary (USD)

YOUNG ABRAHAM

A young Abraham Lincoln awoke with a (12)jolt, excited to pick up where he had left off with his reading. He had chores to complete in the morning, of course, but he loved those days when he could fit in a couple hours of studying before he had to begin with his work.

11. At this point, the writer is considering adding the following sentence:

By taking advantage of apprenticeships or advanced educational opportunities, aerospace engineers can increase their chances of advancement in their field.

Should the writer make this addition?

A) Yes, because it emphasizes the possibility of career advancement for aerospace engineers and provides some insight into how that advancement is earned.

B) Yes, because it provides important information about additional requirements that an entry-level aerospace engineer might have to complete.

C) No, because advancement is most likely not a significant factor for graduates entering the field of aerospace engineering.

D) No, because individuals who are interested in aerospace engineering should not be worried about advancement so early in their career.

12. A) NO CHANGE
B) jolt, being excited
C) jolt and excited
D) jolt; excited

(13)

13. At this point, the writer is considering adding the following sentence:

He was especially looking forward to the quiet time on this particular morning: he was reading a book about his hero, George Washington.

Should he/she make this addition?

A) Yes, because it gives the reader insight into who Lincoln admired as a young boy.

B) Yes, because it provides information about the events that are about to unfold.

C) No, because it distracts the reader from the main point of the paragraph.

D) No, because the detail is irrelevant to the narrative.

Young Abe (14)<u>rolled over, stretches his arms, and reaches toward the wall</u>, where he had lodged his book between two of the logs that constructed his family's cabin. *Oh no*, he thought as he felt the book's binding.

14. A) NO CHANGE

B) rolls over, stretching his arms, and reaches toward the wall,

C) rolling over, stretching his arms, and reaching toward the wall,

D) rolled over, stretched his arms, and reached toward the wall,

It was noticeably (15)<u>sopping</u> and had been warped

15. A) NO CHANGE

B) drenched

C) damp

D) soaking

by the moisture: (16)evidently it had rained most of the previous night. He pulled the book from its slot in the wall and set it down in front of him.

Oh no, he repeated to himself. Young Abe was a dedicated and diligent reader, but because of his family's financial situation, he could not afford to buy his own books. He read only when he could find a book to borrow, (17)which unfortunately was not often.

(18)This book, *The Life of Washington*, was one of his favorites. He had borrowed this wonderful book from his teacher, Andrew Crawford, by whom he had been instructed in manners and composition. He knew he had to tell Crawford the truth about his book, but he was petrified by the thought of admitting his mistake. Still, Abe decided, it was the right thing to do. He attempted to dry the book's pages as best he could and set it aside.

16. Which choice provides the most relevant detail at this point in the narrative?
    A) NO CHANGE
    B) Evidently the pages were thinner than Lincoln had realized.
    C) Evidently the book was a popular one.
    D) Evidently the book had not budged at all while young Lincoln slept.

17. Which choice most effectively illustrates the young Abe Lincoln's commitment to learning?
    A) NO CHANGE
    B) and he had a fine reputation for being cautious with the books he borrowed
    C) so he had only read a handful of books
    D) sometimes walking miles to retrieve it

18. The writer is considering deleting the underlined sentence. Should he/she make this deletion?
    A) Yes, because it gives away the ending of the narrative.
    B) Yes, because it attributes undue importance to the book itself.
    C) No, because it provides important insight into why the incident was so disappointing.
    D) No, because it sheds light on who Lincoln was as a child.

19. For the sake of logic and coherence, the preceding paragraph should be placed—

A) where it is now

B) at the beginning of the narrative

C) after the first paragraph

D) after the second paragraph

Later that afternoon, young Abe stepped out into the crisp autumn air to make the journey to the Crawford home, (20)wear he would have to deliver the news about the ruined book. He took a deep breath and began to walk.

20. **A)** NO CHANGE

B) where

C) were

D) whir

Before long, he found himself at the door of the Crawford home, talking to the man himself. "So you see," Young Abe stammered, "I intended to take good care of your book, but it seems I made an error in judgment. I hope you will allow me to repay you for my blunder." Crawford and Abe both knew that (21)he had no money and that the only way he could pay was through work.

21. **A)** NO CHANGE

B) they

C) the boy

D) him

"Give me three (22)day's work on the harvest," said Crawford, "and the manuscript is yours."

22. **A)** NO CHANGE

B) days

C) daze

D) days'

Young Abraham Lincoln was jubilant. Of course the three days of harvesting corn in the Crawford's field would not be ideal, but at the end of it, he would be the proud owner of a shabby—but readable—copy of *The Life of Washington*.

GLOBAL FOOD PRODUCTION

Environmental concerns have been at the center of ongoing debate in the 21st century: we are going green in both our homes and our offices, and discourse around renewable energy sources, responsible recycling, and threatening pollution (23)are commonplace. Still, according to acclaimed environmental scientist Dr. Jonathon Foley, for all of our concern about the environment, we often

(24)overlook one of the most significant threats to our planet: global food production.

(25)Though we must make food in order to survive as a species, we do not have to do it irresponsibly.

The threat of global food production is manifest in many forms. Greenhouse gases such as methane, nitrous oxide, and carbon dioxide are released in larger amounts by farming and agricultural practices (26) than all the world's transportation vehicles combined. Additionally, the world's limited water supply is both depleted and polluted by farming and agricultural techniques.

23. **A)** NO CHANGE
    B) were
    C) is
    D) was

24. **A)** NO CHANGE
    B) oversee
    C) disregard
    D) overview

25. **A)** NO CHANGE
    B) Incidentally
    C) Until
    D) When

26. **A)** NO CHANGE
    B) than are all the
    C) than by all the
    D) than do all the

(27)The further clearing of land for crops poses a threat to indigenous wildlife in some areas and has, in some cases substantially, contributed to species extinction.

27.
A) NO CHANGE

B) Further, the clearing of land for crops in some areas poses a threat to indigenous wildlife and has contributed, in some cases substantially, to species extinction.

C) In some cases substantially, the clearing of land for crops poses a threat in some areas to indigenous wildlife and has contributed to species extinction.

D) In some areas, the clearing of further land for crops has contributed, in some cases substantially, to species extinction and poses a threat to indigenous wildlife.

(28)

28. At this point, the writer is considering adding the following sentence:

Altogether, the threat that is posed to our planet by our own food production practices is one that we can no longer afford to ignore.

Should the writer make this addition?

A) Yes, because it ties together the author's ideas about sustainability and affordability.

B) Yes, because it provides a brief summary of the previous paragraph and an effective transition into the next paragraph.

C) No, because it distracts the reader from the main point of the paragraph.

D) No, because the tone does not align with the author's purpose.

Fortunately, researchers like Dr. Foley have committed (29)his career to finding solutions to these challenges. In fact, Foley has refined a clear, five-step system that he believes will lead to significant positive change.

First, says Foley, we must halt agricultural expansion. Globally, (30)land devoted to food productions accounts for an area as large as South America and Africa combined. Moving forward, we must commit to preserving natural habits where they currently exist. Second, we must seek to expand production on the lands we have already committed to farming.

(31)Especially in those areas where crop yields are low, new technologies have the potential to significantly increase yields and improve efficiency. Third, we must learn to make better use of our precious, non-renewable resources like water. By borrowing techniques from commercial and organic farming,

29. A) NO CHANGE
    B) there careers
    C) their careers
    D) they're careers

30. A) NO CHANGE
    B) land devoted to food production account
    C) lands devoted to food production account
    D) lands devoted to food production accounts

31. A) NO CHANGE
    B) Significantly, in those areas where crop yields are low, new technologies especially have the potential to increase yields and improve efficiency.
    C) New technologies have the potential where crop yields are significantly low to improve efficiency and increase yields.
    D) Where crop yields are significantly low, new technologies especially have the potential to improve efficiency and increase yields.

(32)farmers around the world can begin to make more conscious choices about efficient water use and protect water sources from contamination.

Fourth, we must reconsider the structures of our diets. Today, more than thirty-five percent of the world's crops are used to feed livestock, but only a small percent of the calories consumed by these animals make it into human diets. By designing diets that are less reliant on meat proteins, we can return some of those crop yields, and calories, to the global food bank. Finally, we must work to minimize food waste worldwide by buying and using food products more consciously.

32. **A)** NO CHANGE

B) farmers around the world can begin to make more conscious choices about using water efficiently and protecting water sources from contamination.

C) farmers around the world can begin to make more conscious choices about efficient water use and protecting water sources from contamination.

D) farmers around the world can begin to make more conscious choices about efficient water use and protect water sources from contamination.

(33)

33. At this point the writer wants to add a concluding statement. Which of the following provides a conclusion that is appropriate to both the tone and purpose of the passage?

A) These changes will be especially challenging in developed countries, where food production costs are high and meals are easier to come by.

B) By following these simple steps in countries all around the globe, we can begin to make positive changes that will feed our population while protecting our environment.

C) While these changes will no doubt be challenging for us as a population, we can definitely make them work for us.

D) By taking these simple steps in countries around the globe, we can ensure that there will be enough food to feed the entire human population.

Go On

The Origins of Humanity?

(34)Charles Darwin wrote *The Origin of Species* over one hundred years ago, in 1859. However, musings on the beginnings of human existence are by no means unique to our modern

mind. (35) Indeed, creation myths are numerous and varied. Despite their differences, however, the universal theme of

34. Which of the following most effectively introduces the topic of the article by relating to the modern reader?

A) NO CHANGE

B) There is currently no way for us to know where our species came from or how we were when we first appeared.

C) Philosophers have, for centuries, pondered the meaning and origins of human life on Earth.

D) In today's technologically advanced world, scientists are spending more time than ever asking questions about the origins of our planet and our species.

35. At this point, the writer wants to add additional support for the paragraph's main point. Which choice most effectively accomplishes this goal?

A) Even centuries ago, the earliest human civilizations sought to understand where they came from.

B) In fact, modern sciences also seek to understand how our universe itself came to be.

C) Scientists have never been clearer about where the human species came from.

D) Still, it is important to be content with one's own understanding, so as not to become dependent on others for one's ideas.

(36)this story highlights the instinctive desire that exists in all cultures to understand how our species came to be.

Some early civilizations subscribed to beliefs about man's evolution from nature. According to Sanchuniathon, an ancient Phoenician mythographer, all things on Earth, including humanity, evolved from the winds themselves. The winds swirled around each other to produce Desire, which eventually took form as a slimy substance called Mot. From Mot (37)was born simple creatures that eventually evolved into conscious human beings.

(38)However, the early peoples of southern California believed humanity evolved from animals—coyotes in particular. According to the legend, coyotes began their evolution when they started sitting up to bury their dead. (39)Over time, their tails were worn down, their paws lengthened, and their snouts shortened into human noses.

36. **A)** NO CHANGE
B) these stories highlights
C) this story highlight
D) these stories highlight

37. **A)** NO CHANGE
B) were born simple creatures
C) was born a simple creature
D) were born a simple creature

38. **A)** NO CHANGE
B) Consequently,
C) Regardless,
D) In a similar manner,

39. At this point, the writer is considering deleting the underlined sentence. Should he/she make this deletion?
A) Yes, because it distracts the reader from the main point of the paragraph.
B) Yes, because the reader already understands that humans evolved from coyotes.
C) No, because it provides further detail about how the early tribes of southern California believed humans evolved from coyotes.
D) No, because it provides a humorous detail that helps readers to relate to the people who believed this myth.

The early Borneo people had their own myth about (40)humanities beginning: they believed that humanity was born out of a

40.
A) NO CHANGE
B) humanity's
C) humanity
D) the human

rock, which (41)one day opened her mouth to let the first humans walk out. Those humans, through their hard work and sacrifices, grew the rest of the earth and its inhabitants.

41.
A) NO CHANGE
B) his
C) it's
D) its

(42)Still, not all ancient peoples believed humans evolved from nature. Some mythologies included stories of humanity's creation by deities. According to Mesopotamian myth, for example, Marduk, the fierce god of the sun, created humanity out of the body of another god, Tiamat,

42. Which choice provides the most effective, appropriate transition from the previous paragraph to this one?
A) NO CHANGE
B) Regardless of their location, many primitive populations used these kinds of myths to make sense of their world.
C) If humanity's evolution from nature was not crazy enough, other cultures believed even crazier myths.
D) In spite of information to the contrary, myths about humanity's evolution from nature were not especially popular.

(43)who he had defeated in an epic battle.

According to the mythology of the Hopi Indians, Tawa, the Sun Spirit, was responsible for the creation of humanity. Their legend stated that Tawa created the first world, which to his disappointment was inhabited only by insects that could not understand the meaning of life. To elevate his creation, he formed a second world and forced the insects to climb to it. Over the course of this challenging journey, they

43.
A) NO CHANGE
B) who it had defeated
C) whom he had defeated
D) whom it had defeated

evolved into more complex creatures and eventually into humans.

Other civilizations believed humanity was (44)neither a descendant of the earth or a creation of the gods: these peoples believed that humanity descended directly from the gods themselves. According to the Hindu creation myth, for example, the deity Purusha, who was both man and woman, was split in half. The two halves of the deity united and continued to reunite in different forms until all of the creatures on Earth had been created.

44. **A)** NO CHANGE

B) neither a descendant of the earth nor a creation of the gods

C) either a descendent of the earth or a creation of the gods

D) both a descendent of the earth and a creation of the gods

Mathematics

For questions 1 – 15, work the problem and choose the most correct answer. For questions 16 – 20, work the problem and write in the correct answer in the space provided.

FORMULA CHART

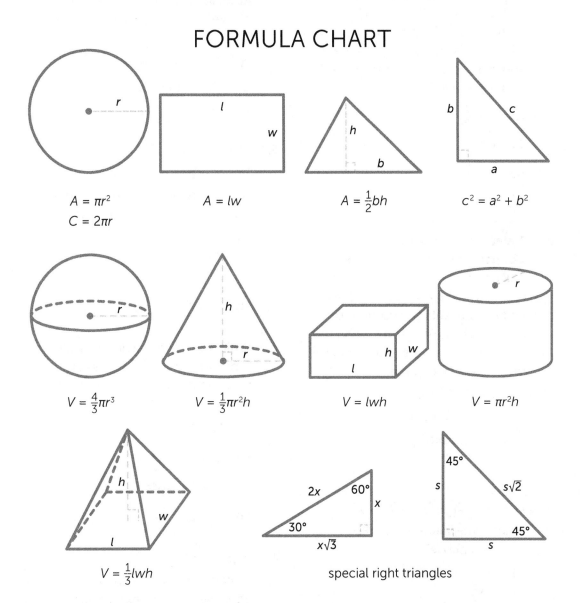

$A = \pi r^2$
$C = 2\pi r$

$A = lw$

$A = \frac{1}{2}bh$

$c^2 = a^2 + b^2$

$V = \frac{4}{3}\pi r^3$

$V = \frac{1}{3}\pi r^2 h$

$V = lwh$

$V = \pi r^2 h$

$V = \frac{1}{3}lwh$

special right triangles

▶ The number of degrees of arc in a circle is 360.

▶ The number of radians of arc in a circle is 2π.

▶ The sum of the measures in degrees of the angles of a triangle is 180.

1. If m represents a car's average mileage in miles per gallon, p represents the price of gas in dollars per gallon, and d represents a distance in miles, which of the following algebraic equations represents the cost (c) of gas per mile?

   A) $c = \frac{p}{m}$

   B) $c = \frac{p}{m}$

   C) $c = \frac{mp}{d}$

   D) $c = \frac{m}{p}$

2. A cleaning company charges $25 per hour per room. Added to this charge is a 7% sales tax. If t represents the number of hours and r represents the number of rooms, which of the following algebraic equations represents the total cost c of cleaning?

   A) $c = 25.07(t)(r)$

   B) $c = 32.00(t)(r)$

   C) $c = 26.75(t)(r)$

   D) $c = \frac{26.7(t)}{(r)}$

3. $10y - 8 - 2y = 4y - 22 + 5y$

   What is the value of y in the equation above?

   A) -30

   B) $-4\frac{2}{3}$

   C) 14

   D) 30

4. If $z = \sqrt{(x^{-1})4x}$, what is the value of z when $x = y + 3$ and $y = 14$?

   A) -2

   B) $\frac{1}{\sqrt{2}}$

   C) 2

   D) 34

5. $x^3 - 3x^2 + (2x)^3 - x$

   Which of the following is equivalent to the expression above?

   A) $20x$

   B) $x^3 - 3x^2 + 7x$

   C) $7x^3 - 3x^2 - x$

   D) $9x^3 - 3x^2 - x$

6. $4x + 3y = 10$

   $2x - y = 20$

   What is the solution (x,y) to the system of equations above?

   A) $(3,-4)$

   B) $(6,-7)$

   C) $(7,-6)$

   D) $(3,-2)$

7. Which of the following equations represents a line that passes through the points (2, 7) and (6, 10)?

   A) $y = \frac{3}{4}x + 5\frac{1}{2}$

   B) $y = \frac{4}{5}x - 5\frac{1}{2}$

   C) $y = 1\frac{1}{3}x - 4\frac{1}{2}$

   D) $y = 1\frac{1}{3}x + 2$

8. $\frac{(x^a y^b)(z^b y^a)}{z(xy)^a}$

   Which of the following is equivalent to the expression above?

   A) $y^b z^{(b-1)}$

   B) $xy^b z^{(b-1)}$

   C) $xy^{ab}z$

   D) $\frac{y^b}{z^b}$

9. $64 - 100x^2$

Which of the following is equivalent to the expression above?

A) $(8 + 10x)(8 - 10x)$

B) $(8 + 10x)(8x + 10)$

C) $(8 - 10x)^2$

D) $(8 + 10x)^2$

10. If $\frac{x}{y} = 7$, what is the value of $\frac{21y}{x}$?

A) 0

B) 1

C) 3

D) 7

11. You are buying supplies for your class cookout. You are expecting 32 students and 2 teachers to attend. You estimate that for every 3 people, you will need 5 hamburgers. The hamburger patties come in packs of 6. How many packs should you buy?

A) 4

B) 8

C) 9

D) 10

12. The county is instituting a new license plate system. The new plates will have 6 digits: the first digit will be 1, 2, or 3, and the next 5 digits can be any number from 0 – 9. How many possible unique combinations does this new system offer?

A) 53

B) 3×10^5

C) 1×10^6

D) 3×10^6

13. If x represents the proportion of 9th graders in a particular school who are female, and y represents the proportion of students in the school who are 9th graders, what is the expression for the proportion of students in the school who are female 9th graders?

A) $x + y$

B) $\frac{x}{y}$

C) xy

D) $\frac{y}{x}$

14. If x is the proportion of men who play an instrument, y is the proportion of women who play an instrument, and z is the total number of men, which of the following is true?

A) $\frac{z}{x}$ = number of men who play an instrument

B) $(1 - z)x$ = number of men who do not play an instrument

C) $(1 - x)z$ = number of men who do not play an instrument

D) $(1 - y)z$ = number of women who do not play an instrument

15. Put the following fractions in order from smallest to largest: $\frac{2}{16}, \frac{1}{24}, \frac{3}{32}, \frac{3}{16}, \frac{5}{48}$

A) $\frac{1}{24} < \frac{3}{32} < \frac{5}{48} < \frac{2}{16} < \frac{3}{16}$

B) $\frac{1}{24} < \frac{5}{48} < \frac{3}{32} < \frac{2}{16} < \frac{3}{16}$

C) $\frac{1}{24} < \frac{3}{32} < \frac{2}{16} < \frac{3}{16} < \frac{5}{48}$

D) $\frac{1}{24} < \frac{2}{16} < \frac{3}{32} < \frac{3}{16} < \frac{5}{48}$

16. In a neighborhood, $\frac{2}{5}$ of the houses are painted yellow. If there are 24 houses that are not painted yellow, how many yellow houses are in the neighborhood?

17. Find the slope of a line parallel to the line given by the equation $3y - 1 = 2x$.

18. Line l_A is perpendicular to line l_B and line l_C is parallel to line l_D. If l_A intersects l_C at a 15° angle, at what angle does l_B intersect l_D?

19. A restaurant employs servers, hosts, and managers in a ratio of 9:2:1. If there are 36 total employees, how many hosts are there?

20. Points B and C are on a circle, and a chord is formed by line segment $\overline{BC}$. If the distance from the center of the circle to point B is 10 centimeters, and the distance from the center of the circle to the midpoint of line segment $\overline{BC}$ is 8 centimeters, what is the length of line segment $\overline{BC}$?

CALCULATOR
Multiple Choice

For questions 1 – 30, work the problem and choose the most correct answer. For questions 31 – 38, work the problem and write in the correct answer in the space provided.

1. Consider the equations $|3x - 5| = 23$ and $|10 + 4y| = 12$. If x and y are both negative numbers, what is $|y - x|$?

A) 0.5

B) 4

C) 7.33

D) 8

4. Consider the bar graph below. Which of the following would be an appropriate title for this graph?

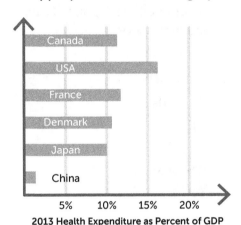

2013 Health Expenditure as Percent of GDP

A) Average Annual Expenditures as Percent of GDP by Country

B) National Health Expenditures in 2013 as Percent of GDP

C) National GDP as Percent of Total Health Expenditure by Country in 2013

D) Total Health Expenditure per Capita in 2013 by Country

2. A microsecond (μs) is equal to 1×10^{-6} seconds. Strobe lights typically send out 1 pulse of light every microsecond. If a strobe light is left on for 5 minutes, how many pulses of light would it send out?

A) 3.0×10^{-4} pulses

B) 1.8×10^{-3} pulses

C) 5.0×10^{6} pulses

D) 3.0×10^{8} pulses

3. $16 - x \leq 7x$

$2x - 40 < 6$

Find all possible values of x given the equations above.

A) $2 < x \leq 23$

B) $2 \leq x > -10$

C) $2 \leq x < 23$

D) $2\frac{2}{3} \leq x < 23$

5. 5 subtracted from 3 times x is greater than x subtracted from 15. Which of the following could be a value of x?

A) −12

B) −7

C) 7

D) 4

6. Consider the chart shown below for cumulative snowfall during a blizzard. During which period of time was the rate of snowfall the fastest?

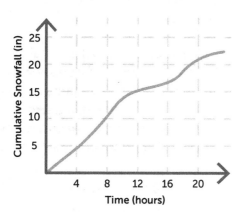

A) 0 to 4 hours

B) 8 to 12 hours

C) 12 to 16 hours

D) 12 to 20 hours

7. The histogram below shows a person's visits to a doctor over her lifetime. From age 0 through age 3, how many times per year (on average) did this person go to the doctor?

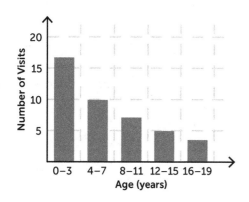

A) 4

B) 5.3

C) 8

D) 16

8.

Test Scores	
CLASS A	**CLASS B**
63	75
82	85
72	76
95	63
74	63
68	80
81	76
76	69
72	63

The table above shows test scores for students in 2 classes. Which of the following would change if the teacher added 5 points to each student's score?

I. mean

II. median

III. mode

A) I

B) II

C) II and III

D) I, II, and III

9. If $|8x - 2| < 4$, which of the following is true of x?

A) $-0.75 < x < 0.25$

B) $-0.25 < x < 0.75$

C) $0.25 < x < 0.75$

D) $x > 0$

10. If $f(x) = x^2 + 3$ and $g(x) = 3x - 12$, then $f(g(5)) =$

A) 3

B) 12

C) 28

D) 72

11. Suppose Mark can mow the entire lawn in 47 minutes, and Mark's dad can mow the entire lawn in 53 minutes. If Mark and his dad work together (each with their own lawnmowers), how long will it take them to mow the entire lawn?

A) 15.6 minutes

B) 24.9 minutes

C) 26.5 minutes

D) 50 minutes

12. There are 3 red, 4 blue, and 6 black marbles in a bag. When Carlos reaches into the bag and selects a marble without looking, what are the chances that he will select a black marble?

A) 0.23

B) 0.31

C) 0.46

D) 0.86

13. $(2x + 6)(3x - 15) = 0$

Which of the following is a possible positive value for x in the equation above?

A) 2

B) 3

C) 5

D) 6

14. Average winter temperatures have increased approximately 4.5% over the past 100 years. If the average winter temperature in 2015 is 34°F, what was the average winter temperature, in degrees Fahrenheit, in 1915?

A) 1.5

B) 29.5

C) 32.5

D) 35.5

15. $A = P\left(1 + \frac{r}{n}\right)^{nt}$

The amount of money in an account, A, is given in the equation above in terms of the initial investment, P, the interest rate, r, the number of times interest is compounded per year, n, and the time in years, t. Andre puts $5000 in a savings account for which interest is compounded monthly at a rate of 0.125. What will be his account balance be after 3 months?

A) $187.50

B) $189.85

C) $5,187.50

D) $5,157.88

16. Solve for x: $15x - 4y + 4 = 3x - 2(2y + 1)$

A) $x = -6$

B) $x = -\frac{1}{2}$

C) $x = \frac{1}{2}$

D) $x = 6$

17. If a rare gene mutation is present in $\frac{1}{1500}$ of the population, and $\frac{1}{4}$ of those with the mutation show symptoms, what proportion of the population shows symptoms associated with this mutation?

A) $\frac{1}{6,000}$

B) $\frac{1}{4,500}$

C) $\frac{1}{375}$

D) $\frac{4}{375}$

18. $x^2 + y^2 - 144 = 0$

What is the radius of the circle given by the equation above?

A) 0

B) 12

C) 24

D) 144

19. A courtyard garden has flower beds in the shape of 4 equilateral triangles arranged so that their bases enclose a square space in the middle for a fountain. If the space for the fountain has an area of 1 square meter, find the total area of the flower beds and fountain space.

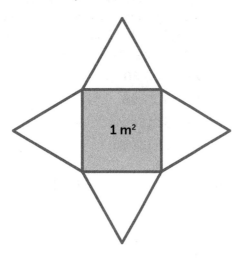

1 m²

A)   1.73 m²
B)   1.43 m²
C)   2.73 m²
D)   3 m²

20. During a recent storm, it snowed at a rate of 2 centimeters per hour for 190 minutes, 4 centimeters per hour for 40 minutes, 1 centimeter per hour for 280 minutes, and 3 millimeters per hour for 50 minutes. What was the total snowfall to the nearest centimeter?

A)   10
B)   13
C)   14
D)   16

Questions 21 and 22 refer to the following information.

$$K = \frac{1}{2}mv^2$$

The kinetic energy, K, of an object is given in terms of its mass, m, and velocity, v, as shown in the equation above.

21. Which of the following expresses the velocity of an object in terms of its mass and kinetic energy?

A) $v = \sqrt{\frac{2k}{m}}$

B) $v = \sqrt{\frac{k}{2m}}$

C) $v = 2\sqrt{\frac{k}{m}}$

D) $v = 2\sqrt{\frac{m}{k}}$

22. Object A and object B have the same mass. If object A is moving at half the velocity of object B, the kinetic energy of object A is what fraction of the kinetic energy of object B?

A) $\frac{1}{2}$

B) $\frac{1}{4}$

C) $\frac{1}{16}$

D) $\frac{1}{64}$

23. Jesse rides her bike 2 miles south and 8 miles east. She then takes the shortest possible route back home. What was the total distance she traveled in miles?

A) 7.75

B) 8.25

C) 17.75

D) 18.25

24. Gym A offers a monthly membership for 80% of the cost at Gym B; the cost at Gym B is 115% the cost at Gym C. What percentage of the cost at Gym C does Gym A charge?

A) 35%

B) 70%

C) 92%

D) 97%

25. Which of the following expressions is equivalent to $(4 + i)$ $(6 - i)$? (Note: $i = \sqrt{-1}$)

A) $24 - i^2$

B) $24 + i$

C) $25 - i$

D) $25 + 2i$

Questions 26 and 27 refer to the following information.

	Number of Participants			
EVENT	YEAR			
	2011	2012	2013	2014
Kids 5 km	73	121	212	250
Adult 5 km	243	355	502	656
Kids Half-Marathon	12	25	100	105
Adults Half-Marathon	1063	1506	1997	2510
Adults Marathon	352	357	412	503

The data in the table above shows the number of runners who participated in each of 5 races for the years 2011–2014.

26. Which of the following best approximates the rate of change of the number of participants in the Adult Half-Marathon from 2011 – 2014?

A) 50 participants per year

B) 250 participants per year

C) 500 participants per year

D) 1000 participants per year

27. Of the following, which event's percent increase in participation from 2011 to 2012 was closest to the percent increase in participation in the Kids Half-Marathon?

A) Kids 5 km

B) Adult 5 km

C) Adult Half-Marathon

D) Adult Marathon

28. If ∡C measures 112°, find ∡F.

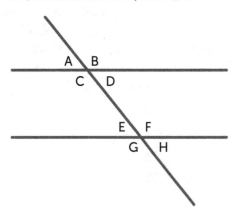

A) 22°

B) 68°

C) 112°

D) 158°

29. 5 pennies are dropped into a fountain. If each penny measures 19 millimeters in diameter and is 1.5 millimeters thick, how much water has been displaced?

A) 2.1 cm³

B) 4.3 cm³

C) 425.3 mm³

D) 676.9 mm³

30. $f(x) = \frac{x-2}{x^2 - 3x - 18}$

For what value of x is the function f above undefined?

A) 2

B) 3

C) 6

D) 18

GRID-IN
Calculator

31. A radio station plays songs that last an average of 3.5 minutes and has commercial breaks that last 2 minutes. If the station is required to play 1 commercial break for every 4 songs, how many songs can the station play in an hour?

32. A runner completes a 12 mile race in 1 hour and 30 minutes. If her pace for the first part of the race was 7 minutes per mile, and her pace for the second part of the race was 8 minutes per mile, for how many miles did she sustain her pace of 7 minutes per mile?

33. A material's specific heat capacity is the amount of energy needed to increase the temperature of 1 gram of that material by 1 degree Celsius. If the specific heat capacity of aluminum is $0.900 \frac{J}{(g \cdot °C)}$, how many joules of energy does it take to increase the temperature of 2 grams of aluminum by 4 degrees Celsius?

34. If $f(x) = 0.5x + 1$, what is the value of $f(-2)$?

35. $15x + 2y = 3$

$12x + y = -3$

Give a possible value of x given the equations above.

36. If a spherical water balloon is filled with 113 milliliters of water, what is the approximate radius of the balloon in centimeters?

37. $4x2 - 2x > 6$

Give a possible value of x for the inequality above.

38. A landscaper is building a garden that will be made from 4 equilateral triangles arranged so that their bases form a square courtyard as shown in the figure above. He plans to line the perimeter of the garden with a fence. If the area of the square courtyard is 2 square meters, how many meters of fencing will he need?

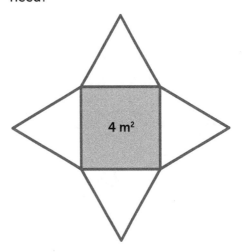

4 m²

Essay

As you read the passage below, consider how Secretary of Education Arne Duncan uses evidence, such as facts or examples, to support claims; reasoning to develop ideas and to connect claims and evidence; and stylistic or persuasive elements, such as word choice or appeals to emotion, to add powers to the ideas expressed.

ADAPTED FROM FORMER SECRETARY ARNE DUNCAN'S SPEECH AT THE CONGRESSIONAL HISPANIC CAUSUS INSTITUTE, 2014.

In 1961 my mother started an inner-city tutoring program on the south side of Chicago. It was actually only about two miles from where we lived. And she raised my sister and brother as part of her program. And what I saw all my life growing up—I was going to an after-school program before I ever went to regular school. I saw children who happened to come from a very violent community; who happened to all be African-American; who happened to be very poor. Despite many real challenges, many went on to do extraordinary things…

In my first real job in 1992—when I stopped playing basketball for six years—I ran an "I have a Dream" program along with my sister, and we ended up working in the same church basement as my mother. And for six years, we worked with a group of sixth graders. And at the end of that, 87 percent graduated from high school.

The class ahead of ours, from Shakespeare Elementary School, had a 33 percent high school graduation rate.

Thirty-three percent versus 87 percent. Same families, same communities, same socioeconomic challenges, very different set of opportunities.

When I led the Chicago Public Schools, we doubled the number of black and Latino students passing AP classes. And while we celebrated that accomplishment, I reminded our staff every day that our children weren't twice as smart as before, we simply had increased opportunity for them.

And the reason I give you these little stories is that all my life, I've seen what our young people do, despite very real challenges, when we as adults have the highest of expectations for them and present them with a real educational opportunity.

Low-income students and students of color have made real progress in recent years. Particularly in high school graduation rates, reducing dropout rates, and college enrollment rates.

High school graduation rates for the nation—I'm pleased to report—are at an all-time high—80 percent. Dropout rates are down significantly. Black dropout rates cut by about 45 percent. Latino dropout rates cut literally in half. And that is translated from 2008 to 2012 with over a million more black and brown young people going on to college. That's a huge step in the right direction.

And we should absolutely celebrate and revel in that progress and that increase in educational opportunity. But despite those very real improvements, everyone here knows that significant gaps remain, especially in academic efficiency.

Justice, and our nation's economic health, require that we close what I call the opportunity gaps by ensuring quality education for all.

If we want to increase upward mobility, we must increase educational opportunity.

If we want to reduce income inequality, we must increase educational opportunity.

If we want to build a growing and a thriving middle class, which is what this conference is all about, we must increase educational opportunity.

I'm absolutely convinced that so many of society's challenges would literally be solved if we simply increased educational opportunity.

This work is about so much more than education. It's a daily fight for social justice…

We believe that the key to improving the lives of all of our youth is to make sure communities are investing in them. And that means everyone.

In far too many of our nation's communities, gaps in essential resources exist, and too often, as we all know, it's students of color that receive less, not more.

These inequities are unjust and they violate the law…

Sixty years ago, the Supreme Court declared in *Brown vs. Board of Education* that public education "is a right which must be made to all on equal terms."

And despite major progress in some areas, many students today—as we all know—continue to lack the opportunity to receive a quality education.

It has never been more important to ensure that all children, not just some, receive a world-class, well-rounded education.

As President Obama has said, education is no longer just a pathway to opportunity and success, it's a prerequisite for success.

This fight is a fight to strengthen families, strengthen communities, and ultimately to build a stronger nation.

Fighting for equity in education is our mission. It's why we come to work each day and what fuels our passion.

And I promise all of you, we will not slow down or tire in that struggle.

PROMPT

Write an essay in which you explain how Secretary Arne Duncan builds an argument to persuade his audience that equity in education should be a national priority. In your essay, analyze how Secretary Duncan uses one or more of the features listed above (or features of your own choice) to strengthen the logic and persuasiveness of his argument. Be sure that your analysis focuses on the most relevant features of the passage. Your essay should not explain whether you agree with Secretary Duncan's claims, but rather explain how he builds an argument to persuade his audience.

Practice Test Two Answer Key
READING

1. C)	**14.** B)	**27.** A)	**40.** B)
2. C)	**15.** C)	**28.** B)	**41.** B)
3. D)	**16.** A)	**29.** D)	**42.** A)
4. B)	**17.** C)	**30.** C)	**43.** D)
5. B)	**18.** D)	**31.** B)	**44.** A)
6. A)	**19.** A)	**32.** B)	**45.** B)
7. C)	**20.** A)	**33.** D)	**46.** B)
8. A)	**21.** B)	**34.** A)	**47.** A)
9. B)	**22.** C)	**35.** D)	**48.** D)
10. C)	**23.** C)	**36.** B)	**49.** D)
11. D)	**24.** D)	**37.** C)	**50.** B)
12. D)	**25.** A)	**38.** D)	**51.** B)
13. B)	**26.** C)	**39.** C)	**52.** C)

WRITING and LANGUAGE

1. A)	**8.** C)	**15.** C)	**22.** D)
2. C)	**9.** B)	**16.** A)	**23.** C)
3. D)	**10.** D)	**17.** D)	**24.** A)
4. C)	**11.** A)	**18.** C)	**25.** A)
5. B)	**12.** A)	**19.** A)	**26.** C)
6. B)	**13.** B)	**20.** B)	**27.** B)
7. A)	**14.** D)	**21.** C)	**28.** B)

29. C)	33. B)	37. B)	41. D)
30. C)	34. D)	38. D)	42. A)
31. A)	35. A)	39. C)	43. C)
32. B)	36. B)	40. B)	44. B)

MATHEMATICS
No Calculator

1. B)	6. C)	11. D)	16. 16
2. C)	7. A)	12. B)	17. $\frac{2}{3}$
3. C)	8. A)	13. C)	18. 75°
4. C)	9. A)	14. C)	19. 6
5. D)	10. C)	15. A)	20. 12

MATHEMATICS
Calculator

1. A)	11. B)	21. A)	31. 15
2. D)	12. C)	22. B)	32. 6.0
3. C)	13. C)	23. D)	33. 7.2
4. B)	14. C)	24. D)	34. 5
5. C)	15. D)	25. C)	35. −1
6. A)	16. B)	26. C)	36. 3.0
7. B)	17. A)	27. A)	37. $x < -1, x > 1.5$
8. D)	18. B)	28. C)	38. 16 meters
9. B)	19. D)	29. A)	
10. B)	20. C)	30. C)	